A

CRITICAL AND EXEGETICAL

COMMENTARY

ON

THE BOOK OF LEVITICUS,

WITH A

NEW TRANSLATION.

BY

JAMES G. MURPHY, LL.D., T.C.D.,

PROFESSOR OF HEBREW, BELFAST, AUTHOR OF COMMENTARIES ON GENESIS AND EXODUS.

PUBLISHERS
Eugene, Oregon

Wipf and Stock Publishers
199 W 8th Ave, Suite 3
Eugene, OR 97401

A Critical and Exegetical Commentary on the Book of Leviticus
With a New Translation
By Murphy, James G.
ISBN: 1-59752-240-6
Publication date 6/8/2005
Previously published by Warren F. Draper, 1874

PREFACE.

IN the present state of man, human reason, if without bias and without revelation, would arrive at three inevitable conclusions: I am guilty, God is holy, and therefore I am doomed to die. It would be easy to put these three propositions into the form of a regular syllogism, of which the last would be the legitimate conclusion. They contain the sum of all natural theology; and it is obvious that they constitute a philosophy of despair.

There is a whole class of the most important truths involved in these few statements. It is well to bring some of these distinctly before the mind. That human reason is under a manifold bias, different in different men and circumstances, and extremely difficult to escape, is a proposition that will not be denied by any one at all conversant with the history of opinion in philosophy and religion. The degree in which certain threads of pure revelation have been woven into the many-figured texture of the imagination, and have influenced the course of reason on questions of the highest moment to man, has not been so fully considered or freely conceded; and it is impossible here to do more than indicate this important point. Yet notwithstanding the acknowledged existence of prejudice, even on the loftiest themes, it is a settled conviction with us, that intellect is indestructible as long as the soul endures, and that reason has the power of cognising first principles, ascertaining elementary facts, and drawing legitimate conclusions, if the wilful vagrancy of the fancy were kept in check. This is the first postulate of all human philosophy, without the admission of which all further pursuit of knowledge is hopeless and unprofitable.

Having adopted the postulate that reason, if true to itself, is a faculty by which knowledge may be acquired, we are prone to investigate the highest problem of man — his moral relation to God, and are led at length to the three fundamental propositions already given. At first sight some will object to their meagreness, others to their comprehensiveness. Let them at all events be put to the test of a thorough and impartial examination. Our business here is to do no more than elucidate them so far that their meaning may not be mistaken. The first proposition affirms two things — that man is of a moral nature, and that when this moral nature is developed he is conscious of sin and guilt; and it implies that right reason is capable of discovering these facts. These conclusions have been all more or less debated by some; yet they are what we hold to be the finding of reason on this question.

The second proposition affirms the moral nature of God, and along with this the perfection of that nature; and involves the idea and the existence of the Creator of all things. Many will hesitate long before they accept these momentous averments, with all that they imply, as the actual or possible deliverance of reason at its best estate from the ordinary sources of intuition, experience, or logical sequence. But the longer we meditate on this transcendent theme the more fully shall we be convinced that they are the probable, if not demonstrable, result to which all the expatiations of human reason inevitably lead.

The third proposition asserts that the doom of sin is death, and that I, being guilty of sin, am doomed to die. This is the conclusion following from the premises already stated, and, like every other conclusion, is simply the evolution of that which is involved in the previous facts. It raises the question of the meaning of death, and of its counterpart, life, and of the general principles of administrative justice on the part of the Moral Governor of the universe. But there is nothing in all this which reason is not competent to investigate, if it have already achieved the results involved in the premises of this argument. Having arrived at this unavoidable conclusion, reason has no more that it can do. By the inexorable logic of facts it has been compelled to draw a dark picture of human destiny. It is not able to cast a single ray of hope on the gloomy scene. Thus ends the book of fallen nature.

On this dark ground we open the book of revelation. It also, we find, contains three cardinal articles of faith, which are the counterparts of the propositions of reason, though in a different order. The fundamental utterance of revelation is, that GOD IS MERCIFUL. This unfolds itself into three elements of evangelical truth: God pardons, redeems, and sanctifies. All this is more fully conveyed in the three following sentences: the Father in mercy appoints an atonement and accepts the returning penitent; the Son makes the required atonement by fulfilling all righteousness and dying for sinners; the Holy Spirit sanctifies the soul, begetting in it faith in Jesus Christ and repentance toward God. We may set these over against the former three propositions thus, God is holy; but he is also merciful: I am doomed to die; but the Word made flesh has died for me: I am guilty of sin; but the Holy Spirit comes with these glad tidings to quicken me to repentance. This is the sum and substance of all revealed religion; and it is plain that it forms the only basis of a philosophy of hope.

These elements of the theology of revelation involve a long series of truths of the utmost moment and interest to man. Antecedent, however, to the entertainment of any or all of these doctrines is the question of revelation itself, with the kindred topics of creation, miracle, inspiration, and prophecy. Dr. Kalisch in a long dissertation on "Theology of the Past and the Future," prefixed to his Commentary on Leviticus, renounces creation, miracle, prayer, revelation, inspiration, and prophecy, and in consistency with these views denies the existence of types in the Old Testament. He therefore naturally remarks; "It is not sufficient to appeal from the letter of the Bible to its spirit; indeed, the one kills, but even the other is no longer life and truth to us. The spirit of the Bible is not the spirit of our times; it is not the light that illumines our path, or points to our goal." It is not surprising that a Jew should write thus, when we consider the precursors he has had among the philosophers and divines of the Christian as well as of the Jewish church, whose interpretation of Scripture he has rashly taken for the letter and the spirit of the Bible. As a natural result of this bewilderment he has betaken himself for guidance and comfort to reason, unaided reason, developing itself successfully in science and philosophy, and proudly sitting in judgment on the Bible as one of the curious products of the ancient mind.

No thinking man will venture to undervalue reason. The progress it has made in the mathematical and experimental sciences, and in their thousandfold application to the arts of life proclaims its power. But its scope, however comprehensive, is limited to intuition, experience, and inference. It cannot by any telescope or microscope of its own invention go beyond these. It cannot look even on the heart of man, much less can it penetrate the thoughts and intents of God. In this field of inquiry the utmost that I can descry is the momentous syllogism, I have sinned against the holy God; he that has sinned against him is doomed to die; I am therefore doomed to death. All that is not involved in this lies beyond the horizon of reason. If Dr. Kalisch had once fairly faced the cheerless and solitary prospect which is presented by this farthest step of reason in the line of man's moral relation with God he would have been slow to hand us over to Baruch Spinoza, and other masters or vaunters of reason, however splendid in intellect or unimpeachable in morals. At this dark abyss without revelation reason can only stand aghast.

Many of those who are in doubt about a written revelation will demur to the account here given of the testimony which reason has to offer with respect to the relation of God with man. Some will affirm that it is overstated ; others that it is understated. We have at present, it is obvious, no pressing concern with those who think it is overstated, inasmuch as the less reason can testify, the more our need of revelation. But those who think it is understated assure themselves that reason suggests, if it does not vouch, that there is mercy with God. If reason actually vouched for all that this implies, the need of revelation, it must be confessed, would not be great. This is the turning-point of the whole question. And the nearer we draw to it, the more sensible we become that it is the most grave and serious theme that can engage the attention of man. Now it is impossible for us to get over the conviction that reason, so far from even hinting at mercy, feels itself constrained to yield unreservedly to the full demand of justice. For it must be borne in mind, that mercy, to be at all to the present purpose, must involve the forgiveness of sin. Now it is most willingly agreed that the sight of suffering, that is presumably the suffering of an innocent being, will awaken pity in the Divine bosom. But on the altogether different question whether the Most High will or can forgive sin, reason can only be silent. All that it can positively asseverate is, that sin deserves its doom, and that justice requires that the punishment be adequate to the offence. If I wrong my neighbor he has a right to redress. And he that is in authority is bound not only to enforce the right, but to vindicate the law by condign punishment. Reason can go no further. I cannot say that my neighbor must or ought or will pardon me. I can by no means say that the magistrate is at liberty to pardon me without redressing my neighbor.

Whence, then, comes the conception of pardon that so readily suggests itself to the mind in this awful predicament? Simply, we submit, from the voice of revelation, a revelation as early as the fall, entwining itself with the memories of the race, descending as a tradition from father to son, and cherished as a fountain of hope in the valley of the shadow of death. But apart from all revelation, reason could only assure us of the sentence of death upon the sinner; and we know not whether imagination could even suggest the possibility of pardon. But even if it could, the bare suggestion would be of no avail for our light or peace against the inevitable doom pronounced by reason upon the guilty. Only a plain and palpable attestation could give comfort to the mind. Hence the line is clear to us that marks off the distinct spheres of reason and revelation in the matter of our relation to God. Reason, at the most, can only tell us of justice and doom. Revelation, when its voice is heard at all, speaks of mercy and peace. Hence also appears to us the absolute necessity of revelation, if hope is ever to have a place in the breast of the fallen.

When a revelation from heaven is made, however, reason has as much to do with it as with any other matter that comes within its ken. First, it acknowledges its possibility. If my fellow-man can tell me of the thoughts and feelings that are within his heart, much more can my Maker unveil to me the purpose of mercy that has lain hid within his breast. I ask not the mode of doing so. He who made me after his own image has, I question not, divers manners of making known to me his mind. Next, reason hears, understands, and estimates the credibility of the revelation. All these processes we hold and admit to be quite competent to right reason. Again, when a revelation comes to be written, it affords still further exercise for reason. We then have the best means not only of preserving it, but of judging of its value and its authority. A written revelation gives rise to the questions of the inspiration and of the canon of Scripture.

The possibility of a revelation involves the wider possibility of a miracle, and this of creation and prophecy. A logical mind, accepting revelation, will be found accepting with equal readiness all these kindred facts, not perhaps in the popular, but at all events in the scriptural sense. On the other hand, he who rejects revelation will feel himself bound in consistency to reject the miracle in all its phases. This single point of revelation, then, divides thinking men into two sharply defined classes, those who acknowledge the miraculous in the scriptural sense, and those who repudiate it in some other assumed sense. It is fitting to express the divergence in this modified form, because the reasoning of one truly thoughtful man is not, and cannot be, in direct antagonism with that of another.

To guard against misconception it is necessary to observe that the inspiration of the Scriptures must be, by the very nature of the thing, verbal, simply because the Scripture to which this property is ascribed consists of words. Dean Alford, than whom few men, if any, in the British Empire are more deserving of thanks from the churches for his labors in the field of New Testament exposition, distinguishes verbal and plenary inspirations as two diverging theories, and gives a definition of the former, on the ground of which he rejects it as unworthy and destructive of the credibility of the Gospels. We regret that he has taken this course, which we think unworthy of his discrimination and his candor. We adhere to the phrase "verbal inspiration," but we must decline to adopt his definition of it. Verbal inspiration is simply *the inspiration of a writing*, which of necessity consists of words. We agree with this eminent expositor, that "We must take our views of inspiration, not from a priori considerations, but ENTIRELY FROM THE EVIDENCE FURNISHED BY THE SCRIPTURES THEMSELVES. Now one express part of the evidence furnished by Scripture is that "Scripture," that is, the written document composed of words, is "given by inspiration of God." We take shelter under this statement, and refuse to be dislodged from it on the insufficient ground that certain advocates, or certain opponents, of the doctrine have given an untenable or unscriptural definition of it. The question of the inspiration of the Scriptures is not merely who are inspired, but what is inspired.

As the evidence of a miracle rests ultimately on the testimony of the senses, so it is with the canon of Scripture. We are inconsiderately looking for too much, when we expect preternatural evidence of a preternatural event. The supernatural must, in the long run, come to our knowledge by natural evidence. To come to the case in point, the last books or book of revelation must be received on the evidence of sense or testimony. For if this evidence were miraculous, it would itself be a part of the canon, and would need its own natural attestation. Hence it is contrary to sound sense to demand inspired evidence of the last contribution made to the volume of inspiration. The Israelites had natural evidence merely, the evidence of experience and testimony to the Divine revelation given to Moses for their instruction. Incidentally we have preternatural evidence, the evidence of the New Testament, for the canon of the Old Testament. But we have simply natural evidence, that of credible testimony, for the canon of the New Testament. And it would be well for us always to bear in mind that, in the nature of things, this is all we can have, unless and until there be a third Testament containing an inspired voucher for the second. This evidence of sense is all we need to have, as it would be all we should still have for another instalment of revelation, if it were to come.

Though reason can formulate the sum total of its own conclusions concerning the relation of man to God, it cannot prescribe, but only accept, the form in which the matter of revelation will come from God. But when it has the volume of revelation before it, it falls within its province to apprehend and to exhibit the substance of the Divine communication in a sentence or system. The sentence is, "There is forgiveness with thee, that thou mayest be feared." The system has been already given in its most condensed shape: The Father pardons, the Son propitiates, the Spirit purifies. The first of these three propositions involves the other two. Because it is the Father's purpose to remit sin, he sends his Son to redeem and his Spirit to regenerate. The first has two seemingly insurmountable obstacles to encounter. How can God, being just, forgive sin; and, how can man, being evil, return to God? The former is overcome by the atonement, in which the Son of God becoming man obeys the law and dies the death, that the sinner who trusts in him with penitent heart may escape death and enter into life. The latter is overcome by the regenerating work of the Holy Spirit, who by the gospel makes the sinner aware of the mercy of the Father and the mediation of the Son, and willing to lean on the Saviour and return to the Fountain of mercy. These three fundamental articles of faith manifestly involve two others of co-ordinate importance, the trinity of persons in the Godhead and the incarnation of the Eternal Word. These may be called the five cardinal points of revelation. The questions of predestination and free-agency lie on the common ground of reason and faith, or of observation and revelation.

To make our way clear, it is expedient to make a few remarks on some of these points. Pardon is by its very nature free: "Freely by his grace," as the Scriptures almost pleonastically express it. Yet pardon is in effect bound by two indispensable conditions, first that the Mediator satisfy the law for the offender, and next that the offender, relying on the Mediator, return to the Father. Propitiation implies expiation, the latter denoting the payment of the penalty due to sin, the former including also, and chiefly, the performance of the obedience due to the law. Purification is a process begun in the new birth and continued in the new life. As long as there is a remnant of sin or of the old man we must present the petition " Forgive us our debts," and plead for acceptance the merits of the Substitute. Incarnation involves not only death on account of sin, but resurrection unto life on account of righteousness. The revelation of the three persons or relatives in the essentially one God unfolds to us the possibility of salvation. None but the essentially Divine can pardon, redeem, or regenerate; and yet the Forgiver, Redeemer, and Sanctifier must be relatively or personally different.

The Book of Leviticus is the figurative exhibition of the way of salvation. It is the central book of the Pentateuch. After the history of the whole human race in relation with God given in the Book of Genesis and, the growth of the seed of Abraham into a free and holy nation recorded in the Book of Exodus, we have in this highly remarkable and singularly interesting book the first full and particular development of the way of salvation for man, in a series of symbolic forms suited to the primeval stage of the human race, and fitted to edify the infant people of God, unfold to their mind and conscience the first principles of reconciliation with God and renovation after his image, and prepare them for the coming of the substance of all these shadows in the fulness of time. Nothing can exceed the interest of this book for the age in which it made its appearance ; and the attentive study of it will contribute much to the confirmation and comfort of us who live in the light of the gospel which it foreshadows, after the advent of the Mediator whom it represents.

Dr. Kalisch, in his Introduction to this book, has a section on its "illogical arrangement," which he founds upon a crude and superficial digest of its contents. It is the easiest thing in the world to make a book appear illogical. We have only to misapprehend the author's principle of arrangement, and the thing is done. Many an author suffers from this sort of treatment on the part of the critic. The more faithful he is to his real plan, the more incongruous will his work appear to the critic who sees no plan in it, or imagines a wrong one. He applies the wrong key, which is sure not to fit. He pronounces the lock out of order ; but it is the key that is wrong, not the lock. Dr. Kalisch has not been at the pains to discover the true principle of arrangement in the Book of Leviticus. It will appear, when due attention is paid to the structure of the book, that the order of its various topics is the very best that could be devised by an author who had a series of distinct communications intrusted to him, not to work into a treatise, but simply to arrange in a book.

The book treats of propitiation and purification. Propitiation involves the priest who mediates and the offering which makes atonement. Besides the priest and the offering that come between, are the almighty, eternal, holy Creator and the fallen creature, between whom they come. It is requisite, for the sake of clearness, to direct our attention to each of these important objects in turn.

The most holy and wise God alone determines what is the nature of the mediation between himself and his fallen creatures, what are the characteristics and functions of the Mediator, and what is the special significance of each kind of offering. It is not of the slightest consequence, therefore, for the illustration of these matters, what were the manners and customs of other nations concerning the worship of the Deity; as they only contain some traces of revealed truth mingled up with a mass of human error. For any certain information, therefore, concerning the priests and their functions, the offerings and the import of their several kinds, and the feelings and intentions with which the worshippers came forward to present them, we must have recourse to the Scriptures which are handed down to us as the revelation of God concerning the mode of his worship.

The priest has two functions to discharge—the offering of sacrifice, and the making of intercession. In the former of these functions, he has two parts only to perform; the application of the blood and the burning of the fat, the flesh, or the memorial of the oblation or meat-offering. These two parts are expressive of expiation and propitiation, or the payment of the penalty and the performance of the righteousness due by the transgressor. It is not necessary to dwell on these, as they will receive their illustration from the explanation of the various offerings.

The various kinds of offerings described in the first five chapters have tasked the ingenuity of expositors from the earliest times; and much depends on the elucidation of their true meaning for the right understanding of the book itself, and of the way of salvation for the lost family of man which the Bible unfolds. It is manifest that there are three primary and stated offerings, and two secondary and occasional. The former are the burnt-sacrifice, the oblation, and the sacrifice of peace, expressing atonement, the benefit of atonement, and the enjoyment of this benefit; the latter, the sin-sacrifice and the trespass-offering, expressing the expiation and the satisfaction for an occasional sin of inadvertence. This is the result of a careful and patient examination of their nature and import.

The burnt-sacrifice represents the great propitiation for sin, to be offered up once only on behalf of a sinful world. This is manifest from the description of it. It is "for the acceptance" of the worshippers; it is " accepted for him to atone for him"; and it is " a fire-offering of a sweet smell unto the Lord." The blood that expiates is sprinkled on the altar; and the burning of the whole upon the altar is the symbol of a full propitiation. The oblation sets forth the fruit of righteousness, which is life. For bread is the staff of life. The memorial of it is burnt by the priest upon the altar, as " a fire-offering of a sweet smell unto the Lord." This denotes a propitiation, which is made by fulfilling all righteousness. It presupposes expiation by the blood of the burnt-sacrifice. The sacrifice of peace includes the three stages, the blood of expiation, the fat of propitiation, and the feast of communion, in which the benefits of redemption are actually received and enjoyed by the worshipper. Subordinate and occasional are the sin-sacrifice and the trespass-offering. They express the application of the great propitiation to the inadvertent sins that are committed by the children of God after repentance and adoption; the former giving prominence to the punishment due for the wrong done, and the latter to the redress due for the right left undone. According to the circumstances, the one or the other is used, or both are offered for the same offence.

The prominent feeling that animates the worshipper is different, according to the nature of the offering. In the burnt-sacrifice he comes to express his faith in God and in the divinely appointed propitiation for sin; in the oblation his acknowledgement of the blessings of life; and in the sacrifice of peace the joy of salvation which fills his soul when he partakes of those blessings. The re-awakening of faith and hope after the sorrow and self-condemnation of inadvertent sins prompts to the sin-sacrifice and the trespass-offering. Hence it appears that the motives which these offerings, in their diversity and mutual relationship, call forth, afford a fine illustration of the process of salvation in the inner man. To lay the hand upon the head of the burnt-sacrifice for the first time, represents the turning-point in the history of the soul. In that representative act is set forth, in a figure, the act of being born of God and adopted into his family, by which sanctification is begun and justification takes place. Justification has two sides, a negative and a positive; it includes the pardon of sin in us, and the acceptance of righteousness for us. These have their corresponding two sides in the atoning sacrifice, which embraces, not only the payment of the penalty, but the performance of the righteousness due to the law of heaven. The same two-sidedness comes out in the definition of the burnt-sacrifice, makes itself very distinct in the sin-sacrifice and the trespass-offering, and appears in the two parts the priest has to perform in the offering of sacrifice. To present the oblation alone, or in conjunction with the sacrifice proper, in which there is the shedding of blood, is practically to acknowledge the good works or righteousness of the mediator as the meritorious ground of the blessings of the life that now is and of that which is to come. The same principle applies to the offering of the first-fruits, which is a confession that the fruits of the earth are the gift of God on the ground of a merit not our own. Hence we perceive that the oblation presupposes, even when it is not immediately preceded by, the sacrifice of propitiation. This is the ultimate ground on which it is accepted, and the benefits which it symbolizes are realized. To partake of the feast on the sacrifice of peace, is to celebrate, not merely the blessings of salvation, but our actual enjoyment of them in fellowship with our heavenly Father. This is a divinely instituted emblem of the Christian living with Christ. It is the symbolic expression of the fact that, "if we walk in the light, as he is in the light, we have fellowship one with another, and the blood of Jesus Christ his Son cleanseth us from all sin." There is, however, another aspect of the experience of a Christian which is presented in the following verse: "If we say that we have no sin we deceive ourselves, and the truth is not in us." Hence the singular aptitude of the sin-sacrifice and the trespass-offering to express the application of the atonement which our humiliating experience requires us to make even after we have with penitent heart laid our hand upon the head of the great atoning sacrifice. The traces of the old man betray themselves in us, which need a fresh sprinkling of the blood of atonement, and a long and persevering effort for their complete obliteration. These are the sins of inadvertence, more or less grave, which mar the spiritual beauty and wound the conscience of the child of God. The sin-sacrifice and the trespass-offering thus symbolize the fresh application of the blood of sprinkling, which the sin-vexed soul has to make, while humbly confessing the easily-besetting sin which he has not yet been able entirely to lay aside, and uttering the often needful supplication, " forgive us our debts as we forgive our debtors." In this twofold form of offering for sin, as has been already said, the Christian expresses his regret for walking in any respect after the flesh, and his longing to walk in all respects after the Spirit.

To bring out more clearly the full scope of this interpretation of these offerings, it is requisite to notice some of the interpretations which have been recently presented to the public. Kurtz sums up his view of the proper sacrifices in the following sentence : " The same progressive stages, therefore, which distinguish redemption and its symbolical correlate, the complete idea of sacrifice, incorporated themselves, as it were, in these three *varieties* of sacrifice : the stage of atonement, of *justificatio*, in the sin-offering ; that of *sanctificatio* in the burnt-sacrifice ; and that of sacramental fellowship, of the *unio mystica*, in the peace-offering." A faithful adherence to the text of Scripture will show the inaccuracy of this representation of the sacrifices. First of all, as a whole it is an incongruous mixture of justification, sanctification, and the mystical union. Now proper sacrifice signifies only one thing, atonement, in two branches, expiation and propitiation. Corresponding to this is justification with its two corresponding parts, pardon and acceptance. This is the act of the Father on the ground of the atonement, which is the act of the Mediator. But sanctification and the mystical union do not stand in the same category with justification, and have no similar relation to sacrifice. Hence the arrangement violates all the laws of good division. And next in detail the sin-sacrifice denotes, not justification, nor strictly its correlative, atonement, but expiation, and that not for sin in general or as a state, but for an occasional sin of inadvertence. Hence it has no right to the first place, nor even to a co-ordinate place with the burnt-sacrifice or the peace-sacrifice. Again, the burnt-sacrifice is not symbolic of sactification. It is not " the sacrifice of entire, full, unconditional self-surrender." There is nothing of all this in the scriptural account of it, as any one may see. It is simply a means of atonement and acceptance, a fire-offering of a sweet smell unto the Lord. These are the only indications of its meaning, and they are plain unmistakeable marks of atonement. To make any sacrifice denote *self-surrender* is to confound the feeling of the offerer with the meaning of the offering. The former is not self-surrender, but faith. The latter is the self-surrender, not of the offerer, but of the victim. These distinctions are obvious to the thoughtful reader. The sacrifice of peace closes with a feast upon a sacrifice, which gives it its distinctive character. The sacrifice, as usual, represents propitiation, the foundation of peace; and the feast at its close exhibits the participation of the redeemed in the blessings of salvation.

The following passage contains a like summary of the views of Keil : " The sacrificial law, therefore, with the five species of sacrifices which it enjoins, embraces every aspect in which Israel was to manifest its true relation to the Lord its God. Whilst the sanctification of the whole man in self-surrender to the Lord was shadowed forth in the burnt-offerings, the fruits of this sanctification in the meat-offering, and the blessedness of the possession and enjoyment of saving grace in the peace-offerings, the expiatory sacrifices furnished the means of removing the barrier which sins and trespasses had set up between the sinner and the holy God, and procured the forgiveness of sin and guilt, so that the sinner could attain once more to the unrestricted enjoyment of the covenant grace." Here is the same violation of the laws of good division. The parts should contain neither more nor less than the whole. But sacrifice does not contain sanctification among its parts. The meat-offering represents the fruit, not of sanctification, but of propitiation: the expiatory sacrifices, by which are meant the sin-sacrifice and the trespass-offering, are only both expiatory, if expiation be identical with propitiation, and only the one expiatory and the other propitiatory, if we distinguish these terms; and they properly open the way for the forgiveness of sins of inadvertence. There is nothing in the scriptural account of the burnt-sacrifice to show that it means the self-surrender of the worshipper. It is the victim that is in every case surrendered to the doom of death, after having established its claim to life. It is not the feeling of the offerer, but that of the priest and victim, that is expressed in the sacrifice.

Kalisch exhibits his view of the sacrifices in the following terms: " The sacrifice may either be designed to evince the offerer's absolute submission to the divine sovereignty and to acknowledge God's unlimited sway over the destinies of man; or it may be intended as an expression of gratitude for blessings enjoyed; or it may serve to implore forgiveness and expiation for offences committed; or, lastly, it may mark the return of a state of purity after a period of uncleanness, as after the recovery from the leprosy or a running issue. In the first case, it was a *burnt-offering;* in the second, a *thank-offering* or *praise-offering;* in the third, a *sin-offering* or a *trespass-offer-*

ing; and in the last, a *purification-offering.*" There is here some forcing of preconceived notions on Scripture, and considerable confusion of things that differ. In the view of the sacred writer the sacrifice expresses not the subjective feelings of the worshipper in presenting it, but the atonement which the victim is to make in the purpose of God. The burnt-sacrifice represents, not the absolute submission of the offerers to the divine sovereignty, nor God's unlimited sway over the destinies of man, ideas which are foreign to the notion of sacrifice, and only akin to that of predestination, but the making of *atonement* and the opening of the way for pardon and *acceptance.* The sacrifice of peace is not necessarily a thank or praise offering, an expression of gratitude for blessings received, but primarily a symbolic enjoyment of the blessings procured through an accepted atonement. The sin-sacrifice or trespass-offering does not exactly " serve to implore forgiveness and expiation for offences committed," but exhibits the penalty paid, or redress made, for the faults of inadvertence in which holy men are overtaken. The sacrifice does not "implore," but atone; and " forgiveness and expiation " are not parallel, but the latter is the condition of the former. And it must be understood that a " purification-offering " may be so called, not because it purifies, since its proper effect is to propitiate, but because it is offered when purification has taken place. It is also one of the kinds of sacrifice already specified.

 A few remarks only will be added in conclusion. The writer has been sparing of philological and grammatical remarks, as they are within the reach of all who have a good grammar and a good lexicon. He has also arranged them in the form and place of notes, so that the English reader may peruse the comment without interruption or difficulty. He has indulged in some occasional repetition to avoid the trouble of reference. He has generally avoided going far beyond the stand-point of the men for whom the book was originally written, inasmuch as it was intended for the present instruction and edification of the early church. After the general view of the sacrifices above given, it is unnecessary to enter here into the distinctions between the sin-sacrifice and the trespass-offering, the nature of the sacrifices of the two birds and the two goats, and other debated points, which will be treated in their proper places. Reflections of an admonitory nature are seldom offered, as they will come more freshly and profitably from the thoughtful reader's own mind. No difficulty occurring to the writer has been left without an attempt at a full explanation. The pleasure and benefit he has reaped from the study of this book have been to him a great reward. If the result of his study affords any gratification or illumination to any of his readers, his labor will not be in vain.

In the arrangement of the text and notes the amended version is placed over the comment for the sake of reference. The paragraph may be advantageously read over before beginning to peruse the comment on it. The figures refer to the few philological notes at the end of the chapter. The ordinary reader may examine these by omitting the Hebrew words.

INTRODUCTION.

X. LEVITICUS.

The third fifth of the law, called familiarly וַיִּקְרָא, from its initial word, is designated by sundry other names, which are more or less indications of its nature and contents. It is entitled in the Talmud תּוֹרַת הַכֹּהֲנִים, the law of the priests, and סֵפֶר תּוֹרַת הַקָּרְבָּנוֹת, the book of the law of offerings, and in the Septuagint and the Vulgate Λευιτικὸν (βίβλιον) and Leviticus (liber).

Leviticus and Numbers are the complement of Exodus. The first of these three books records the constitution of the holy nation; the second supplies the account of its chief religious institutions; and the third mainly that of its civil institutions. Hence the latter two form the counterparts of one whole. The religious and civil concerns of a nation, however, are so interwoven that they cannot be entirely severed. There is therefore a slight intermingling of these themes in the two books.

Leviticus treats of the ritual of the chosen people. In the preceding book the departure of Israel out of the land of bondage, the publication of the moral law in ten commandments, and of the civil law in seven sections of ten clauses each, and the erection of the tabernacle for the worship of God after the pattern shown in the mount, had been placed on record. This is naturally followed by a treatise prescribing the ceremonial observances, by which communion between God and the people, among whom he had chosen to dwell, might be maintained. This book is accordingly a divinely instituted code of worship. If there had been no fall, a ritual of worship would have been unnecessary. The knowledge of God would have remained unclouded. The way of approaching him would have been obvious and familiar. Every word would have been a note in the psalm of life, every deed a step in the path of rectitude, and every thought a link in the never-ending chain of truth; and all together would have been the unbidden presentation of a reverent homage to the Father of all. But with a fallen being all is changed. Guilt is upon his conscience, and doom is before his eyes. Of the mercy of God, or of the mode in which it may be exercised, he can form no anticipation. Only a positive revelation from God can afford any ground of certainty or comfort on these points. The main fact, that there is mercy with God for the returning penitent, had been communicated to the family of man immediately after the fall. And some hints had been given of the mode in which it could alone be conveyed. But now that a peculiar people has been selected to receive the Divine favor, and keep up the knowledge of God and his mercy on the earth, it is full time that a more complete and definite account should be given of the way in which the returning penitent may draw near to God with acceptance. This is the topic of the Book of Leviticus. The worship of a fallen being returning to God is here prescribed. This worship must take its start from an atonement provided by God and accepted by man. Hence the priest and the sacrifice have a prominent place on the scene of worship; and the book which describes it is appropriately termed, the law of the priests, and the law of offerings. The priestly family were of the tribe of Levi, and the Levites were given to them in place of the first-born, to be their attendants and ministers in the service of the sanctuary. Hence the book of the law of offerings is not unsuitably styled Leviticus; though the Levites are only once mentioned in it, and that incidentally in a regulation concerning their cities and houses, contained in the twenty-fifth chapter.

As the tabernacle and its furniture had a typical significance, so the priest, the offering, and the various observances of a ritual nature comprised in this book are shadows of good things to come, symbolic representations of that real atonement which was eventually to be made by the High Priest for the sin of mankind. Its leading object is to interest the mind in the doctrines of redemption, and direct the will to faith in a Redeemer. The infant race had to be trained to the only mode of returning to God and abiding with him. The moral and intellectual capacity of fallen man had to be developed by the exhibition in a tangible and intelligible form of the ways and means by which reconciliation to heaven might be effected in harmony with the eternal principles of truth and holiness. And the theory of the atonement thus lodged in the mind was to be enforced by the practice of the enjoined rites; which, if it had any meaning, was the formal acceptance of the Divine mercy on the only terms on which it could be offered.

There are two ends contemplated in forming the regulations for the conduct of the chosen nation; the one being the welfare of the little commonwealth itself, and the other the ultimate reconciliation of the whole human race to their Maker. The former is evidently subordinate to the latter. It gives rise to the civil code, which is intermingled with the more general enactments, and helps to give shape even to those which aim at the restitution of all things in this fallen world. The very smallness of the nation rendered it more easy to give a practical realization of the kingdom of God on earth; inasmuch as the people were enabled to convene for the purpose of common worship three times a year at the centre of the community. The one temple in the holy city was the meet figure of the one heaven, where he resides who is at the same time King of the kings of earth and Monarch of the universe of things. And the theocracy of Israel was the germ and type of that kingdom of righteousness and peace which was eventually to be set up on earth, and thenceforward never to be moved.

To this grander end the main body of the peculiar institutions of Israel had regard. The moral law was proclaimed to bring home again to the understanding and the conscience of man the great principles of rectitude and personal responsibility to his Maker. The sense of guilt having been in this way awakened, craved some relief from the dark prospect which loomed in the future. The institutions of Leviticus are calculated to satisfy this need. The principle of redemption, as the only legitimate method of reconciliation to God, is hereby implanted in the human breast. The minister of atonement is set forth in the priest; the means of atonement in the sacrifice, which is the shedding of blood, or the giving of life for life. Compliance on the part of the sinner with the prescribed ritual, coming to God in his sanctuary, availing himself of the good offices of the high priest, and presenting through him the appointed exchange for his own life; these form the entrance into the life of reconciliation with God. The life itself corresponds with the birth, as it has its legal standing in the same substituted righteousness, and its essential validity in the same inborn faith and repentance. The penitent stands only in the righteousness of the Redeemer, who makes satisfaction where he has failed, and lives only in the strength of the Sanctifier, who has enabled him to accept the legal standing thus mercifully vouchsafed, and thenceforth to walk with his God in newness of life.

On examining the Book of Leviticus, we find it contains two series of regulations: the former, concerning entrance into communion with God; the latter, concerning preparation for entrance into the land of promise. Hence the former relates to the process of reconciliation, affording natural scope for faith and repentance, the first moments of the new-born soul; the latter, to the state of reconciliation, calling into exercise those graces and endowments which grow out of faith in God and repentance towards him. These parts correspond, in some measure, with redemption and salvation, or with the new birth and a holy life, as the beginning and continuance of a state of salvation. The first part contains sixteen chapters, which fall into three sections. Section I. (ch. i.–vii.) treats of the various kinds of offerings; Section II. (ch. viii.–x.) of the consecration of the priests and the accompanying events; Section III. (ch. xi.–xvi.) of the several arrangements pertaining to purity in diet (xi.) and in person (xii.–xv.), and culminating in the day of atonement (xvi.), which had direct and emphatic reference not only to propitiation, but also to purification. There is, therefore, a perfectly logical arrangement in this part — the first seven chapters relating to propitiation, the next three to the appointment of the propitiator, the next five to purification, and the remaining one to a peculiar ordinance which combines propitiation and purification as the two counterparts in the whole of salvation. In the second part, also, there are three subdivisions. Section IV. (ch. xvii.–xx.) refers to the civil life of the regenerate people; Section V. (ch. xxi.–xxiv.) to the religious life; and Section VI. (ch. xxv.–xxvii.) to the matters that affect both the civil and the religious life. The civil matters are abstinence from blood, chastity, holiness, and the sanctions by which the regulations concerning them are enforced. The religious matters are the priests, the offerings, the days, and the house of God. The mixed matters are the Sabbath, the jubilee year, and the vow. Thus we discern a logical principle running through the second part, as well as the first.

It is obvious, from this glance at its contents, that this book is collateral with that of Exodus. Its object is not to advance the narrative, but to embody the ritual, which was necessary for the service of the tabernacle. It records not more than two facts. The first of these is the consecration of Aaron and his sons, which appears to have taken place during the seven days before the first day of the second year of Israel's deliverance. The second is the stoning of the blasphemer, which is recorded after the directions concerning the oil for the lamps and the bread for the table of the Lord (xxiv.), and therefore may have occurred before the erection of the tabernacle. The enactments which form the main substance of the book were most probably communicated to Moses before the formal commencement of the ceremonial worship on the first day of the second year. The only clear exception to this is the portion from the consecration of the priests to the end of the sixteenth chapter (ch. xi.–xvi.). There are three obvious reasons for this conclusion. First, some of the regulations contained in it were necessary for the due performance of the ordinances commenced on the first day of the second year, such as the sacrificial rules (i.–vii.) and the directions concerning the lamps and the shew-bread (xxiv.). Secondly, the consecration of the priests during eight days, the offerings of the princes occupying the twelve or fourteen days after the tabernacle was set up, the celebration of the passover extending over the next eight days, the arrangements of the census, or mustering of the host, and the celebration of the second passover, were sufficient to occupy Moses from the twentieth of the last month to the twentieth of the second month, when they decamped from Mount Sinai; whereas, during the six or seven months of the construction of the tabernacle he must have been at leisure to receive the divine communications recorded in the present book. Thirdly, the Book of Numbers goes back to the day on which Moses had fully set up the tabernacle, which implies that no absolute progress had been made in the narrative up to chapter vii. of that book. Leviticus is, therefore, mainly taken up with those collateral topics which were left out in Exodus in order to allow the stately march of the narrative to come to a fitting close in the setting up of the tabernacle and the solemn inauguration of the national worship.

The communications thus reserved for this book were eminently worthy of being embodied in a separate treatise. The ceremonial observances of ancient Israel were all significant of higher things than themselves, and of the highest things in reference to man. "Wherewithal shall I come before the Lord, and bow myself before the high God?" is the question of transcendent interest for fallen man. The present section of the law is a full and explicit response to this question from the stand-point of the church in the wilderness. The institutions here prescribed place it in the clearest light in which it was capable of being presented to the mind of that day. They are so many lessons, introducing into the sphere of rational contemplation the fundamental principles of salvation by a mediator. They establish a sacrificing priest, presupposing sin and doom in man, proclaiming mercy and grace in God; acknowledging, at the same time, his holiness, justice, and truth; revealing the method of propitiation wherein the deliverer undertakes to fulfil the demands of the law for the transgressor; and implying the change of regeneration, whereby the fallen spirit is raised up again, accepts the Saviour, and turns from enmity to love. The momentous importance of this exposition of the way of salvation to the men of Israel in the days of Moses can scarcely be exaggerated. And its historical value to us, now that it is touched with the hoar of a venerable antiquity, is unquestionably great. It is the ancient text, of which the New Testament is the practical and exegetical commentary. In the Gospels we have the fourfold history of that atonement actually accomplished which its ordinances prefigure; in the Acts of the Apostles we read of the first steps of that new life which is shadowed forth in its second part; and in the Epistles, especially the Epistle to the Hebrews, we have the inspired interpretation of those typical acts and things in it which point to that great event whereby eternal redemption was obtained. This book is therefore exceedingly helpful to us, not only from the intrinsic value of its contents, but from the historical account which it renders of a remarkable stage in the development of that system of symbolic ordinances by which the way of reconciliation with God was exhibited and prognosticated.

We append a scheme of the contents of the book:

Entrance into Life.	Section I. Sacrifices,	Chap. i.-vii.
	Section II. Consecration of the Priests,	viii.-x.
	Section III. Cleansing. Atonement,	xi.-xvi.
Progress in Life.	Section IV. Rules in Matters Civil,	xvii-xx.
	Section V. Rules in Matters Religious,	xxi.-xxiv.
	Section VI. Rules in Matters Civil and Religious,	xxv.-xxvii.

COMMENTARY ON THE PENTATEUCH.

PART IV.

SECTION I.—OFFERINGS.

I. THE BURNT-SACRIFICE.

ON the first day of the second year from the exodus the tabernacle was set up. On the twentieth day of the second month (Num. x. 11) the sons of Israel set out on their journey from Mount Sinai through the wilderness to the land of promise. In the interval most of the following highly important events must have taken place: The consecration of Aaron and his sons to the priesthood, occupying eight days (Lev. viii.-x.); the preparation of the water of purification (Num. xix.); the dedication of the Levites (Num. viii.); the offerings of the princes of the tribes, occupying twelve days (Num. vii.); the passover, extending over seven days, at least (Num. ix.); the numbering of the people (Num. i.); and the second passover (Num. ix.). The last two events are sufficient to occupy the nineteen days of the second month; and it remains to be seen whether the preceding occurrences can be satisfactorily distributed over the first month. It is natural to suppose that the offerings of the princes were presented on twelve successive days, without any interruption, unless it were the Sabbath. In that case, they should be placed in the fourteen days before the passover. It is possible to arrange the consecration of the priests and the dedication of the Levites for the nine days after the passover at the close of the first month. But this interval would be necessary to prepare for the census, which was to be commenced on the first day of the second month (Num. i.). Moreover, it seems proper to proceed with the consecration of the priests, either before or as an integral part of the formal dedication of the tabernacle, as they were required to discharge some of their highest functions on that occasion and on the following twenty days; and the concurrence of the former with the latter event accords best with the directions given in Ex. xl. 12–15, and the particulars recorded in Lev. ix. The omission of any detail of this incidental ceremony in the account of the setting up of the tabernacle arises from the natural desire of the narrator not to embarrass the record or disturb the grandeur of the leading event of the day. The report of this subordinate circumstance is reserved for another occasion (Lev. viii.–x.). But this is quite consistent with its commencement on the same day with the solemn process of the erection and dedication of the tabernacle. In like manner the offerings of the princes are not mentioned until we come to Num. vii., although it is there stated that they began to be offered on the day on which the tabernacle was set up. Hence the order of events may have been the following: In the process of setting up the tabernacle, which is carried on for seven days, and consummated on the first day of the second year, the consecration of the priests takes place as an essential and concurrent part of the whole ceremony. On the day of its consummation the princes appear prepared with their offerings. The waggons and oxen may have been accepted then and there, and the arrangement made for the successive presentation of their sacrifices on the twelve or thirteen following days. Hence their offerings will have been completed on the fourteenth day of the month, if we allow the Sabbath to be a day of intermission. As the Levites are said to be sprinkled with water of purification, it is most natural to suppose that the preparation of this water (Num. xix.) took place on the second day of the month. The dedication of the Levites, narrated in Num. viii., after the offerings of the princes, and before the account of the passover (Num. ix.), may thus have taken place on the third of the first month, so that they would as soon as possible be regularly qualified to assist the priests in the extraordinary duties they were now called on to perform. Thus everything would be duly arranged for the orderly celebration of the passover on the proper day. We cannot affirm that this was the precise order of all these events; but it seems the most probable, and it serves, at all events, to give a clear and definite conception of the interesting proceedings that took place in the first month, and for some days before and after it.

LEVITICUS I. 1-9.   33

We are here reminded, by some very striking examples, of the law of Hebrew composition, according to which one train of events is brought to a fitting close before the writer pauses to go back for a concurrent train of events that had been omitted for the sake of perspicuity. The setting up of the tabernacle is summarily recorded in Ex. xl. A contemporaneous event — the consecration of the priests, is narrated afterwards, in Lev. viii.-x. It is obvious that this record, with all its attendant circumstances, would have marred very much the effect of the simplicity and beauty of the statement in Ex. xl. An immediately consecutive event — the offerings of the princes — is deferred until the seventh chapter of the following book. The dedication of the Levites, probably concurrent with this, and the celebration of the passover, consequent upon it, are reported in Num. viii. and ix. And all these three events are related after the account of the census (Num. i.) which took place in the beginning of the following month. From all this we learn that Leviticus and a considerable part of Numbers form the needful supplement to the closing chapters of Exodus, and are disposed according to an order of thought, and not of time. It behooves the expositor to discover, as far as possible, this order, if he is to give a fair interpretation to the author. It is plain, at first sight, that the whole narrative in Leviticus may not go beyond the beginning of the first month.

The first section of this book, which is now before us, treats of the different kinds of offerings in seven chapters. The first five lay down general rules concerning the burnt-sacrifice, the oblation, the sacrifice of peace, the sin-sacrifice, and the trespass-offering, for the instruction of the worshipper. The remaining two prescribe certain special rules for the guidance of the priests in regard to these several offerings.

The first chapter relates to the burnt-sacrifice. It contains three paragraphs: the first treating of the ox (1-9); the second, of the sheep or goat (10-13); and the third, of the turtle-dove or pigeon (14-17).

1-9. The ox for a burnt-sacrifice. 1. *Called.* It is not stated who immediately called, whether Joshua, the minister of Moses, or not. But the call was ultimately from the Lord. This phrase occurs here for the fifth and last time. The occasion on which it is employed is always important. In Ex. iii. 4, God called unto him out of the

I. 1. AND he called unto Moses, and the LORD spake unto him out of the tent of meeting, saying, 2. Speak unto the

midst of the bush, and gave him his great commission. In Ex. xix. 3, 20, the Lord called to him to enforce the keeping of the covenant, and to prepare for the giving of the law. In Ex. xxiv. 16, he called unto him out of the midst of the cloud to show him the plan and specifications of the tabernacle and its appurtenances. Here he is called once more to receive another series of regulations concerning the intercourse of the chosen people with the God of mercy. These are contained in the seven following chapters and other parts of the books of Leviticus and Numbers. Hence we perceive that this is a suitable beginning for a new book of the law. *Spake unto him.* This book consists mainly of oral communications from the Lord (see on v. 2) to Moses, usually alone, but, after the consecration of the priests, sometimes in conjunction with Aaron. To understand the book it is necessary to bear this in mind. These are not dated, in respect of time (except xvi. 1), though the place is sometimes given. It is manifest that Moses, having these separate communications by him in a written form, at length put them together, as we find them in Leviticus and Numbers, according to a plan suggested by circumstances, not of time, but of use. Without a knowledge of the use, we cannot judge of the plan. *Out of the tent of meeting.*[1] Commentators usually explain this of the newly erected tabernacle. This is, at least, doubtful. We know there was a tent which Moses took and pitched without the camp afar off, and called the tent of meeting (Ex. xxxiii. 7). We learn from Lev. vii. 38 that Moses received these directions concerning the offerings in Mount Sinai. Now, the tabernacle was not erected on the mount; but the tent of meeting, which Moses pitched afar off from the camp, may have been on the slopes of Sinai. It may have been near, if not on, the spot where the elders waited forty days, until Moses and his minister Joshua returned (Ex. xxiv. 14). These communications would thus be made on mount Sinai. Moreover, these ordinances must have been given to Moses before the setting up of the tabernacle. For the burnt-sacrifice, the sin-sacrifice, and the peace-offering, which had to be presented on the grandest of all occasions when the tabernacle was in process of erection and for

sons of Israel, and say unto them, If any man of you make an offering unto the LORD, of the cattle, of the herd, and of the

twenty days after, are here described for the first time. And in particular the oblation to be presented by Aaron and his sons at their consecration in the same solemnity is specified in this very section (Lev. vi. 12–16). Hence we infer that these seven chapters contain a series of communications which must have been made to Moses in the period antecedent to the erection of the tabernacle and the consecration of the priests, while Bezalel and his assistants were engaged in preparing its various parts and furnishings. This was an interval of comparative leisure to Moses, during which he might receive and commit to writing the successive directions from the mouth of the Lord, which would be requisite at, as well as after, the setting up of the tabernacle. Having in his sublime narrative given the place of prominence to this principal event, he now according to the Hebrew usage, returns to the previous time to record an order of events which was going on parallel with the preparation for the rearing up of the Lord's house.

2. *Any man*, any descendant of fallen Adam. *An offering*.[2] This is the general term for anything presented to the Lord by the intelligent creature. It is a thing brought nigh. It therefore implies an approach to the Creator on the part of the rational creature, a presenting of something to him, and therewith and therein an acknowledgement that he himself belongs to the Lord, a dedication of himself to the Lord. The dedication is the main act of the worshipper expressed by the general term offering, though it is not at all the meaning or essential principle of sacrifice, which is indeed not an act of the worshipper. Such dedication implies regeneration, faith, and all that revival of right feeling in the heart of the sinner towards his merciful God, which is involved in a right approach to him. *The Lord.* It is to be remembered that the original term thus rendered throughout the book, is Jehovah, the self-existent Author of all things and events, and hence the Performer of promise and the Keeper of covenant. This is accordingly the appropriate divine name for a book treating of peace, propitiation, and purification. The name Elohim occurs in it about fifty times, and invariably in relation to some person

flock shall ye make your offering. 3. If his offering be a burnt-sacrifice of the herd, a perfect male he shall offer: at whose God he is said to be, never in an absolute sense. Jehovah occurs about two hundred and six times. *Of the cattle.* Some connect this with the opening (apodosis) of the sentence, thus, "If any man make an offering of the cattle," thereby affording room for the alternative in vs. 14, "If his offering be of the fowl"; but we hold by the Masoretic pointing, and attach it to the close (epitasis) of the sentence, which thus prescribes the standard form of the offering; for which, however, a less costly substitute is afterwards admitted. So in chaps. ii. 2, iv. 28, and v. 6, we have the usual material prescribed first, without any hint of the alternative that is afterwards allowed. A second reason, however, is, that the author is as yet speaking of offerings in general, and his observation, therefore, applies to the whole of the animal offerings, whereas the alternative in vs. 14 refers to the burnt-sacrifice in particular. Cattle are suitable for sacrifices because they are domestic, or home-reared, and thus in some measure connected with man. The same reason applies to poultry. On the other hand, grain and fruits, being products of human industry and therefore, so far, a species of property, are suitable for oblations, which express gratitude or self-dedication on the part of the offerer.

3. *A burnt-sacrifice.*[3] We adopt this variant of the English version for what is usually called the burnt-offering, partly to avoid the frequent use of the word offering in this book, but chiefly to get somewhat nearer to precision. The term whole-burning or holocaust is preferable, so far as it is still more expressive of its real nature; but habit recoils from so much innovation. This is emphatically the sacrifice, the animal sacrifice, the whole sacrifice, the wholly-burnt sacrifice. We meet with the burnt-sacrifice on two interesting occasions in Genesis. Noah, standing once more safe on dry land, took of all clean cattle and of clean fowl, and offered burnt-offerings (Gen. viii. 20). Abraham, having his unreserved obedience put to the test, offered the ram caught in the thicket for a burnt-offering instead of his son (Gen. xxii). From the remark of Isaac to his father, "Behold the fire and the wood, but where is the sheep for a burnt-offering?" it is plain that the burnt-sacrifice was familiar to the mind of that day. It is the earliest of all

LEVITICUS I. 3. 37

the door of the tent of meeting he shall offer it for his acceptance before the LORD. 4. And he shall lay his hand upon

proper sacrifices, and inclusive of them all. Its essential characteristic is propitiation. It therefore presupposes sin and guilt on the part of the creature for whom it is offered, and holiness and mercy on the part of the Creator whom he has offended. And it involves expiation, or the suffering of the punishment incurred, as the indispensable concomitant of propitiation, or the full performance by a mediator of the obedience that had been withheld; expiation made by the death, and propitiation by the perfect and uniform righteousness, of the substitute, warranting the pardon and acceptance of him for whom the substitute has undertaken. The particulars follow. *Of the herd.* A life, a soul, in the wide sense of the animal principle, is needed when propitiation is to be made. Hence the mediator must be a person, a moral being, a voluntary or free agent. The animal soul is but the symbol of what the propitiatory sacrifice must be. As a human life has been forfeited, a human life must be laid down. Not a fallen soul, however; for that needs itself expiation, not to speak of propitiation. Hence the vanity of all merely human sacrifice. The Son of man who is to propitiate must be himself free from the taint of sin. *A perfect*[3] *male.* A male is the complete and all-inclusive sex. So it was with the first Adam, out of whom Eve sprang. This male must be without blemish, to symbolize the moral integrity of the personal victim. Righteousness, perfect obedience, is the antecedent part he must have performed. It is the only ground of propitiation. This is the undeniable reason why a fallen creature can make no atonement. *He shall offer.* By this act the sinner becomes partaker of the benefit of the sacrifice. This implies in him a knowledge of the appointed and revealed way of salvation, a voluntary trust in it and acceptance of it, with all the dispositions which befit such an act — shame, regret, repentance, gratitude, good-will. *For his acceptance;*[3] that he may be accepted. This is the rendering of the Sept., Onkelos, and Jerome. The phrase must be so rendered in Leviticus xxiii. 11; and this rules other cases. "Of his own voluntary will"[3] would be otherwise expressed. The acceptance includes the pardon as well as the acquittal. It comes in here appropriately, where the moral perfection, which is its ground, is intimated.

the head of the burnt-sacrifice: and it shall be accepted for him to atone for him. 5. And he shall slay the steer before

It is the crowning characteristic of propitiation. *Before the Lord.* At the door of the tent of meeting, of the Father's home; at the throne of grace, though it may be afar off, and by a mediator, he appears to present the atoning sacrifice.

4. *Lay[4] his hand.* The verb, to lean upon, does not seem to have any stress upon it here. It does not mean to press upon, but simply to lay. Laying the hand on is the solemn act of designating or destinating to a certain purpose. Thus Joshua is formally destined to be the successor of Moses (Num. xxvii. 8, 23). So here the ox is destined to be symbolically all that is implied in the burnt-sacrifice. This significant act has come down to us from a hoary antiquity. Jacob lays his hands on Joseph's sons to bless them (Gen. xlviii. 14). When the English phrase represents the verb denoting to stretch forth, violence is often meant by it (Gen. xxii. 12; Ex. vii. 4). The laying on of the offerer's hand is expressive of his faith, his trust in the revealed mercy of God, and his acceptance of the ransom which he has provided. *It shall be accepted for him.* This is the positive part of justification, and is prominent and emphatic in the burnt-sacrifice. *To atone[4] for him.* Literally, to cover, to place a covering over him, sheltering him from the penal consequences of sin, as well as investing him with the endowment of righteousness by the suffering and obedience of another in his stead. Atonement is of the same import with propitiation, which is thus expressly ascribed to the burnt-sacrifice. The positive part of justification always involves the negative, which is pardon.

5. *He shall slay.[5]* Slay is a more general word than sacrifice, which is limited to the slaying of victims. The taking of life from the victim is the expiation. The moral law is summed up in the eighth commandment, Thou shalt not steal (see on Ex. xx. 15), that is, Thou shalt not take by force or guile that which is not thine. If this law be violated, the transgressor is bound to restore the property stolen. This is satisfaction. But this is not all the law of right demands of the wrong-doer. It requires this and something more of the borrower, who has done no wrong. This is therefore no punishment. To understand what the punishment must be, let us come to the ultimate case, that of the

the LORD; and Aaron's sons, the priests, shall offer the blood, and sprinkle the blood upon the altar around, which is at

creature disobeying the Creator. Whatever may be the amount of self-beguiling here practised, there is at the root of all such disobedience the determination to thwart the will, the uniformly and wholly good and holy will, of the Author of his being on the part of the creature. Such a fixed determination, by its very existence, it is evident, forfeits the life that was given, even before the attempt is made to carry it into effect. ʽ When it is actually executed, therefore, the offender by the very act forfeits life. Death, be it remembered, however, is not annihilation. As life is not mere existence, but a holy and happy state of being, so death is not mere loss of existence, but the wreck of all the joys and hopes of a rational and susceptible being, an unholy and unhappy state of being. Death alone, then, can avenge defiance of the Creator. This is expiation, the penalty incurred by sin. Hence, if we are to have expiation by another, by a mediator, it must be by death. The slaying of the victim, then, is the real expiatory sacrifice. *The steer*, literally the son of the herd. This includes the calf[5] of a year old and the bullock or ox of greater age. *And Aaron's sons, the priests.* Any one of them was sufficient for the duty. The high priest himself merely presided on these occasions. The previous acts, it is to be observed, are performed by the offerer himself. The priest now comes forward. He has to appear, because the brute creature is not sufficient to signify all that is done by a mediating act, which can only be effected by a person. Even the merely human priest, though a person, is only a figure of the real mediator in this process, since he is disqualified by his fallen nature, as well as otherwise, for actual mediation. As mediator he has two parts to perform, one for the offender and another for the offended. These come out in the sequel. *The blood*, which is the life of the victim (Gen. ix. 4), is solemnly presented by the priest for the life of the offerer, and accepted by the God of mercy who has appointed the atonement. This is the first act of the priest, as distinct from the worshipper. In the primeval state the head of the house was priest for himself and his household. The priests are not only to present the blood, but to sprinkle it on the altar of God, to indicate palpably that the expia-

the door of the tent of meeting. 6. And he shall flay the burnt-sacrifice, and cut it into its pieces. 7. And the sons of Aaron the priest shall put fire upon the altar, and lay wood upon the fire. 8. And Aaron's sons, the priests, shall lay the

tion is made to him. In this act the priest represents the sinner, tendering a positive and negative satisfaction to the law on his behalf. The blood is the negative satisfaction; the freedom from blemish in the victim whose blood is shed expresses the positive satisfaction. *The altar*,[5] literally the place of slaughter, because the victim was sometimes laid bound on the altar, and there slain (Gen. xxii. 9, 10). *Around*, on all sides, in token of completeness. *At the door of the tent of meeting.* The space in front of the door of the tabernacle was a square of fifty cubits, or about seventy-five feet. The altar was situated probably about twenty-five feet from the gate of the court, and the laver half way between it and the door of the tabernacle (Ex. xxvii. 18; xxx. 18). At the distance of fifty feet, therefore it was said to be at the door of the tabernacle.

6. *And he*, the worshipper. *Shall flay.* It is not necessary to seek a meaning in every minute detail of the process. Yet, the flaying of the victim presents a striking figure of the moral nakedness produced by sin. It also points to the coats of skin with which our first parents were clothed. *Its pieces*, the pieces into which the animal was usually cut for consumption as food. These were said to be twelve in number. 7. *And the sons of Aaron.* The second act of the priests was to burn the sacrifice on the altar. Preparatory to this they put the fire and wood upon the altar. This mechanical part might have been performed by an inferior priest or a Levite, had it not been connected with the altar. At all events when the fire was once kindled, it was kept perpetually burning (Lev. iv. 6), so that this act had only to be performed once. 8. *And Aaron's sons.* This is apparently a third part, but in strict reality, the second part, of the priest's office, for which the putting on of the fire was a mere preparation. Abarbanel, indeed, states that as the worshipper had five things to do, namely, to lay his hand on the victim, kill, flay, cut it up, and wash the inwards, so the priest had five things to do, namely, to receive the blood in a vessel, to sprinkle it, to put fire on the altar,

pieces, the head, and the tallow upon the wood that is on the fire which is upon the altar. 9. But its inwards and its legs shall he wash with water: and the priest shall burn the whole

lay on the wood, and lay the pieces on the wood. This is important, as it indicates to whom the several parts were assigned in the estimation of the Jewish Rabbis.[8] *The pieces, the head, and the tallow.*[8] The head is here distinguished from the pieces, because it was removed before the division into pieces. The tallow is a word that occurs only three times, twice in this chapter and once in the eighth. It is so rendered simply to distinguish it from the usual word for fat. This was taken in a mass from the inwards. In all sacrifices it was consumed by fire on the altar. 9. *Its inwards and its legs.* These parts are washed, because it was meet and customary to wash them before they were used for food. The hind legs,[9] which are chiefly meant by this word, are particularly liable to be defiled in animals. *Shall he,* the worshipper. *Wash.* All the acts that are not connected with the altar are performed by the worshipper himself. *And the priest.* At the close of the process it is said that the priest shall burn the whole upon the altar, which is merely the completion of the second function he has to discharge. This second part he performs as the representative of the merciful God, who by this significant act accepts the death and obedience of the substitute on behalf of the penitent offender. This is manifest from the fact that the Lord on certain great occasions kindles the altar-pile without the intervention of the priest (Lev. ix. 24; Judg. vi. 21; 1 Kings xviii. 38). Thus we see there are four parts in the great work of atonement: the righteousness and the death of the victim, and the presentation and the acceptance of these by which they become a propitiation. Righteousness can only be rendered and penal death can only be suffered by a moral agent, and for a man by a man. Hence the true victim can only be a person. This same person it is who intervenes to present satisfaction from himself to God, and receive acceptance from God to himself for the penitent, believing offerer. With equal certainty it may be affirmed that the latter two parts can only be performed by a divine person. It is not competent to any mere creature to present his obedience or his death for another, simply because he has not the requisite independence.

upon the altar, a burnt-sacrifice, a fire-offering of a sweet smell unto the LORD.

He who owes all to his Maker cannot by any possibility answer for another. And this is the condition of every creature. Much less can any creature take upon himself to accept on the part of God the service of the substitute on behalf of the penitent. *Shall burn,*[9] turn into smoke and odor. Fire here performs the part of the digestive organ in man. Hence the sacrifice is called bread or food (Lev. iii. 11; xxi. 6). It resolves the sacrifice into its elementary parts, which mingle as gases and flavors with the air of heaven. It thus comes as a grateful perfume before the sense of smell. *The whole.* The whole victim is burned upon the altar to represent the full propitiation for sin. The burnt-sacrifice is also the model and complex of all sacrifices, and on this account it is fitting that the whole should go up on the altar. But a further reason is that it is the propitiation not for a particular transgression, but for a sinful state, with all its outward manifestations. *A burnt-sacrifice,* a lifting, a thing going up on the altar, a general name for a sacrifice. If taken from another root denoting wrong or moral evil,[9] it would mean a propitiation for moral evil, and would still be a term of broad and deep significance. It points to the great propitiation by which atonement is made, once for all, on behalf of returning, hoping, penitent man. This he pleads at the beginning of his new life, and continues to plead as long as he is subject to sin and temptation. *A fire-offering*; a firing or offering made by fire. This belongs to the burnt-sacrifice but not exclusively. It is common to all offerings that were laid on the altar. *Of a sweet smell.*[9] The sense of smell is akin to that of taste. It is naturally introduced here, where the offering by fire has diffused itself through the air in savory fumes. It is a refined species of taste, and therefore the fitter to symbolize a spiritual feeling. The sweetness, acquiescence, or satisfaction is expressive of the intense pleasure which is derived from the odor which scents the air. *Unto the Lord.* This lifts us up from the region of sense, and reminds us that we are on the heights of the moral consciousness. By the highly expressive figure of an exquisite perfume is conveyed to us the pure delight, the supreme complacence, with which the Lord regards and receives the propitiation

10. And if his offering be of the flock, of the sheep or of the goats, for a burnt-sacrifice, a perfect male shall he offer. 11. And he shall slay it at the flank of the altar northward before the LORD: and Aaron's sons, the priests, shall sprinkle

for the sins of man made by the all-sufficient Mediator. This atonement springs from the benign purpose of his own merciful breast. It has been tendered by one who is infinitely able and worthy and willing to interpose. And it is gladly accepted by him who is merciful and gracious, as well as holy and true.

Such is the burnt-sacrifice. It is the sum and substance of all sacrifice. It includes expiation and satisfaction, which are combined in propitiation. The trembling sinner who lays his hand on the head of the victim is fully aware that its whole intent and content is the Mediator doing and dying, bleeding and interceding, feeling and bearing, for the sinner, and that the sinner's feeling in presenting it is altogether external to its intrinsic significance. They gravely err who imagine that the sacrifice of Scripture is the expression of self-surrender on the part of the offerer.[a] It is the offering of it that expresses the feeling of the offerer. The sacrifice itself expresses solely the feeling and dealing of the Mediator for the trustful penitent who ventures, in the tumult of his spiritual emotions, to lay his hands on it. Let us carefully distinguish here. In the burnt-sacrifice we have on the part of the offerer, penitence and trust; on the part of the Mediator, expiation and propitiation; and on the part of the Accepter, pardon and acceptance. The first may be expressed by the single word faith, the second by atonement, and the third by justification. It is obvious to the judicious reader that the atonement is the direct theme of this chapter, and that the feelings of the offerer and the Accepter lie comparatively in the background.

10–13. The sheep or goat for a burnt-sacrifice. This was designed for the middle class, who could not afford the steer. The regulations are in substance the same as before. 11. *At the flank*[11] *of the altar, northward.* The place where the victims were to be slain is now indicated for the first time. The one specification supplies what is wanting in the other. This affords room for a little variety in the statement. The place assigned for the slaughter of the burnt-sacrifice

its blood upon the altar around. 12. And he shall cut it into its pieces, with its head and its tallow; and the priest shall lay them upon the wood that is on the fire which is upon the altar. 13. And the inwards and the legs he shall wash with water; and the priest shall offer the whole, and burn it upon the altar; it is a burnt-sacrifice, a fire-offering of a sweet smell unto the LORD. ¶

14. And if his offering to the Lord be a burnt-sacrifice of the fowl, he shall make his offering of the turtles or of the pigeons. 15. And the priest shall offer it at the altar, and pinch off its head, and burn it on the altar: and its blood

is expressly extended to the sin-sacrifice and the trespass-offering, and serves no doubt for all sacrifices. The north, according to Tholuck, is selected because it is the cold and dark region, and therefore akin to death. The altar was no doubt regarded as facing the tabernacle. The place of slaughter was in that case at the right hand, which is strong to smite. The place of offering was, according to Jewish tradition (Joseph. Jewish Wars, V. 5, 6), at the left hand, which is near the heart, and is often employed in giving. The cup-bearer presented the cup on his left hand. The place of ashes was in the rear, and the place of the laver in the front. Ezekiel, indeed (xliii. 17) states that the steps in his symbolic altar are to look toward the east. But this probably means that the ascent, though on the south side, was not at right-angles, but parallel to it, and rising from the east, a not unusual and much more convenient arrangement for those who officiated. The prohibition of steps to the altar (Ex. xx. 26), seems to refer to the open ladder which was in use at the time, and not to the earthen slope or the boarded or enclosed stair. 12. *With its head and its tallow.* The preceding verb is used in a pregnant sense, to signify taking off the head and tallow, as well as dividing the body into its pieces.

14–17. The dove or pigeon for a burnt-sacrifice. The fowl is allowed as a burnt-sacrifice for the poorest class. The turtle-dove and the pigeon were common in Palestine. They were suitable emblems of innocence. 15. *Pinch off its head.* The head seems to have been immediately laid on the altar, as it had to be burned along

shall be poured out on the wall of the altar. 16. And he shall take away its crop with its dirt, and cast it beside the altar eastward in the place of the ashes. 17. And he shall cleave it with its wings, but not divide it; and the priest shall burn it upon the altar, on the wood that is on the fire: it is a burnt-sacrifice, a fire-offering of a sweet smell unto the LORD. §

with the body. The blood is to be squeezed out on the wall of the altar. 16. *Its crop with its dirt.*[16] The first "its" refers to the fowl; but the second refers to the crop, and hence its contents, and not the feathers, as the Sept. has it, must be the meaning of the word in the original (Rosenm.). This is to be cast on the ash-heap at the east end of the altar. 17. *Cleave it with its wings.* He is to split it up the middle, so that a wing is on each side, but not to complete the separation.

In all these victims we see the four essentials of the burnt-sacrifice, the perfection and the death of the victim, the sprinkling of the blood and the burning of the body upon the altar. The slaying and the sprinkling of the blood symbolize the expiation for sin. The perfection and the burning of the whole shadow forth the satisfaction made by a perfect obedience. The two combined constitute the propitiation in its symbolic form. This sacrifice comprehends the essence of all the sacrifices. It was presented on account of sin as a habitude of the fallen soul at the commencement of a religious profession as the only mode of access to God, and at fitting seasons as the sole ground of its continuance, in the morning and evening of every day on the national altar, in all the great festivals, and on other suitable occasions. It is thus distinguished from the sin-sacrifice and the trespass-offering, which referred to particular acts or occasions of sin, and from the sacrifice of peace, which was expressive of the blessings of fellowship with God. It was distinguished from the oblation, as a sacrifice for sin is distinct from a mere gift of gratitude or acknowledgment.

NOTES.

1. *Tent,* אֹהֶל, it consists of a haircloth awning. It is different from מִשְׁכָּן, *the mansion,* consisting of the wall of boards with an inner

curtain of linen (Ex. xxvi. 1, 12). In the tabernacle the former covered the latter.

2. *Offering*, קָרְבָּן, a thing brought near; the general name for any thing presented to the Lord. There were three classes of Corbanim: 1. Dedication gifts for the sanctuary; 2. Taxes for the maintenance of worship (first-fruits, tithes, first-born), and 3. Altar-offerings (Kurtz on Sacrifice). The word is here applied to the latter alone.

3. *Burnt-sacrifice*, עֹלָה, that which goes up, to wit, on the altar. כָּלִיל, *whole*, is applied to it in 1 Sam. vii. 9, and is presumed to denote it in Deut. xxxiii. 10. In Ps. li. 2 it seems distinct from it. It is also applied to the priest's oblation (Lev. vi. 15) and to many other things. *Perfect*, תָּמִים, having no blemish or defect in health or parts. " This freedom from blemish symbolizes the sinlessness and holiness of the true sacrifice " (Keil), but not at all the sanctification of the worshipper, who is not the burnt-sacrifice, nor that of which it is the symbol. *For his acceptance*, לִרְצֹונֹו, to gain for him acceptance with God. This demonstrates the propitiatory nature of the עֹלָה against all who deem it a mere expression of devotion. It is corroborated by the following verse. *Of his own will*, כִּרְצֹנוֹ, or rather in the present connection לִנְדָבָה (Lev. vii. 16; 2 Chron. xxxv. 8).

4. *Lay*, סָמַךְ, literally *lean*. It cannot denote "a transfer of the feelings of the offerer to the victim," because it is not the present disposition of the worshipper that *propitiates*, which is here declared to be the end of the burnt-sacrifice. *To atone*, לְכַפֵּר, to cover another, by standing over him to bear what he has incurred and do what he has failed to do, that he may not only escape the penalty of his sin, but obtain the reward of obedience. This is a term of fundamental importance in this book. The plain statement that the עֹלָה, *atones* proves that it does not denote the " self-surrender " of the offerer, as Keil and others think.

5. *Slay*, שָׁחַט, is very often used of the slaying of victims, though זָבַח is the technical word for sacrifice. *Calf*, עֵגֶל; *ox*, פַּר. *Altar*, מִזְבֵּחַ, place of sacrifice.

8. The five acts of the priest are reducible to two; the former including the receiving and sprinkling of the blood, and the latter the laying on of the fire, the wood, and the pieces of the victim. These two acts might, after the first occasion, be decorously performed in two

minutes by one priest, and in one minute by two. *Tallow* פֶּדֶר, *adeps a carne sejunctus* (Boch.), the mass of fat separable from the intestines.

9. *Legs,* כְּרָעַיִם, the hind legs, with which the locusts leap (xi. 21); r. כָּרַע, *bend*, crouch as the lion on his hind legs (Gen. xlix. 9). *Burn,* הִקְטִיר, burn as incense. קְטֹרֶת, that which is burned as incense on the altar. This makes a point of connection between the brazen altar and the golden altar. *Burnt-sacrifice,* עֹלָה sometimes עוֹלָה; which may be compared with עַוְלָה, *wickedness*. This would be like חַטָּאת, *sin* and *sin-sacrifice,* אָשָׁם, *trespass* and *trespass-offering*; But see on vs. 3. *A sweet smell,* רֵיחַ־נִיחוֹא, a savor or odor of acquiescence or complacence. This proves that the fire-offering denotes propitiation by the victim, not self-surrender by the worshipper. It concurs also with previous statements to show that the sprinkling of the blood and the burning of the flesh are related, not as the justification and sanctification of the saved (Keil), but as the *obedientia passiva et activa* of the Saviour. The former would be a strange mingling of the outward work of the mediator with the inward disposition of him for whom he mediates in the one sacrificial process.

11. *Flank,* יָרֵךְ, literally *thigh*, and hence the hinder part of the side.

16. *Its dirt,* נֹצָתָהּ, from יָצָא, *go forth*. The suffix is feminine, and therefore refers to מֻרְאָה, *crop*. If it meant feathers, it would be from נָצָה, *flee*.

II. THE OBLATION.

The oblation, or meat-offering, is simply a gift or donation consisting of some vegetable product, mainly grain or meal in some form, to the Lord as expressive of good works as the ground of the means of life, of this life primarily, and ultimately of eternal life. It either accompanied a proper sacrifice or implied a previous atonement, on the ground of which alone it could be acceptable. Of these there are three kinds here mentioned, the second admitting of three varieties. The show-bread and other forms of oblation will present themselves afterwards.

1–3. The oblation of flour. 1. *An oblation.*[1] This term we may use to denote the meat-offering as a special kind of the more general

48   THE OBLATION.

II. 1. AND when a soul makes an offering of an oblation unto the LORD, his offering shall be flour; and he shall pour oil upon it, and put frankincense upon it. 2. And he shall bring it to Aaron's sons, the priests, and he shall take thence his neaf-ful of its flour and of its oil with all its frankincense; and the priest shall burn the memorial of it upon the altar, a

offering; namely, the offering of grain, as a vegetable product, which had a propitiatory, but no expiatory, significance. *Flour*, fine wheaten meal. *Oil*, the pure extract of the olive tree. *Frankincense*. Olibanum, the *thus* or frankincense of the ancients, is said to be a gum-resin exuded from the Boswellia thurifera or libanus, of the natural order Burseraceae, which grows in Arabia and India. The three ingredients which thus enter into the oblation are significant of the perfect obedience and entire consecration that are due to God. The oil is the emblem of a hallowed mind, illuminated and purified by the Spirit of truth; the frankincense, of a holy will rising to heaven in prayer and intercession (Rev. v. 8); and the flour, of the active and productive power of a spiritual nature. These are the qualities of him who is at once the Righteousness and Intercessor of the penitent believer.

2. *And he shall take thence.* From v. 12 it appears that it was the part of the officiating priest to take the handful. This is in keeping with the previous clause. When the worshipper brings it to the priest, we expect the latter to act. Such an act accords also with the priest receiving the blood. *His neaf-ful.*[2] This old word enables us to give a distinct term in the version for the distinct term in the original. It means the hand made hollow for the purpose of grasping and holding it full. The Rabbis describe it as the three fingers bent over the palm, and the thumb and the little finger closing the aperture above and below. It is probable the original handful was larger than this seems to be. It was to include part of the meal and oil and the whole of the frankincense. *And the priest.* This is the principal and properly sacerdotal act, to which the taking of the handful was merely preparative. Hence the writer is careful to mention expressly that the priest burns the handful on the altar. *The memorial of it,* the portion which brings to remembrance the whole offering itself, and

LEVITICUS I. 2–5. 49

fire-offering of a sweet smell unto the LORD. 3. And the remnant of the oblation shall belong to Aaron and his sons: it is a thing most holy of the fire-offerings of the LORD. §
4. And if thou make an offering of an oblation baken in the oven; it shall be of flour, sweet cakes mingled with oil, or sweet wafers anointed with oil. §
5. And if thy offering be an oblation on a pan, it shall be of flour, sweet bread mingled with oil. 6. Thou shalt break it in pieces, and pour oil thereon; it is an oblation. §

therewith him who offered it before the Lord; not, as some say, the odor of it, which is mentioned afterwards. *A fire-offering of a sweet smell.* It is hence to be regarded as itself propitiatory in its nature, and presupposes the sacrifice that both expiates and propitiates. 3. *And the remnant.* The whole belongs to the Lord to whom it has been presented. The memorial is gone up as a perfume into the air of heaven. The remnant is assigned by the Lord to his priests. *A thing most holy.* This extraordinary holiness pertains, it seems, to that which makes atonement or is consecrated or devoted to God, which therefore belongs entirely to him, and hence to the oblation, the sin-sacrifice, the trespass-offering, the vow, and the thing devoted. The burnt-sacrifice is not expressly distinguished as most holy, probably because no part of it was to be eaten. Eating by the priest was a mode of acceptance as well as consuming by fire on the altar.

4–13. The oblation of cakes or baked meat. Of this there are three varieties. 4. The first is cooked in the oven. *Baken*, or cooked. This kind of oblation is thus distinguished from the former, which consisted merely of undressed flour. *In the oven*, the portable oven, or large baking vessel, which is still used in the East. *Sweet*,[4] unleavened, the one a positive term like the original, the other a negative. *Cakes*,[4] perforated or round, of a convenient thickness for a substantial meal. *Mingled with oil.* The oil is not poured on them when shaped, but mingled with the flour, and kneaded up in it. *Wafers*, pan-cakes, or thin cakes. *Anointed*, spread or smeared with oil after being shaped.

5, 6. The second kind of baked flour is prepared *on a pan*, an iron

7

THE OBLATION.

7. And if thy offering be an oblation in a pot, it shall be made of flour with oil. 8. And thou shalt bring the oblation that is made of these unto the LORD: and he shall present it to the priest, and he shall bring it unto the altar. 9. And the priest shall lift from the oblation the memorial of it, and burn it upon the altar, a fire-offering of a sweet smell unto the LORD. 10. And the remnant of the oblation Aaron and his sons shall have: it is a thing most holy of the fire-offerings of the LORD. 11. No oblation which ye shall offer unto the LORD shall be made with leaven; for ye shall burn no leaven

plate (Ezek. iv. 3), still used by the Arabs and other Orientals for baking round cakes or bannocks. It is also mingled with oil and unleavened. 6. *Break it in pieces.* Such fritters soaked in oil or butter are common among the Bedouins.

7–13. The third kind is boiled *in a pot*, a deep vessel used for boiling. Hence this oblation was a kind of pudding. The ingredients are flour and oil. 8. *Thou shalt bring.* It is to be brought unto the Lord, into the court of the tabernacle, the dwelling-place of the Lord. *He shall present it.* The person is here changed from the second to the third; a deviation not unusual. Here it serves to generalize the rule. *Bring it to the altar.* The agent here is usually considered to be the priest. If, however, it be the offerer, he merely brings it to the priest who stands by the altar. In this case it simply completes the previous statement. 9. *And the priest.* His agency now certainly begins. *Shall lift.*[9] This is the word from which the *terumah*, or heave-offering, is derived. But it seems to be used in the ordinary sense of raising or taking up (Keil; see Lev. iii. 3; iv. 8). *The memorial of it*, not now a handful, but a single cake, or a spoonful of the fritters or pudding. The frankincense is wanting in the second kind of oblation.

11–13. Two general directions concerning the oblation are here given. It is to contain leaven never and salt always. 11. *No oblation .... made with leaven.* Leaven is a portion of sour dough, which, when mingled with the fresh mass, sours it also. *No leaven nor*

nor honey in any fire-offering unto the LORD. 12. An offering of first-fruits ye may make of them unto the LORD; but they shall not go upon the altar for a sweet smell. 13. And every offering of thy oblation shalt thou season with salt; and thou shalt not stop the salt of the covenant of thy God from thy oblation. On all thine offerings thou shalt offer salt. §

honey.[11] The latter word certainly denotes the honey of bees (Judg. xiv. 8). A kind of syrup is made in the East from the grape or the date which the Arabs call *dibs.* Some suppose this was also denoted by the Hebrew word. The honey of bees is gathered from the cups of flowers, and is therefore mainly a vegetable product, and partakes of the qualities of the plants from which it is taken, and hence it is sometimes poisonous. It is capable of the vinous fermentation, and therefore may, like leaven, cause the fermentation of dough. Fermentation is a kind of decomposition, and consequently of corruption. It therefore symbolizes evil, and that which is capable of this significance is excluded from the offerings of the altar. 12. *An offering of first-fruits.*[12] First-fruits here is the first of any product of the field. The first-fruits of both sour dough and honey are to be accepted. But they *shall not go up on the altar* as a fire-offering, as they cannot be accepted as a sign of propitiation or consecration. 13. *Season with salt.* Salt, in contrast with leaven, has the quality of preserving from corruption or putrefaction. It serves, therefore, to typify integrity and security, qualities which comport with salvation. *Of the covenant.* The covenant is the compact, expressed or understood, which necessarily arises from the co-existence of moral beings standing in some tangible relation to one another. In the present case it is the compact between Jehovah and man, the terms of which are exhibited in the law, or the written revelation communicated by Moses and enlarged by successive prophets. One term of the covenant of grace is, that a mediator and substitute for fallen man should fulfil the law and suffer the penalty of its breach. A covenant so fulfilled on behalf of man can never fail him who relies on it. It is a covenant of salt forever (Num. xviii. 19). The use of salt to indicate the stability and perpetuity of the covenant was known among all nations. *On all*

14. And if thou offer an oblation of early fruits unto the LORD, ears parched in the fire, grits of the first grain thou shalt make the oblation of thy early fruits. 15. And thou shalt put oil upon it, and lay frankincense thereon: it is an oblation. 16. And the priest shall burn the memorial of it,

thine offerings. This shows that the use of salt was not confined to the oblation, but was common to all kinds of offerings.

14–16. The third kind of oblation, that of early fruits. The early fruits were the first portion of the fruits of the earth presented to the Lord, as an acknowledgement that the whole came from him, in order that all the after-fruits gathered in might be blessed and consecrated for the use of the pious owner. 14. *Ears* [14] of corn, fully formed, but still tender. This gave the name of Abib to the first month of the sacred year, which contained the vernal equinox, and was therefore the month of green ears in Palestine. *Parched in the fire.* The Syrians, Arabs, and Kopts were wont to broil or toast the soft ears in the blaze of the fire. *Grits.*[14] The grits, or scorched grains, were then separated from the straw and chaff. *The fresh grain.*[14] This word means a fruitful field or cultivated garden, and then the vegetable product which grew on it. Here it denotes the full grown, but still tender, wheat. The grain thus prepared was roasted on a pan and regarded as a very palatable dish. 15. The frankincense here appears again along with the oil. 16. This oblation is treated in the same way as the first.

The offerer presents these means of nourishment and enjoyment as the fruit of perfect obedience on the part of the Mediator between himself and his God. Representing this obedience they are accepted. The Creator confirms the worshipper in the possession of all earthly blessings, and in these as types of greater things, even of all heavenly blessings needful for the soul. It is manifest that the oil is the emblem of the Spirit's influence, as the incense is the symbol of the Redeemer's work. The bread also bears a relation to the Father, who giveth bread to his children. It is obvious, also, that the Messiah, as a prophet, gives light to the mind, as a priest, makes intercession for the soul, and as a king, bestows the bread of life on his people. In these two

of its grits and of its oil, with all its frankincense, a fire-offering unto the LORD. ¶

chapters we have the two great classes of offerings expounded to us in their primitive form. The oblation was apparently at first comprehensive of both the bloodless and the bleeding offerings, as the offerings of both Cain and Habel were called by this name (Gen. iv. 4, 5, When the burnt-sacrifice received a distinct name (Gen. viii. 20), the oblation came to be limited to the vegetable offering. In a fallen world where an atonement is needed, the oblation comes in merely as the companion or humble follower of the sacrifice, which represents the full propitiation for sin.

NOTES.

1. *Oblation*, מִנְחָה, gift, tribute, offering. This is an early word, occurring in Gen. iv. 3, 4. It is there inclusive of both animal and vegetable offerings. Its special meaning as a vegetable offering appears first in Ex. xxix. 41. *Flour* סֹלֶת, fine, sifted wheaten meal. *Frankincense*, לְבֹנָה, the *luban* of the Arabs. Hence, Olibanum.

2. *Neaf*, קֹמֶץ, the hand closed upon its contents. It occurs only three times, here and in Lev. v. 12; vi. 8. The verb means to take a handful.

4. *Sweet*, מַצָּה, compact, close in the grain, and not raised or swollen by leaven. The cognate מָצַץ means *to squeeze* or *suck out*. Sweet is a secondary quality retained in the absence of leaven. *Cake* חַלָּה, from חָלַל, *perforate* (Ges.) *be round* (F.).

9. *Lift*, חֵרִים, whence תְּרוּמָה, *a lifting, heaving*.

11. *Honey*, דְּבַשׁ. The root probably means to knead or press together (Ges. F.).

12. *First-fruits*, רֵאשִׁית, now of vegetables; but sometimes also the firstlings of cattle.

14. *Early-fruits*, בִּכּוּרִים, in this form always applied to vegetable products. *Ears of Corn*, אָבִיב, from אָבַב, *bud* or *shoot*, as grain. *Parched*, קָלוּי, also, קָלִי. *Grain*, כַּרְמֶל, a fruitful field, and hence the fruit of the field, whether of the tree or the herb. כֶּרֶם, *vineyard*, and also *choice vine*.

III. THE SACRIFICE OF PEACE.

The sacrifice[1] is distinguished from the burnt-sacrifice by this, that, while the burnt-sacrifice was a victim wholly consumed upon the altar, the sacrifice was a victim of which the flesh was eaten by the offerer, and those whom he invited to partake of it. In this we have a kind of sacrificial feast, very familiar to all ancient nations. Mention is made of it as early as Gen. xxxi. 54, where Jacob made a sacrifice on the mount, and called his brethren to eat bread. Here the sacrifice ends in a common meal, representing the blessings of the new life of reconciliation with God. In like manner Jethro offered sacrifices to God, and Aaron and all the elders of Israel came to eat bread with him before God (xviii. 12). On this ground the passover is a species of the sacrifice (Ex. xii. 27; xxxiv. 25), in which the whole family shared as heirs together of the benefits of redemption. The same characteristic, namely, of a solemn feast of the worshippers upon the victim, appears more or less distinctly in all the notices of the sacrifice; for example, in 1 Sam. ii. 13; ix. 12; xx. 29, and 2 Chron. vii. 4, 5. In accordance with this, the sacrifice is often added as a distinct thing from the burnt-sacrifice, as in Ex. x. 25; Lev. xvii. 8; Num. xv. 3–5; 2 Kings v. 17; Josh. xxii. 28. We find also the three kinds of offering discussed in the first three chapters of our book enumerated as a triad in Josh. xxii. 29, and Jer. xvii. 26. From all this we are warranted to infer that in the sacrifice, strictly so called, the believing, hoping worshipper eats the flesh of the victim as a solemn feast before the Lord, in token of his participation in the rights and means of eternal life flowing from the propitiation for sin. It reaches beyond the burnt-sacrifice therefore, as the benefits resulting from propitiation reach beyond the propitiation itself. By the holocaust the sinner enters into the kingdom of grace; by the sacrifice he enjoys all the privileges and blessings of the kingdom into which he has entered.

The ordinary species of this sacrifice is the sacrifice of peace.[1] This phrase appears first in the time of Moses (Ex. xxiv. 5; xxxii. 6), after the redemption from Egypt and the renewal of the covenant. It is rendered sacrifice of salvation (Sept.), of sanctities (Onk.), of the pacific (Jer.), of thanksgiving (Trem.), or of the perfect (Gerund.).

III. 1. And if his offering be a sacrifice of peace, if he offer of the herd, whether male or female, he shall offer it perfect before the LORD. 2. And he shall lay his hand upon

The reasons are even more various than the renderings. We may combine most of the renderings by understanding that it is the sacrifice of those who are already saved, sanctified, at peace with God, thankful for his grace, and perfect in the substitute he has provided. The burnt-sacrifice is the propitiation by which the worshipper is reconciled to God; and hence it stands at the beginning of the new life, and refers to the ground and rise of that life. The sacrifice of peace is an act and expression of fellowship with God after he has been reconciled. It is strictly a symbolic realization of the blessings of salvation. Hence it follows the burnt-sacrifice, and attests the freedom of access, which the children of God have to him in all the joys and sorrows of life on earth (Lev. vii. 13; Judg. xx. 26). This is its leading characteristic. Still it is a bleeding sacrifice, to intimate that access to God is only and always through the intercession of a mediator who has opened the way by a true and full propitiation. Thus we perceive that the burnt-sacrifice signifies propitiation, the oblation intercession, and the sacrifice of peace communion consequent upon propitiation and intercession. As the holocaust expresses that which is necessary for all, provision is made in the dove or pigeon for its being open to the poorest. As access to God is the privilege of his people without the speciality of another offering, the sacrifice of peace is voluntary. It is, therefore, a male or a female, of the herd or of the flock only, because a dove or pigeon would not suffice for the social meal. Three kinds of sacrifice of peace are mentioned in Lev. vii. 12-16. The chapter before us contains regulations for one of the herd (1-5), or of the sheep (6-11), or a goat (12-17), as a peace sacrifice.

1-5. One of the herd for a sacrifice of peace. 1. *A sacrifice of peace.*[1] This is the usual phrase in Leviticus. *Male or female.* The liberty of choice arises partly from the spontaneous nature of the offering. *Perfect.* It is to be remembered that it is a sacrifice, and every victim represents the mediator, who must be himself of spotless integrity. 2. All the particulars here mentioned are the same, and

THE SACRIFICE OF PEACE.

the head of his offering, and slay it at the door of the tent of meeting; and Aaron's sons, the priests, shall sprinkle the blood upon the altar around. 3. And he shall offer of the sacrifice of peace a fire-offering unto the LORD, the fat that covereth the inwards, and all the fat that is upon the inwards. 4. And the two kidneys and the fat that is on them, which is by the flanks; and the caul upon the liver, with the kidneys he shall take it away. 5. And Aaron's sons shall burn it on

have the same meaning as in the whole sacrifice. The slaying of the victim and the sprinkling of the blood denote expiation, which is one part of the prelude to fellowship. 3, 4. *And he shall offer.* This refers to the worshipper. The whole victim is not here to be laid on the altar. The completeness of the sacrifice has been already indicated by the burnt-sacrifice. *The fat.* The pieces that consist of fat are here selected for the fire-offering. The fat is expressive of the holiness which pertains to the substitute, as the blood is significant of the penal death which he has undertaken to suffer. The two go to make up what is called righteousness, or active and passive obedience to the law for the sinner. The fat is sufficient to shadow forth the satisfaction made by an active obedience, and the flesh is reserved for another purpose (Lev. vii. 11–18). This purpose is not here mentioned, because this chapter is entirely devoted to the sacrificial part of the service. *That covereth the inwards.* Quain informs us that " the fat is collected in large quantity round certain internal parts, especially the kidneys. It is deposited beneath the serous membranes, or is collected between their folds, as in the mesentery and omentum." The fat that covers the inwards appears to be that connected with the gastro-colic or great omentum which covers the bowels. The fat upon the inwards is connected with the mesentery and the adjacent parts. *The flanks,*[4] the inner muscles of the loins in the region of the kidneys. *The caul*[4] *upon the liver* seems to be the small omentum which bounds part of the liver and the stomach, and comes into the region of the kidneys, which is itself surrounded with the tunica adiposa, a bed of fatty matter. *He,* the offerer, shall take it away. 5. Aaron's sons now come forward to perform the second part of their office. *On*

the altar upon the burnt-sacrifice which is upon the wood that is on the fire, a fire-offering of a sweet smell unto the LORD. ¶ 6. And if his offering for a sacrifice of peace unto the LORD be of the flock, male or female, he shall offer it perfect. 7. If he make his offering of a lamb, he shall offer it before the LORD. 8. And he shall lay his hand upon the head of his offering, and slay it before the tent of meeting: and Aaron's sons shall sprinkle its blood upon the altar around. 9. And he shall offer of the sacrifice of peace a fire-offering unto the LORD; the fat of it, the entire tail, hard by the spine he shall take it off; and the fat that covereth the inwards, and all the fat that is upon the inwards; 10. And the two kidneys, and the fat that is upon them, which is by the flanks, and the caul upon the liver, with the kidneys he shall take it away. 11. And

the burnt-sacrifice. Not after the manner of the burnt-sacrifice, but upon it (Lev. vi. 5). The daily burnt-sacrifice was offered every morning, and upon this was placed the fat parts of the sacrifice of peace. This is in keeping with the relation subsisting between them. After, and upon the sacrifice of propitiation, comes that of communion. *A fire-offering.* The fire-offering is always propitiatory; that is, it affords a legal ground of acceptance, as appears from the qualifying words "of a sweet smell unto the Lord." The blood, then, expiates, the fat propitiates; the two form the condition of access to God and fellowship with him. The disposal of the flesh which remains to complete this important form of sacrifice is afterwards determined (Lev. vii. 11–21).

6–11. The lamb for a sacrifice of peace. The process here is the same as before. 8. *Before the tent of meeting;* before the Lord. 9. *The entire tail.*[9] The tail of the broad-tailed sheep (ovis laticaudia) weighs at least ten or twelve pounds, and consists almost wholly of marrowy fat. *Hard by the Spine.*[9] This word is found only here, and must denote the end of the backbone or rump. 11. *The food.* This corresponds with the "sweet smell," the one pointing to the sense of taste, and the other to that of smell. It is properly introduced

the priest shall burn it upon the altar, the food of the fire-offering unto the LORD. ¶

12. And if his offering be a goat, he shall offer it before the LORD. 13. And he shall lay his hand upon its head, and slay it before the tent of meeting: and Aaron's sons shall sprinkle its blood upon the altar around. 14. And he shall make of it his offering, a fire-offering unto the LORD, the fat that covereth the inwards, and all the fat that is upon the inwards; 15. And the two kidneys, and the fat that is upon them, which is by the flanks, and the caul upon the liver, with the kidneys he shall take it away. 16. And the priest shall burn them upon the altar; all the fat is the food of the fire-offering for a sweet smell unto the LORD. 17. It is a perpetual statute for

here where an account is given of the sacrifice of access to God and fellowship with him. The breaking of bread is the act of communion. Food is the appropriate emblem of all that is delightful in itself or conducive to happiness. When transferred to moral things it denotes perfect obedience to the moral law (Jno. iv. 34; vi. 35), which is the object on which God looks with the utmost complacence. This is the very thing which is represented by the fat on the altar of propitiation. The food, or bread of God, is that which is burned on the altar or reserved from it to be eaten by the priests (xxi. 21, 22).

12–17. The goat for a sacrifice of peace. The ritual here is a repetition of the former. 14. *Make of it his offering.* He shall offer a portion of it, namely, all the pieces of fat already specified. 16. *All the fat.* The fat, as we have seen, is that which represents holiness of heart and life in the substitute and mediator. All the fat that is formed into separate masses is therefore to be reserved for the altar. Here the "food" and the "sweet smell" are combined in the same sentence; and the senses of taste and smell are so akin as to be parts of a greater whole. 17. *A perpetual statute.* The covenant is an everlasting covenant; and the mode of its exhibition lasts as long as the existing state of things continues. *For your generations,* from generation to generation, until a new order of things demand a new

your generations in all your dwellings. Ye shall eat no fat nor blood. ¶

economy, and of course, until the substance comes, of which all these sacrifices are the shadows (Ex. xii. 14). *In all your dwellings.* Not only at the tabernacle in Shiloh and the temple of Jerusalem, but in the towns and villages and homes where ye dwell shall this statute, as far as possible, be observed (Ex. xii. 20). *No fat nor blood.* This is the part of the statute that is to be of universal obligation. No blood or fat is to be eaten. The blood shed, the cause of death, is set apart to denote expiation and foreshadow the death of the great Expiator. The fat burned, the emblem of righteousness, is in like manner reserved to signify satisfaction and prognosticate the righteousness of the Holy One and the Just, who is to magnify the law by his perfect obedience. The two combined form the symbol of propitiation.

We have not yet exhausted the meaning of the sacrifice of peace. We have merely contemplated the part of it which is properly a sacrifice; and in this respect it corresponds with the burnt-sacrifice in denoting propitiation. It is, therefore, so far the echo of the burnt-sacrifice. It will come before us in its proper and full light as an act of communion when we arrive at chap. vii. Meanwhile, the three kinds of offering already described have been occasionally noticed in the previous books of the law, and in this respect differ from those which follow. They have also a unity in themselves, as they refer to the beginning and progress of a life of reconciliation with God. The burnt-sacrifice, the oblation, and the sacrifice of peace are the three great offerings which are presented with an obvious reference to the fallen state of man, but without reference to any particular instance of transgression. By this they are distinguished from the sin-sacrifice and the trespass-offering, which refer to particular offences. They cover the whole experience of the man of God; the burnt-sacrifice always referring to the propitiation, by which he is reconciled to God, the oblation to the intercession, on the ground of which the confession of dependence and gratitude and the consecration of himself and all that he has to the Author of his being and his hope are accepted, and the sacrifice of peace to the access to and fellowship with his Heavenly Father, which have been opened up to him by the whole-sacrifice of propitiation. This ritual proves itself by its whole significance to be a type awaiting the antitype, a shadow forecasting the coming substance. In this respect it is eminently adapted to the nature of man, who stands with his back to the past and his face to the future, and expects the childish things of sight to give way to the loftier things of hope. Man, like his Maker, is the former of purpose.

From all these considerations it is obvious that the first five chapters fall into two distinct parts, three referring to offerings which constitute in themselves a complete whole, and two concerning offerings which are occasional and secondary, and of themselves form a minor unity. Accordingly a new communication begins in the fourth chapter.

NOTES.

1. *Sacrifice*, זֶבַח — *Feast*, δαῖτα. Thus, according to Homer, the blameless Ethiopians entertained the deities at a feast for twelve days; in which, of course, the inviting worshippers feasted on the flesh of the victims offered to the celestials (Iliad, I. 423), and thus Agamemnon sacrificed a fat five-year-old ox to the supreme deity of the Greeks, and invited a party of the chieftains to partake of the good cheer (Iliad, II. 402). A very graphic account of such a sacrificial feast is given in Iliad, I. 446–476. *Sacrifice of peace*, זֶבַח שְׁלָמִים, sacrifice of or concerning the rights, hopes, and duties of peace with God. Also, זְבָחִים שְׁלָמִים (Ex. xxiv. 5), or שְׁלָמִים alone (Ex. xxxii. 6 ; Num. vi. 8). In Sept. θυσία σωτηρίου, in Vulg. *hostia pacificorum*.

4. *Flanks*, כְּסָלִים. Here and in vs. 10, 15 ; iv. 9 ; vii. 4. In this sense the word occurs elsewhere only in Job xv. 27 ; Ps. xxxviii. 8. *The caul*, יֹתֶרֶת, that which is over and above. It occurs twice in Ex. xxix. and nine times in Leviticus, always in connection with כָּבֵד, *the liver*.

9. *The tail*, אַלְיָה. Root, not in use, *be stout, thick, fat*. This word occurs for the first time in Ex. xxix. 22, and hereafter only in Lev. vii. 3 ; viii. 25 ; ix. 19. *The spine*, עָצֶה, only here. עָצָה, *make firm*.

IV. THE SIN-SACRIFICE.

In the next two chapters are three communications, of which the first (iv. 1–v. 13) refers chiefly to the sin-sacrifice, and the remaining two (v. 14–26) to the trespass-offering. Both of these offerings are special sacrifices provided for particular offences. They are called sin-sacrifices or trespass-offerings, according as the sin or the trespass comes into the foreground. Sin[1] is the deviation in intent, act, or disposition from the path of rectitude, the transgression of the law. Trespass[1] is the moral wasteness, the failure, the guilt in the sense of indebtedness to the party wronged for the positive right which has been infringed and ought to have been rendered. The transgression of the law has a twofold aspect; the right undone and the wrong done. If the transgressor were to do afterwards the right which had been undone, he would only have done what the righteous man had all along done, and was bound to do. To demand therefore no more of him than such amends or compensation would be to treat him as well as the righteous man who had never deviated from rectitude or had injured his neighbor by accident without ill-intent. This cannot be the law of equity. Hence, we are constrained to admit that a penalty is incurred by the transgressor, distinct from mere amends, proportional to the gravity of the offence. The offender is bound not only to do the right, but to undo the wrong. Amends, then, and punishment are the two legal claims against the transgressor. This is a conclusion from the first principles of morality, altogether apart from the interpretation of the sin-sacrifice and the trespass-offering. But this essential distinction finds its counterpart in these two kinds of offering. The penalty stands in the foreground in the sin-sacrifice; the compensation in the trespass-offering. The negative requital or suffering deserved is regarded in the former; the positive righteousness required is contemplated in the latter. Hence expiation takes the lead in the sin-sacrifice; propitiation in the trespass-offering. And so they often accompany one another, to denote the more emphatically a full propitiation, including both expiation by an adequate penalty and positive satisfaction by a perfect obedience. The grounds of this interpretation will come out in the course of the exposition. Meanwhile it may be observed that the same offence is called a sin and a trespass, and for the same offence both a sin-sacrifice and a trespass-offering are often provided, and that death is prominent in the former and compensation in the latter.

The fourth chapter treats of the sin-sacrifice, strictly so called, and deals first with the high-priest (1–12), then with the whole assembly

IV. 1. And the LORD spake unto Moses, saying, 2. Speak unto the sons of Israel, saying, If a soul sin in error against any of the commandments of the LORD, as to what should not be

(13–21), then with the prince (22–26), and lastly, with one of the people (27–35). It is addressed to Moses, and designed for the people whose conduct it is to regulate.

1–12. The sin-sacrifice for the high-priest. 1. *And the Lord spake.* This formula is now introduced the second time, indicating a new communication and a second topic. The sacrifices in these two chapters differ from the former in referring to special acts of sin. 2. This verse contains a general heading, which applies to the whole chapter. *The sons of Israel.* Israel is the prince that had power with God and prevailed (Gen. xxxii. 28), and the sons of Israel are, therefore, the people of God with whom he has entered into a covenant of peace. This is of moment for the right understanding of what follows. *If a soul.* A moral and responsible being, susceptible of pleasure and pain and liable to temptation. *Sin.* In this fallen world there is no man that sinneth not. Certainly not David nor Solomon. And certainly not the professors of faith and repentance in the present day, though they may be free from the grosser offences of a more uncultivated age. Those who, it is here supposed, may fall into sin are within the commonwealth of Israel, having received the sign of circumcision and offered the sacrifice of propitiation. If the latter have been an act of genuine faith, they are born from above and partakers of a spiritual nature. Yet they are liable through remaining infirmity and under temptation to commit sins of inadvertence. *In error.*[2] This is an important word in this and the following chapter. The sins of God's people cannot go beyond errors into which they fall through want of watchfulness or consideration. On the other hand, sins committed with a high hand, a defiant pride, or a deliberate knowledge and intent are marks of a heart still estranged from God, and prove those who are guilty of them, notwithstanding their profession, to have no claim to be reckoned among the people of God (Gen. vi. 5; Num. xv. 30; Deut. xvii. 12). Such persons have either made no profession of return to God, or if they have, are either self-

done, and do against any of these. 3. If the anointed priest sin to the guilt of the people, then he shall offer for his sin which he hath done a bullock of the herd perfect unto the

deceivers or hypocrites. Such is the criterion of godliness. Such is the serious lesson to professors of religion, intimated in this significant word. Witting and wilful transgressors are by the very fact excluded from the covenant for the time being, whatever change of mind may come afterwards. *Against any of the commandments*[2] *of the Lord.* This is a very comprehensive phrase, which may denote any part or the whole of his revealed will. There are two sorts of obligation to a particular duty, that of intrinsic equity, and that of extrinsic authority. A law is binding either in itself or from its source. The former is called a moral law or ethical principle, which carries its light and force in itself. The latter is called a positive law or authoritative command, which derives its obligation from him who imposes it. The Creator is the ultimate source of all authority, and he alone has a right to claim unreserved obedience to his holy will. The commandments of the Lord have therefore this second ground of obligation, as indeed the very term indicates. When his commandments are distinguished from his charge, his statutes, and his judgments (Deut. xi. 1), they appear to denote specially the moral law, which thus includes the twofold obligation of equity and authority. From the present passage we learn the fundamental characteristic of sin. It is a deviation from the commandment of Jehovah. A wrong done to a neighbor is at the same time an infringement of the command of God, and in this respect partakes of the character of sin. But it is specially to be noted that this chapter throughout refers to sin against God, the covenant God of the people, and not to that committed against a fellow creature. In the former the redress to be made is a minimum, for we cannot really rob God; but the penalty to be endured is a maximum, because he that is wronged is the Author of our being. In the latter the reverse of both these points holds good.

3–12. We come now to the special case. *The anointed*[3] *priest.* This implies that there were priests who were not anointed, or at least not in the same solemn way. The only distinction of importance

LORD for a sin-sacrifice. 4. And he shall bring the bullock to the door of the tent of meeting before the LORD; and lay his hand upon the bullock's head, and slay the bullock before the LORD. 5. And the anointed priest shall take of the bullock's

must be between the high priest and the other members of the priestly order. He was to have a special anointing at his investiture and consecration (Ex. xxix. 7; Lev. viii. 12, 30). And besides, he only had a dignity parallel with that of the whole assembly (vs. 13). The anointed priest therefore appears to mean the high-priest. *Sin.* The very supposition of sin in him implies that we are in the land and time of type and shadow. Here is only a high-priest that hath infirmity (Heb. vii. 27, 28). He serves therefore only unto the example and shadow of heavenly things (Heb. viii. 5). *To the guilt*[3] *of the people.* If the high-priest sin, if he fail in any point, if he be not morally perfect, the propitiation which he mediates is null and void, and so the guilt of the sinful people for whom he is to mediate remains unremoved. They are still naked and exposed to the doom of unexpiated sin. No lower meaning, such as bad example, false teaching, or faulty ministration, conveys the full significance of the phrase. It is not the moral defect merely, but the incompetence of one morally imperfect to make an atonement, that leaves the people helpless in their guilt. To remedy this defect in the type, the law provides an expiation even for the atoner, and thus enables the people to look forward with confidence to the real Atoner. *For a sin-sacrifice.*[3] The old name sin-offering is not altogether wrong. It expresses a truth, namely, that there is an offering. But it is only a secondary truth; while the primary fact, namely, that it is a sacrifice, a life given for my life by another who has not failed like me, and who is entitled to take upon him this office of self-denying love, is left in the back-ground, or rather in the dark. For this paramount reason we must disregard custom and, what we regret still more, old association, and use the less euphonious name sin-sacrifice, if it were only to impress more emphatically, on those who may cling to the old phrase, the real meaning of the thing so designated. That the *chattath* is a sacrifice for sin is obvious from the statement of the text. It is equally obvious that expiation, or the

blood, and bring it to the tent of meeting. 6. And the priest shall dip his finger in the blood, and spatter of the blood seven times before the LORD on the face of the veil of the sanctuary. 7. And the priest shall put of the blood upon the horns of the altar of incense before the LORD, which is in the tent of meeting; and all the blood of the bullock shall he pour at the foot of the altar of burnt-sacrifice, which is at the door of the tent

bearing of the punishment of sin by dying, is the leading characteristic of the sin-sacrifice. 4, 5. He that has sinned inadvertently, as in the case of the burnt-sacrifice, offers, lays on his hand, and slays the victim. *The anointed priest* here officially takes and brings the blood (iv. 16). We learn from this that the taking and bringing of the blood was not the strictly sacerdotal act. This follows in the next verse. 6. *And the priest*, not the high-priest, who was in this case the inadvertent sinner for whom expiation had to be made, but the officiating priest of the day or the occasion. *Dip his finger in the blood.* The blood that expiates is the chief thing in the sin-sacrifice. *And spatter.*[6] This expresses the action of the finger dipped in the blood by which the drops of blood are cast upon the object to which it is to be applied. It is usually performed with the finger, though sometimes with a sprig of hyssop (Num. xix. 18). *Seven times.* Seven is the number of perfection and the signature of the covenant (Gen. xxi. 28). It expresses the fulness and efficacy of the expiation. *Before the Lord.* It is added, "on the face of the veil of the sanctuary." Here we have a threefold use of the blood. First, it is dropped seven times on the veil of the sanctuary before the Lord. The altar of propitiation and the altar of intercession are passed by, because the offerer of the sin-sacrifice has been already accepted through the burnt-sacrifice. Hence, he comes to the mercy-seat with the drops of the victim's blood pleading for the pardon of his inadvertent sin. Still it is only before the veil he stands and spatters. The way into the holiest is not yet made manifest. The type is but an imperfect shadow. And hence though the worshipper is "before the Lord," yet a veil hangs between him and the divine presence. 7. Next the blood is put upon the horns of the altar of incense; and lastly all the blood that remains is

of meeting. 8. And all the fat of the bullock of sin-sacrifice he shall lift from it; the fat that covereth the inwards, and all the fat that is upon the inwards: 9. And the two kidneys, and the fat that is upon them, which is by the flanks, and the caul upon the liver, with the kidneys he shall take it away. 10. As it was lifted from the bullock of the sacrifice of peace: and the priest shall burn them upon the altar of burnt-sacrifice. 11. And the bullock's skin and all its flesh, with its head and with its legs, and its inwards and its dung; 12. Even the

poured at the foot of the altar of burnt-sacrifice. This may indicate the purging of these altars from guilt which the sin of inadvertence on the part of the man of God had occasioned. But it also implies that the propitiation already made is not robbed of its efficacy by the inadvertent sin. Hence it appears that the mercy-seat partakes of the nature of an altar, inasmuch as blood is directed towards and applied to it. We have, then, the altar of propitiation, the altar of prayer, and the altar of mercy, which is the throne of grace. At the first we have the priest sacrificing, at the second the priest-prophet interceding, at the third the priestly and prophetic king pardoning and accepting. 8–10. The fat is burned upon the altar, as in the sacrifice of peace. It expresses satisfaction, and, with the blood, makes up propitiation. 11, 12. The whole of the following differences serves to distinguish the sin-sacrifice for a sin of inadvertence after being received into the covenant of grace from the whole-sacrifice by which propitiation was effected, and from the sacrifice of peace, by which the communion of the saints in the blessings of salvation was symbolized. *The whole bullock*, destitute now alike of all life and of all power, yet still having a palpable hold of existence as a carcass. The blood has expiated, and the fat has satisfied; the two conjoined have propitiated. The whole victim is not burned on the altar, because this sacrifice is not for one in the state and course of alienation from God, but for a particular sin of a regenerate soul that has been already accepted through an atonement. Neither is it to be reverently and thankfully partaken of by the offerer, because it is a symbol of expia-

whole bullock shall he carry forth without the camp unto a clean place at the pouring out of the ashes, and burn it on the wood with fire ; at the pouring out of the ashes it shall be burned.

tion, and not of fellowship. Yet the whole belongs to the Lord, and is most holy, as everything that expiates must in itself be. *Shall he carry forth.* The party for whom the sacrifice is made is to carry it forth, or cause it to be carried forth. *Without the camp.* While in itself most holy, it is as the bearer of sin accursed, and therefore is carried out of the holy precincts. *Unto a clean place.* The residue of the victim being most holy is to be deposited in a place free from defilement and convenient for its destruction by fire. Such is the place of the ashes which have been taken from the altar of propitiation. *And burn*[12] *it.* This is the completion of the death which is the penalty of sin. The word " burn " here is different from that which is used to denote turning into odor or perfume on the altar. It signifies merely to destroy by fire; whereas the other means to incend or consume as incense. The former is the burning of wrath ; the latter the burning of complacence. Hence this act is the deepening and perpetuating of that penal death, which is otherwise simply expressed by the slaughter of the victim. Extrusion from the holy ground and destruction in the place of ashes lend an awful emphasis to that second death which follows the sin that knows no penitence. There is a significance in the sin of the high-priest, or of the whole congregation, which renders this exhibition of the penal consequence of sin peculiarly necessary. By the sin of the high-priest the propitiation fails in its primary condition, that of the perfection of the mediator; and so all is lost for the whole church. Hence the extent of the expiation for his sin is set forth in the most distinct and solemn form ; and its perpetuity is incidentally intimated.

This completes the account of the sin-sacrifice, the main burden of which is the expiation of sin by the death of an adequate substitute. The blood is applied to all the three altars which appear in the sanctuary in the most distinct and formal manner. The fat, indeed, is consumed on the altar of burnt-sacrifice, because propitiation can

13. And if the whole assembly of Israel err, and the thing be hid from the eyes of the congregation, and they have done somewhat against any of the commandments of the LORD, as

never in practice be separated from expiation. But after all, the whole carcass of the bullock is burned, not incensed or turned into a sweet smell on the altar, but consumed by fire in the place of ashes, in token of the utter destruction which sin brings on its subject.

13-21. The sin-sacrifice for the congregation. 13. *The whole assembly.*[13] In the original there are three words, not clearly distinguished in the English Version, which we may render assembly, congregation, and meeting. The *édah*, or assembly, was a regularly-appointed and well-defined body of men. The smallest number that constituted an assembly among the Jews was ten heads of families. The *édah* also denoted the representation of the people in lawful convention, consisting of the princes of tribes, heads of clans or houses, the elders, the judges, and the shoterim, or officers, as they are called in the English Version. This was the public council, the members of which seem to have been the called of the assembly mentioned in Num. i. 16; xvi. 2. The assembly, or largest *édah*, consisted of the men of twenty years and upward, who were called the numbered of the assembly (Ex. xxxviii. 25). The *cahal*, or congregation was simply a multitude or a nation assembled or incorporated with common rights. With the definite article it usually denotes the whole body of the people. The *môed*, or meeting, was a set time of meeting, or a stated festival or convention held at such a time. It is the word constantly used in the phrase which has been rendered tent of meeting. It is obvious that the *édah*, or regularly constituted assembly, is the only body whose act could bring responsibility and guilt on the whole congregation. The act of an individual, however, had the same effect (Josh. vii.). *Err*, commit a sin through inadvertence. Sinning with a high hand, or being still in a state of estrangement from God, requires other handling. The *ôlah*, or burnt-sacrifice, is the way by which a penitent sinner is reconciled to God. *Hid from the eyes of the congregation*, which is different from the assembly, whether this be the council or the legally constituted convention of the nation. The *cahal* includes

to what should not be done, and are guilty, 14. And the sin in which they have sinned be known, then the congregation shall offer a bullock of the herd for a sin-sacrifice, and bring it before the tent of meeting. 15. And the elders of the assembly shall lay their hands upon the head of the bullock before the LORD; and one shall slay the bullock before the the LORD. 16. And the anointed priest shall bring of the bullock's blood to the tent of meeting. 17. And the priest shall dip his finger in the blood, and spatter seven times before the LORD the face of the veil. 18. And he shall put of the blood upon the horns of the altar, which is before the LORD, that is in the tent of meeting: and all the blood he shall pour at the foot of the altar of burnt-sacrifice, which is at the door of the tent of meeting. 19. And all its fat he shall lift from it, and burn upon the altar. 20. And he shall do

the women and children and old men. *And are guilty.*[13] It is evident from this that the word rendered guilt denotes not a distinct class of offences from sin, but merely a different aspect of the same offence. For here the people who have sinned are said to be guilty in regard to the self-same act. Hence the question is not what kind of transgression is a sin and what kind is a trespass, but in a given offence what is the sin and what the trespass. Now in every transgression there are two things, and no more: a wrong done, and a right undone. The wrong done is the sin which demands punishment; the right neglected is the trespass which calls for redress Hence it is plain, as the text states, that he who sins is guilty. 14. *And the sin ..... be known,* that is, when it becomes known. *The congregation shall offer,* by their representatives. 15. *The elders.* These are the primeval representatives of the people (Gen. l. 7; Ex. iii. 16; xii. 21). *And one shall slay.* The original is indefinite. One of the elders by himself or his minister performs this part on behalf of the congregation. 16, 17. *The priest* is different from the anointed priest. Both take part in this solemn rite. 18, 19. The process is here precisely the same as in vs. 7–10 of the foregoing paragraph. 20. *And he shall do,* to the bullock as was done to the bullock of the sin-sacrifice, so shall he do to it: and the priest shall atone for them, and it shall be forgiven them. 21. And he shall carry forth the bullock without the camp, and burn it as the first bullock was burned: this is the sin-sacrifice of the congregation. ¶

22. When a prince sinneth and doeth aught against any of the commandments of the LORD his God, as to what should not be done, in error, and is guilty. 23. If his sin wherein he hath sinned, be known to him, then he shall bring his

the officiating party shall proceed as with the former bullock in all that has been briefly prescribed concerning this. *The priest shall atone for them.* To atone is to propitiate in the full sense, and so it is done here, though the expiation has the chief place. *It shall be forgiven.* Forgiveness is remission of the penalty of sin, the negative part of justification. This corresponds with the end of the sin-sacrifice, which is to expiate for sin. It is the part of the mediator to atone; it belongs to the Being who has been offended to forgive. Propitiation does not preclude the necessity of forgiveness, but only provides for the lawfulness of it. The unconquerable spirit of true forgiveness displays itself in providing and in accepting the ransom. The counterpart of forgiveness is acceptance, which is prominent in the burnt-sacrifice (i. 3, 4). 21. *He shall carry.* The offerer shall do so himself or by his agent. The offerer is here the congregation, who must of necessity act by their representative. *And burn it.* The sin of the whole congregation annuls the covenant, and forfeits its benefits on the part of the whole community. Hence it has the same effect as that of the priest; and this result is exhibited in the burning of the whole carcass of the substitute in the place of ashe This paragraph thus confirms and illustrates the preceding one.

22–26. The sin-sacrifice for the prince. 22. *A prince.* The head of a tribe, clan, or family (Num. iii. 24). 23. *Wherein he hath sinned.* This is a mere variation for "which he hath done" (vs. 28). *Be known* eventually, that is, become known to him. *A kid of the goats.* The kind of offering is suited to the rank of the individual. *Upon the horns*

offering a kid of the goats, a perfect male ; 24. And he shall lay his hand upon the head of the goat, and slay it in the place where the burnt-sacrifice is slain before the LORD. 25. And the priest shall take of the blood with his finger, and put it upon the horns of the altar of burnt-sacrifice ; and shall pour out its blood at the foot of the altar of burnt-sacrifice. 26. And all its fat he shall burn upon the altar, as the fat of the sacrifice of peace: and the priest shall atone for him from his sin, and it shall be forgiven him. ¶

27. And if any soul of the people of the land sin in error, by doing aught against the commandments of the LORD, as to what should not be done, and be guilty ; 28. If his sin which

of the altar of burnt-sacrifice. In the former instances the blood was spattered on the veil, and then applied to the horns of the altar of incense. By this it was intimated that the sacrifice was made on behalf of one already accepted through the burnt-sacrifice of propitiation. The same is now indicated by applying the blood, not to the sides, where the blood of the burnt-sacrifice was sprinkled, but to the horns of the altar, which were nearer heaven. Hence it is manifest that the application of the blood means the same thing to whatever altar it is applied. 26. The flesh of the victim is not directed to be carried out as before, but, as we learn afterward (vi. 19), is to be eaten by the officiating priest in the holy place. This difference arises, no doubt, from the fact that in the case of the priest or the congregation inadvertently sinning the covenant is virtually made void for the whole community of the faithful, whereas the inadvertent sin of the individual only affects himself, and leaves the covenant in full force in regard to all others. The flesh in this case goes with the fat to make the propitiation ; the fat by being consumed on the altar, the flesh by being eaten by the priest in the holy place. *Atone for him from his sin.* This is a pregnant expression, denoting to make atonement for him and deliver him from the penal effects of his sin. Forgiveness follows as before.

27-35. The sin-sacrifice for one of the people. 27. *Any soul.* An

he hath done be known to him, then he shall bring his offering a kid of the goats, a perfect female, for his sin which he hath done. 29. And he shall lay his hand upon the head of the sin-sacrifice, and slay the sin-sacrifice in the place of the burnt sacrifice. 30. And the priest shall take of its blood with his finger, and put it upon the horns of the altar of burnt-sacrifice; and pour out all its blood at the foot of the altar. 31. And all its fat he shall take away, as the fat is taken away from the sacrifice of peace; and the priest shall burn it upon the altar for a sweet smell unto the LORD; and the priest shall atone for him, and it shall be forgiven him. ¶
32. And if he bring a lamb as his offering for sin, he shall bring it a perfect female. 33. And he shall lay his hand upon the head of the sin-sacrifice, and slay it for a sin-sacrifice in the place where the burnt-sacrifice is slain. 34. And the priest shall take of the blood of the sin-sacrifice with his finger, and put it upon the horns of the altar of burnt-sacrifice, and pour out all its blood at the foot of the altar. 35. And all its fat he shall take away, as the fat of the lamb is taken away from the sacrifice of peace; and the priest shall burn

individual of the people. 28. *A perfect female.* The distinction between the sacrifice for the prince and that for one of the people is merely in the gender of the victim. 29–31. The mode of sacrifice is precisely the same as in the case of a prince. The words "for a sweet smell" are inserted here in reference to the burning of the fat on the altar, and are, no doubt, to be understood in all the previous cases.

32–35. *A lamb.* This is an alternation allowed for the kid. The mode is unaltered. 35. *Upon the fire-offerings.* The morning sacrifice is a burnt-sacrifice and a fire-offering; and others may have been presented after it and before the present one. But the expression is significant for the place of the sin-sacrifice, which is for the inadvertent sin of the believer in God after he has been reconciled by

them on the altar upon the fire-offerings of the Lord : and the priest shall atone for him for his sin that he hath done, and it shall be forgiven him. ¶

the burnt-sacrifice of propitiation. Atonement and forgiveness follow as usual.

NOTES.

2. *In error,* בִּשְׁגָגָה, in Sept. ἀκουσίως, *involuntarily.* Commandment, מִצְוָה, when used in a strict sense, *a moral precept.* Charge, מִשְׁמֶרֶת, a function to be discharged by an official. Statute, חֹק, a positive enactment, including any precept of civil or ecclesiastical law. *Judgment,* מִשְׁפָּט, a judicial decision or sentence having the force of common law.

3. *Anointed,* מָשִׁיחַ; hence Messiah. *Guilt,* אַשְׁמָה, indebtedness or liability for a righteousness which should have been, but has not been, rendered, either by the party guilty or by the substitute; r. *be waste.* *Sin-sacrifice,* חַטָּאת, missing the mark, swerving from the line of rectitude, sin, and then sin-sacrifice.

6. *Spatter,* הִזָּה, different from זָרַק, *sprinkle.* The latter denotes a more plentiful diffusion, as it refers to the whole of the blood when it was applied to the sides of the altar of burnt-sacrifice. The former refers only to the few drops which fall from the shaken finger on the veil or the mercy-seat.

12. *Burn,* שָׂרַף, used of the burning of towns, houses, corpses, bricks, lime, and the like. We have not a word in English to distinguish הִקְטִיר, *turn into perfume,* from ordinary burning. Incend is too unfamiliar.

13. *Assembly,* עֵדָה, a stated and regularly summoned meeting, consisting of a definite number of members when fully convened. *Congregation,* קָהָל, a nation or indefinite body, of which the assembly is some legal convention greater or smaller. *Meeting,* מוֹעֵד, appointment, time or place of appointed meeting, meeting. *Be guilty,* אָשֵׁם, become a moral waste, be a debtor for the righteousness which should have been, but was not done; in this sense, be guilty. *Trespass,* אָשָׁם, the defect or want of righteousness toward another, which is therefore a trespass against him; the liability for the positive righteousness which has been left undone; primarily in this sense, guilt.

V. THE TRESPASS-OFFERING.

We have already seen that in propitiation two distinct things are included, expiation and satisfaction. In expiation the mediator bears the penalty of sin, and the sinner who trusts in his mediation is freed from it, or pardoned. In satisfaction, strictly so called, the mediator renders a perfect obedience to the law, and the penitent sinner who relies on his good offices is justified or accepted and treated as righteous, as well as pardoned. The sin-sacrifice represents chiefly the expiation, as we have seen; the trespass-offering chiefly the satisfaction, as we shall see. The former has been already explained; the latter is unfolded in the present chapter. Those who hold that sin is one kind of offence and trespass another are in a difficulty about the first part of this chapter (1–13). Some hold that the sin-sacrifice is continued in this passage, and the trespass-offering treated of in the remainder; others maintain that the trespass-offering forms the subject of the whole chapter. It is quite true that the first thirteen verses are a continuation of the communication begun in chap. iv. But when we understand that every moral offence is both a sin and a trespass, we come to perceive that this chapter refers chiefly to the trespass, while the former dwells upon the sin, involved in every violation of morality. It is to be observed that the previous chapter refers throughout to a deviation from "the commandment of the Lord," to acts "which should not be done," because they were contrary to the Divine will. These, then, are offences against the whole moral law, as commanded by God. On the other hand, in the first part of the fifth chapter the offences are against the civil and ceremonial law, or trespasses arising between neighbors. This is a sufficient warrant for separating this portion, and assigning it to a new chapter. At the same time it unfolds to us the ground for calling the offerings prescribed in this passage by the generic name of trespass-offerings (vs. 6). For in an offence against God the sin is the chief thing, and the trespass is subordinate in importance. The penalty, therefore, is prominent, and the sin-sacrifice, which alludes mainly to expiation, is the first thing needful. And hence the preceding chapter necessarily treats of the sin-offering. But in an offence directly involving my neighbor the trespass is the chief thing, and the sin falls into the

V. 1. And when a soul sins and hears the voice of an oath and is a witness, whether he have seen or known of it, if he tell

shade. The trespass cries for redress, and accordingly the trespass-offering points primarily to the satisfaction which is included in propitiation. The first paragraph, then, of this chapter referring to transgressions of man against man or by man, with no less propriety treats of the trespass-offering. The examination of the whole chapter will be an instructive illustration of these distinctions.

The former chapter treated of particular acts of inadvertent sin, distinguishing the rank of the transgressor and varying the regulations accordingly. This chapter specifies certain classes of offences for which a special mode of atonement is prescribed. It contains three parts, the remainder of one divine communication (1–13), and the whole of two others. In the English Version the second of these forms the beginning of chap. vi., after the Sept. and Vulg., which is an illogical arrangement.

1–13. Four forms of sin for which a special mode of atonement is prescribed. 1. First case: neglecting to give evidence when required. *And when a soul sins.* We must observe that throughout this chapter, as throughout the former, the moral offence is invariably called a sin, (vs. 5, 15, 17, 21). *Hears the voice of an oath,* hears the voice of adjuration, of the judge adjuring him. In some cases the witness did not himself pronounce the form of oath, but heard it addressed to him by the judge (1 Kings xxii. 16; Matt. xxvi. 63). *Or known of it.* Witnesses are here divided into two classes, those who have seen the occurrence in question, and those who have become aware of it in some other way. *If he tell it not.* The adjured, when questioned, is bound to give evidence in a case of law. *Bear his iniquity.*[1] Iniquity, that is, deviation from equity, is a very suitable rendering for the original word. To bear iniquity is to take its legal consequences. The transgressor bears his own iniquity when he suffers the penalty of it, or is still liable to suffer it. The mediator bears the iniquity of another when he takes his place and suffers for him. The party offended bears the iniquity of the other when he accepts the satisfaction made by the mediator, or, in other words, takes it away from the actual offender and lays it on the substitute whom he has

it not, and bear his iniquity, 2. Or if a soul touch anything unclean, either a carcass of an unclean beast, or a carcass of unclean cattle, or a carcass of an unclean creeper, and it be hidden from him, and he be unclean and guilty, 3. Or if he touch the uncleanness of man, according to all his uncleanness wherewith he is defiled, and it be hid from him, and he know of it, and be guilty, 4. Or if a soul swear to utter with the

provided. In this last case it is usually rendered to forgive, though it really means to accept an atonement for the offender.

2. The second case: ceremonial defilement. *Touch anything unclean.* This is a general phrase which may apply to this and the following verse. The uncleanness here spoken of is ceremonial. We know that "there is nothing unclean of itself." Ceremonial uncleanness, then, is typical of moral defilement. It can only have a place or a meaning in a world where sin has entered. Three kinds of unclean animals are here specified, wild beasts, cattle, and creepers. They are not to be used for food. They are described in Lev. xi. Even the carcasses of those animals which are allowed for food defile (Lev. xi. 39). *And it be hidden from him.* This is a hint that all such defiling objects are to be carefully avoided; and if this be done, unclean contact can only happen in some unexpected and unintentional way. *And guilty.* The mention of guilt, which runs through this chapter, is no less obvious in the previous one (vs. 3, 13, 22, 27). Thus the terms sin and guilt or trespass are common to both chapters, and to all the voluntary actions specified in them. This of itself goes to prove that sin and trespass are two aspects of one and the same offence.

3. Third case: this is defilement by contact with one who is unclean. From the completeness of the previous verse it is obvious that this is regarded as a distinct species of offence. The modes of human defilement are various. A living body affected with any flux or issue, or a dead body communicates defilement (Lev. xv.; Num. xix. 11). The putrid matter flowing from a diseased part, or the dead body in which putrefaction sets in is a seat of corruption, and in man is not only a type, but a fruit, of moral pollution.

lips to do evil or to do good, according to all that a man utters with an oath, and it be hid from him, and he know of it, and be guilty in any of these, 5. Then it shall be, when he is guilty in any of these, that he shall confess that he hath sinned in it, 6. And he shall bring his trespass-offering unto the LORD for his sin which he hath done, a female of the flock, a lamb or a kid of the goats for a sin-sacrifice; and the priest

4. Fourth case: rash swearing. *To utter with the lips*, to speak rashly in the hearing of men. *To do evil or to do good*, a general phrase to denote a certain act of any kind whatever (Num. xxiv. 13). This refers to swearing improperly or falsely regarding the act in question, whether past or future. *And it be hid from him;* having forgotten or neglected it. *And he know of it*, and some person or circumstance bring it to his knowledge. The series of cases has now been stated.

5-13. The course to be pursued in these cases. *When he is guilty in any of these.* The epithet guilty is here applied to all the four classes of offenders, and hence we find that bearing his iniquity (vs. 1) and being guilty are equivalent phrases. *He shall confess.* The conduct of the offerer in making confession and presenting his offering is the outward indication of his state of mind, of his inward penitence, trust in God, affection, and obedience. But they make no atonement for his sin. This is the effect of the trespass-offering. 6. *Bring his trespass-offering.*[6] This is the natural rendering. It presents a difficulty only to those who hold that sin and trespass must be different offences. The words will not admit of any other rendering. We cannot say, "bring his trespass or his guilt." *For a sin-sacrifice.* If we were to insist that sin and trespass denoted distinct offences, there would appear a contradiction here. But when we find sin and trespass or guilt uniformly ascribed to one and the same act through these two chapters, we learn simply from this passage that in these cases the trespass-offering and the sin-sacrifice are united in the same victim, or that the one offering serves for both. Nothing can more clearly show, in fact, that the same offence is in one aspect a sin and in another a trespass. *Atone for him from his sin;* as in iv. 26. In

shall atone for him from his sin. 7. And if his hand reach not to enough for a lamb, then shall he bring as his trespass-offering, for what he hath sinned, two doves or two pigeons unto the LORD, one for a sin-sacrifice, and one for a burnt-sacrifice. 8. And he shall bring them unto the priest, and he shall offer that which is for the sin-sacrifice first, and pinch off its head from its neck and not divide it. 9. And he shall spatter of the blood of the sin-sacrifice upon the wall of the altar, and the rest of the blood shall be squeezed out at the foot of the altar: it is a sin-sacrifice. 10. And the second he shall make a burnt-sacrifice according to the manner; and the priest shall atone for him for his sin which he hath done, and it shall be forgiven him. §

11. And if his hand reach not to two doves or two pigeons, then he shall bring as his offering for what he hath sinned the tenth of an ephah of flour for a sin-sacrifice : he shall not add

this case the sacrifice including in itself expressly the sin and the trespass-offering makes a complete atonement. 7. *His trespass-offering.* This is consistent with the statement in the previous verse. *For what he hath sinned.* The original might be rendered simply "which he hath sinned," and so we might suppose that *asham* here meant simply his trespass. But precisely the same phrase is found after "his offering" in vs. 11, where we must render as we have done here. Besides we cannot use the phrase "bring his trespass" here, any more than in the sixth verse. *Two doves.* Here the twofold import of the sacrifice is intimated by the two victims ; the one for a sin-sacrifice, which properly expiates, the other for a burnt-sacrifice, which propitiates, and therein makes satisfaction. 8, 9. *Spatter of the blood.* This makes a difference, as before (iv. 6), between the sin and the burnt-sacrifice. 10. *According to the manner*, the rule already prescribed (Lev. i.).

11–13. A third alternation. *For what he hath sinned.* See on vs. 7. *Flour for a sin-sacrifice.* On the principle that without shedding of

oil to it nor put frankincense upon it; for it is a sin-sacrifice. 12. And he shall bring it to the priest, and the priest shall take of it his neaf-ful, the memorial of it, and burn it on the altar upon the fire-offerings of the LORD: it is a sin-sacrifice. 13. And the priest shall atone for him for his sin which he hath done in any of these, and it shall be forgiven him: and it shall belong to the priest as the oblation.

blood there is no remission, this would be entirely unintelligible, did we not know that the atonement had been already made and accepted for all such inadvertent offenders by the burnt-sacrifice, which represented the great and only propitiation for the sinner who through it returns to God. This burnt-sacrifice had been offered either by the penitent himself or by his parent or people on his behalf. Its virtue was all-sufficient, both for the sinful state antecedent to propitiation, and the inadvertent sins that might afterwards be committed. The sin-sacrifice merely represented a fresh appeal to the one only atonement, symbolized no less by this than by the burnt-sacrifice. But besides, it is to be remembered that this particular sin-sacrifice comes under the head of a trespass-offering (vs. 6), which presupposes expiation by blood indeed, but expresses positive satisfaction or propitiation by a fire-offering on the brazen altar. The flour suffices for this purpose, when the atonement has gone before. *Not add oil to it nor put frankincense upon it.* Inasmuch as this is a trespass-offering (vs. 6), it is propitiatory in its nature, and may even be expressed by flour, part of which is burned as a fire-offering unto the Lord. But as it is in another respect a sin-sacrifice, and in this respect expiatory, the oil and the frankincense are excluded. The bare flour represents life, and therefore deliverance from death, which is the proper effect of the expiation. It is the basis of the oblation, which presupposes the burnt-sacrifice in which expiation is made. *For it is a sin-sacrifice.* Oil expresses sanctification and frankincense intercession, which transcend all that is implied in the mere blood of expiation. 12. *The priest shall take* with his own hand, as in the animal sacrifice he receives the blood in a sacrificial bowl. *Upon the fire-offerings,* as in iv. 35. 13. *In any of these,* literally from any of these, as in iv. 26.

14. And the LORD spake unto Moses, saying, 15. If a soul do wrong and sin in error in the holy things of the LORD, then he shall bring as his trespass-offering unto the LORD a perfect ram of the flock with thy valuation in silver shekels after the

It shall belong. The flour, after the memorial has been burned on the altar, shall be the priest's, as the oblation (ch. ii.).

14–19. The trespass-offering for transgressions in the holy things of the Lord, or directly against his moral law. This is the first distinct communication concerning trespass-offerings. It contains, as we see, two different cases. The first regards any wrong-doing in the holy things of the Lord. 15. *If a soul do wrong,* defraud or in any way injure. The reference now is specially to the damage which has been done to the right or property of another. *And sin.* Every kind of wrong is at the same time a sin. *In error.* This qualification is never to be forgotten. The soul that has repented and been reconciled to God can sin only in error or inadvertence. A wilful or deliberate violation of the command of God marks an impenitent and unreconciled sinner. The lawgiver is careful to mark the distinction. *In the holy things of the Lord.*[15] The original has " from the holy things," which is a pregnant construction for, " in taking from the holy things of the Lord." This refers to the service of the tabernacle, the tithes, or any other requirement of the worship of God. *A perfect ram,* is the constant trepass-offering, without respect to rank or means, to intimate that the recompense should always be an exact equivalent for the damage done. The mode of dealing with the ram of trespass is the same as that with the peace-offering (iii. 2–5), as we learn from vii. 2–5, where this account is supplemented. *With thy valuation.* This cannot with any propriety be referred to the value of the ram, which it is simply impossible to vary in proportion to the damage done. It must therefore refer to a distinct accompanying sum of money, at which Moses or the officiating priest or the high-priest is to estimate the loss. *In silver shekels,* that is, in current coin; silver, the customary medium of exchange, having acquired the meaning of coin or money. *After the shekel of the sanctuary.* As this matter regarded the sanctuary it is natural that the payment should be made in

LEVITICUS V. 15-17.

shekel of the sanctuary, for a trespass-offering. 16. And he shall make amends for the sin that he hath done in the holy thing, and shall add thereto the fifth of it, and give it unto the priest; and the priest shall atone for him with the ram of trespass, and it shall be forgiven him. ¶

17. And if a soul sin and do aught against any of the commandments of the LORD, as to what should not be done, and

the currency of the sanctuary. Some suppose that the *beka*[15] is the common shekel, which would in that case be only half the sacred shekel (1 Kings x. 17; 2 Chron. ix. 16). The sacred shekel [15] would at all events be of full weight, and in value about 2s. 3d. of English money, or half an American dollar. *For a trespass-offering.* Hence we perceive that an equivalent compensation for the right that had been infringed is the fundamental meaning of the trespass-offering. 16. *Make amends,* make good, or replace that which had been lost or taken away or withheld. The idea of restitution in positive value or right runs through the whole account of the *asham* or trespass-offering. *The fifth of it.* This serves to cover all losses or costs contingent on the exchange or replacement. The same addition was to be made when a firstling or any part of the tithe in kind was exchanged for a money value (Lev. xxvii.). The tenth is the customary offering in acknowledgment of the supremacy and benignity of the Most High. In the case of compensation or exchange for that which belongs to him, two tenths or one fifth is the usual addition.

17-19. The trespass-offering in the case of a direct breach of the moral law. This is the second branch of the present communication. 17. *If a soul sin.* On comparison it is manifest that this is precisely the case for which the sin-sacrifice is provided in the preceding chapter, namely, doing anything against any of the commandments of the Lord, as to what should not be done. There it was treated as a sin or wrong done, deserving punishment; here it is regarded as a trespass or right left undone, demanding amends. The penalty and the recompense make up the propitiation. And hence we often find the sin-sacrifice and the trespass-offering accompanying each other, and presented for the same transgression. The trespass-offering, there-

know it not, and be guilty and bear his iniquity; 18. Then he shall bring a perfect ram of the flock, with thy valuation for a trespass-offering unto the priest; and the priest shall atone for him for his error which he committed and knew it not, and it shall be forgiven him. 19. It is a trespass-offering: he hath indeed trespassed against the LORD. ¶
20. And the LORD spake unto Moses, saying, 21. If a soul sin and do wrong against the LORD, and lie unto his neighbor in a trust or in giving of the hand or in theft, or oppress his

fore, now prescribed is simply that which is to be offered along with the sin-sacrifice of the previous chapter. 18. *With thy valuation.* This refers to such material compensation as may be admissible in certain breaches of the moral law. It would be vain for the transgressor to make a trespass-offering if he were not prepared to make all the reparation in his power for the right infringed. *For his error.* The offences for which these sacrifices are offered are invariably acts of inadvertence, and not of the intentional wilfulness that marks an unregenerate heart. 19. *He hath indeed trespassed against the Lord.* The valuation and material compensation following upon it is a matter between man and man; in this instance referring to the priests of the house of God who have been wronged. The transgressor can make no proper compensation to his Creator for the right he has infringed. Hence we need the trespass-offering, which, like the ram caught in the thicket, represents the righteousness of the substitute for the transgressor, by which the law that has been violated is truly magnified and honored. This alone ultimately propitiates and earns eternal life for the penitent who returns, laying his hand on the trespass-offering.

20–26. The trespass-offering for sins against the Lord that are direct offences against a neighbor. This second communication on the trespass-offering refers to direct breaches of the second table of the law. It bears, therefore, the same relation to the former communication which the first paragraph of this chapter bears to the previous chapter. 21. *If a soul sin and do wrong*[21] *against the Lord.* The breach of equity between man and man is an offence against God.

neighbor, 22. Or find that which was lost and deny it and swear to a lie, in aught of all that a man doeth to sin therein, 23. And it be that he sins and is guilty, then he shall requite the thing which he stole, or the oppression that he wrought, or the trust that was delivered to him, or the lost thing that he found, 24. Or all that about which he had sworn to a lie; and he shall make it good in the principal of it, and add to it a fifth of it; to him to whom it belongeth shall he give it in the day of his trespass. 25. And he shall bring his trespass-offering unto the LORD, a perfect ram of the flock, with thy valuation for a trespass-offering unto the priest: 26. And

To do wrong here means to act treacherously or deceitfully, sin always involving a lie in some form. This corresponds with the forms of sin afterwards enumerated. Fraud in a trust or compact, or in property, and oppression are inclusive of most wrong done to a neighbor. 22. Speaking or swearing falsely regarding a thing found. All these result from strong and sudden temptation by which a man entering on the life of faith in God and allegiance to him may be overcome in a moment of heedlessness. 23. *He shall requite,* or make good by an equivalent. 24. Full compensation, that is, an equivalent with a fifth added to it, is to be made for the wrongs done to his neighbor, as an essential part in the re-establishment of a good understanding with his Heavenly Father. *To him to whom it belongeth.* A thorough and genuine integrity is the only satisfactory criterion of a new heart at peace with God. *In the day of his trespass,* on the occasion of his having failed to render to his neighbor any part of his right. If the day is to be taken more strictly, it must refer to the time of his trespass having become known. 25, 26. The process here is quite the same as in the former case (vs. 18).

In these five chapters we have the ritual of the various sacrifices which are needful to meet the exigencies of a godly life on the earth, in the period antecedent to the making of the great propitiation which really takes away sin. The burnt-sacrifice represents the full propitiation for sin, including both expiation and satisfaction proper,

the priest shall atone for him before the LORD, and it shall be forgiven him, for aught of all that he doeth to trespass therein.   25   ¶ ¶ ¶

by which the sinner, coming in faith and penitence, is pardoned and accepted once for all. This has to be offered again and again, as it is merely the shadow of the substance, to call to remembrance the one great propitiatory sacrifice which takes away sin and brings in everlasting righteousness. Next we have the oblation, which serves to accompany and complete the proper sacrifice, or to afford expression on suitable occasions for that gratitude and devotion which characterize the obedience of the soul that has once been ransomed by the blood of atonement. This offering is accepted either on account of the proper sacrifice which has preceded, or of the perfect righteousness of the all-prevalent Intercessor. The sacrifice of peace is the medium of fellowship with the God of mercy and truth for his saints who have been reconciled by the sacrifice of propitiation. As the old man still lingers in the flesh, betraying the penitent soul in unguarded moments into sins that imply, not intentional rebellion, but only moral imperfection, the sin-sacrifice and trespass-offerings afford special means of expiating occasional errors, and making amends for the rights which have been infringed, being, in fact, the symbols of the special application of the one great atoning sacrifice to the relief of the conscience, when distressed with these dregs of a fallen nature. The lessons which these singular arrangements teach will be obvious to the attentive reader.

NOTES.

1. *Iniquity*, עָוֹן, deviation from rectitude; r. עָוָה, *bend, twist*. *Bear iniquity*, נָשָׂא עָוֹן.

6. *Bring his trespass-offering*, הֵבִיא אֶת־אֲשָׁמוֹ.

15. *From the holy things of*, מִקָּדְשֵׁי. *Beka*, בֶּקַע, a dividend, a half; r. cleave. *Shekel*, שֶׁקֶל, a weight of about 220 grains.

21. *Do wrong*, מָעַל, act covertly or treacherously.

VI. LAWS OF THE OFFERINGS.

VI. 1. And the Lord spake unto Moses, saying, 2. Command Aaron and his sons, saying, This is the law of the burnt-sacrifice: that is the burnt-sacrifice upon the hearth on the altar all the night until the morning; and the fire of the

The two remaining chapters on the offerings are occupied with certain regulations to be observed by the priests in the ministrations of the altar. They chiefly refer to the use of the flesh that is not to be burned on the altar, and other details not before settled. These are reserved until now, that the form and character of each offering might stand out clearly to the view, and not be confused by details, which, however essential in themselves, do not enter into their specific nature as offerings. There are in all five distinct communications in these two chapters, of which two and a part of the third are contained in this chapter. It treats of the law or rule of the burnt-sacrifice 1–6, of the oblation 7–16, and of the sin-sacrifice 17–23.

1–6. The law of the burnt-sacrifice. 1. *The Lord spake.* This communication is made to Moses, and concerns the priests. It includes the law of the burnt-sacrifice and that of the oblation made by any of the people. 2. *Command.* Moses is the lawgiver. *Aaron and his sons.* The following regulations apply to the proceedings of the priests in the matter of these offerings. *The law,*[2] properly, doctrine or instruction. Here it refers to the mode of administration, and to the duties and rights of the priests. *The burnt-sacrifice.* This sacrifice gave name to the altar on which it was offered. The morning and evening sacrifices come under this description. And besides these, others were continually offered by individuals. It was, moreover, the sum and substance of all other sacrifices. Hence the propriety of calling the altar of sacrifice by this name. *That is.* The attention is here drawn to the evening burnt-sacrifice, as the one at present in question. *Upon the hearth,*[2] the grating in the middle of the altar where the fire was placed. See on Ex. xxvii. 4. *All the night.* This, then, is the evening sacrifice, which is to burn all the night until the morning. The account of the process begins with the

86   LAWS OF THE OFFERINGS.

altar shall burn on it. 3. And the priest shall put on his linen coat, and linen breeches shall he put on his flesh; and he shall take up the ashes into which the fire consumeth the burnt-sacrifice on the altar, and put them beside the altar. 4. And he shall strip off his clothes and put on other clothes: and carry the ashes forth without the camp unto a clean place. 5. And the fire upon the altar shall burn on it, it shall not go

evening, as the sunset was the beginning of the Hebrew day. The fire would be renewed for the evening sacrifice every day. *Shall burn on it*.[2] The fire thus prepared for the perpetual burnt-sacrifice is to burn all night on it, that is, on the altar. 3. *And the priest*. In the morning the priest is to trim the altar fire that has been burning all the night. *Shall put on*. For this purpose he is to put on linen garments. The breeches are mentioned in particular because he is now to mount the altar. This linen array is the emblem of purity and humility, in which he is for the present purpose to approach the altar. *Take up the ashes*. This manual labor belongs to the priest because it is connected with the altar, and these are the ashes of the burnt-sacrifice. *Beside the altar*. On the east end or rear of it (i. 16). The object of laying the ashes in the rear of the altar is that the priest may renew the fire and offer the morning sacrifice before he takes off his official dress to carry them out of the the camp. *Strip off*. The official garments befit the altar and the court, but not the outer world. *Without the camp*. The residue from the altar is in one sense accursed, as that which bears the iniquity of the sinner, and therefore must have no place in the camp of the holy nation. *Unto a clean place*. In another sense, and in itself, it is holy and without blemish, and has been consecrated unto the Lord, and therefore as a holy thing must not be cast down in a common or unclean place. 5. *Burn on it*,[2] that is on the altar, to which the pronoun refers. *Not go out*. The fire on the altar is to be a perpetual expression of acceptance through an atonement. To keep up this fire the priest shall put on fresh wood, and lay on it the morning sacrifice before he leaves the holy place with the ashes; and all day long, as occasion requires, he shall burn on it the memorials of the oblation, and the fat of the

out; and the priest shall burn wood on it every morning; and he shall lay on it the burnt-sacrifice, and burn on it the fat of the peace-offerings. 6. Fire shall burn always on the altar, it shall not go out. §
7. And this is the law of the oblation : let Aaron's sons offer it before the LORD upon the altar. 8. And he shall lift of it in his neaf of the flour of the oblation and of its oil and all the frankincense which is on the oblation, and burn on the altar for a sweet smell the memorial of it unto the LORD. 9. And the remainder thereof shall Aaron and his sons eat: sweet shall it be eaten, in the holy place, in the court of the tent of meeting they shall eat it. 10. It shall not be baken with leaven ; I have given it as their portion of my fire-offerings ; it is most holy, as the sin-sacrifice and as the trespass-offering.

peace-offerings, and other sacrifices. 6. *Burn always*, as a symbol of the perpetual acceptance of the true propitiation once to be made, and of the perpetual worship of God and fellowship of his people with him. The fire that came down from heaven on the altar was the token of the divine acceptance of the sacrifice offered for his people. It is abundantly manifest from all this that the burnt-sacrifice was the sum and substance of all sacrifice, and the symbol of propitiation.

7–11. The law of the oblation of the people. 7. *Aaron's sons*, that is, one of them, thou of his sons, as the verb is in the imperative. *Upon the altar*, literally, on the face of the altar. 8. This is a recapitulation of ii. 9 for the sake of connection. 9. *The remainder thereof*. Here we have the detail of the disposal of the remainder which in ii. 10 is omitted, not being to the purpose then in hand. *Sweet*, unleavened. *In the holy place*, because it is most holy (ii. 10). The holy place includes the court of the tabernacle, where a suitable place would be provided for the purpose. 10. *Not be baken with leaven* (ii. 11), neither by the worshipper nor by the priest. *I have given it*. The oblation belongs wholly to the Lord. He disposes of it as it pleases him. The memorial is burned on his altar ; the remainder eaten by his priests. *My fire-offerings*. The whole is a

11. Every male of the sons of Aaron shall eat of it: it is a statute forever for your generations of the fire-offerings of the LORD: all that toucheth them shall be holy. ¶

12. And the LORD spake unto Moses, saying, 13. This is the offering of Aaron and his sons, which they shall offer to the LORD in the day when he is anointed, the tenth of an ephah of flour for a perpetual oblation, half of it in the morning and half of it in the evening. 14. On a pan shall it be

fire-offering; hence, after the memorial is burnt, to be eaten by the priests has the same import as to be consumed by fire on the altar. It denotes propitiation. *Most holy*, because it is wholly his, as the sin-sacrifice and the trespass-offering are wholly his. 11. *Every male;* because he is a priest, or will be when he is full-grown. *A statute forever*, continuing until the substance comes of which it is the shadow. *All that toucheth them shall be holy.* This is capable of two meanings. Every one that toucheth them must be ceremonially or essentially holy; or everything that toucheth them thereby acquires the quality of holiness. The latter seems to be the more natural meaning. See on Ex. xxix. 37.

12–16. The daily oblation of the high-priest. This paragraph forms a distinct communication of itself, which Moses puts here in its right place. In the general ordinances concerning the offering in the first five chapters it would have been out of place because of its speciality. In the special rules now given it has its appropriate place. On account of its peculiar importance it forms the subject of a separate communication. It is manifest that this communication must have been made before the consecration of Aaron and his sons, as it forms part of their immediate functions. 13. *The offering of Aaron and his sons.* From this and the following context we learn that this is an offering from the priestly order, and pre-eminently from the high-priest as their head. *In the day when he is anointed.* This refers to the high-priest, who received a special anointing on the day of his consecration. Having been consecrated he was empowered to officiate as a priest. From that day he presents his oblation along with the

made with oil, toasted thou shalt bring it; an oblation of fried crumbs thou shalt offer it for a sweet smell unto the LORD. 15. And the priest anointed in his stead of his sons shall make it: it is a statute forever unto the LORD; it shall be wholly burnt. 16. And every oblation of a priest shall be a whole offering; it shall not be eaten. ¶

17. And the LORD spake unto Moses, saying, 18. Speak

burnt-sacrifice of the people. *A perpetual oblation,* to be offered morning and evening like the daily sacrifice. 14. *On a pan.* The flour is to be kneaded without leaven and baked on a pan. *With oil,* like the other oblations. *Toasted.*[14] This is rendered by some mixed, by others toasted or hardened by fire. *Of fried*[14] *crumbs.* The word rendered "fried" occurs only here. But it denotes exposure to the fire in a pan according to the context. 15. *Anointed in his stead.* His successor in the office of high-priest. This implies that the high-priest made this offering for the priestly family, including himself. *Shall make it.* Not only offer, but prepare it. *Wholly burnt.* The whole, not a memorial of it, is to be placed on the altar, because the offerer partakes not of his oblation, and in this case the offerer is the priest himself. 16. *A whole offering.* This term is applied to any offering that is wholly consumed on the altar by fire, and hence to the burnt-sacrifice (1 Sam. vii. 9). The rule of the preceding verses is here generalized, and applied to all priestly oblations. Thus, along with the whole sacrifice of the people, morning and evening, was presented the whole oblation of the high-priest. As the former represented the one propitiation which was of perpetual avail for the chosen people, so the latter symbolized the unblemished integrity of him who was to mediate between God and man. The whole oblation was consequently the meet accompaniment of the whole sacrifice of every evening and morning.

17-23. The law of the sin-sacrifice. Here begins a new communication, which includes the laws of the sin-sacrifice, the trespass-offering and the peace-offering. A new arrangement of the offerings here makes its appearance. The burnt-sacrifice and oblation take the first place, as before, and the other three are formed into one group. Here

90   LAWS OF THE OFFERINGS.

unto Aaron and to his sons, saying, This is the law of the sin-sacrifice: In the place where the burnt-sacrifice is slain shall the sin-sacrifice be slain before the LORD; it is most holy. 19. The priest that offereth it for sin shall eat it: in the holy place

the principle of division is the constant and the occasional. The burnt-sacrifice of the nation is to be presented every morning and evening. And from Num. xv. and xxviii. we learn that it was invariably accompanied with a meat-offering and drink-offering. Hence these two agree in being constant. And it is obvious that the peace-offering being voluntary, and the sin-sacrifice and trespass-offering referring to particular offences, are by their very nature occasional. The constant go before, the occasional follow after. Moreover, the sin-sacrifice and trespass-offering here precede the peace-offering. This rests on another principle of arrangement adapted to the present object. The burnt-sacrifice, being wholly burnt on the altar, is placed first; the oblation, the sin-sacrifice, and the trespass-offering, being usually burnt in part on the altar, and eaten in part by the priests, come next; and the peace-offering being one part burnt on the altar, one part eaten by the priests, and the main part eaten by the worshippers, stands last of all. 18. *Speak unto Aaron.* The priests have the administration of these laws. *The place* of slaughter is first determined. It is where the burnt-sacrifice is slain, at the north side of the altar (i. 11). *It is most holy.* The sacrifice for sin is the substitute for the sinner. It is holy because it must in itself be unblemished, and it is doubly holy because it is unreservedly devoted to the Lord. 19. *That offers it for sin*, literally, that makes it sin, treats it as that which bears iniquity, not its own, but that of another. We have already seen that the victim must be a moral being, a free and independent agent, and that the priest and the victim must be one and the same. But in type this requires a manifold representation. *Shall eat it.* The priest is mediator between the sinner and his Maker. Hence he represents alternately the former and the latter. To eat the sacrifice is to accept it. Hence the priest in doing so represents God; and for this reason he alone is to eat of it. *In the holy place,* the dwelling-place of God, where he welcomes the returning offender.

LEVITICUS VI. 20-23. 91

shall it be eaten, in the court of the tent of meeting. 20. All that toucheth its flesh shall be holy; and when any of its blood is spattered on a garment, thou shalt wash that on which it is spattered in the holy place. 21. And the earthen vessel wherein it is sodden shall be broken; and if it be sodden in a brazen vessel, then it shall be scoured and rinsed in water. 22. Every male among the priests shall eat of it; it is most holy. 23. And no sin-sacrifice, whereof any of the blood is

20. *All that toucheth its flesh.* Everything that innocently touches the flesh, and inanimate objects can only so touch it, shall be holy, consecrated to the Lord. This indicates the expiatory virtue of the sacrifice to him who with an intelligent purpose lays his hand on it. *On a garment.* It is to be remembered that the victim has a twofold character: in itself holy, and in its act most holy; but in the stead of the guilty accursed, suffering the whole penalty of disobedience. The material touch represents the moral touch, the touch of regretful faith in the mediator. The garment accidentally touched with the blood of expiation is tainted with the uncleanness of the sin which it bears, and cannot be put to a common use unless the contact be broken or undone. Hence the garment spattered with the blood must be washed by the priest or his minister in the holy place. 21. *The earthen vessel,* in which the flesh is sodden is by its porous nature so impregnated with its essence that the contact cannot be broken. And hence it must never be used again. It is broken, because it partakes of the curse of sin on the one hand, and in order that it may not be applied to a common use on the other. The brass or copper vessel is to be scoured and rinsed, as in this way the contact is effectually undone. 22. *Every male;* who even in childhood is prospectively a priest. *Among the priests,* in the priestly family. 23. *No sin-sacrifice,* whereof any of the blood has been brought into the sanctuary to make atonement, shall be eaten. This rests on the principle that the priest's eating of the flesh and the burning of the fat on the altar are alike expressive of propitiation. The latter takes place in every sin-sacrifice, and sufficiently expresses propitiation. The former method cannot be employed when the high-priest is the offerer, because the offerer

brought unto the tent of meeting to atone in the holy place, shall be eaten : it shall be burned in the fire.

does not partake of his own sin-sacrifice, and the other priests are in this case also excluded from partaking on the same ground on which no oblation of a priest is to be eaten (vs. 16). The same rule may be extended to the whole congregation, which is a kingdom of priests (Ex. xix. 6), and therefore the high-priest, its representative, does not partake of its sin-sacrifice. These are the two cases in which the blood is brought into the sanctuary, and the flesh is burnt without the camp. *It shall be burned,* consumed by fire in the clean place, without the camp, where the ashes of the altar are laid. This indicates the second death or perpetual destruction, which is the natural destiny of the sinful.

NOTES.

2. *Law,* תּוֹרָה, doctrine, practical principle; r. in hiph. *teach.* *Hearth,* מוֹקְדָה, place of burning. Found only here; r. יָקַד, *burn.* *On it,* בּוֹ. The pronoun both here and in vs. 5 is masculine, and therefore cannot refer to the עֹלָה (Keil) or the מוֹקְדָה, which are feminine. The altar, which is masculine, affords the natural antecedent.

14. *Toasted,* מֻרְבֶּכֶת, Sept. πεφυραμένην, *mixed* or *kneaded.* It occurs only here, in Lev. vii. 12, and 1 Chron. xxiii. 29. *Fried,* תֻּפִינֵי, from תּוּף, *burn.* (F.) or אָפָה, *bake* (Ges.). The construction is very peculiar, giving as the literal rendering, "fried of an oblation of crumbs," the first word agreeing with the last in number.

16. *Whole offering,* כָּלִיל (Ps. li. 21).

VII. LAWS OF THE OFFERINGS — *Continued.*

In this chapter we have the remainder of the third communication and the fourth and fifth on what may be called the by-laws of the offerings. In the continuation of the third communication are included the law of the trespass-offering (1–10), and that of the peace-offering (11–21). The fourth refers to the prohibition of fat and blood, (22–27) ; and the fifth to the rights of the priests in regard to the peace-offerings (28–36). This is followed by the recapitulation (37, 38).

VII. 1. And this is the law of the trespass-offering: it is most holy. 2. In the place where they slay the burnt-sacrifice shall they slay the trespass-offering: and the blood thereof shall he sprinkle on the altar around. 3. And he shall offer of it all its fat; the tail and the fat that covereth the inwards. 4. And the two kidneys and the fat that is upon them, which is by the flanks; and the caul upon the liver, with the kidneys shall he take it away. 5. And the priest shall burn them on the altar, a fire-offering unto the LORD: it is a trespass-offering. 6. Every male among the priests shall eat of it: in the holy place shall it be eaten; it is most holy. 7. As the sin-sacrifice, so is the trespass-offering; they have one law: the priest that

1–10. The law of the trespass-offering. *It is most holy.* The victim being righteous is holy. Being a voluntary substitute for another it is most holy. 2. *The place* of slaughter, on the north side of the altar, as usual (i. 11). *Sprinkle on the altar around,* as in the whole sacrifice (i. 5). The blood of the trespass-offering makes expiation, as that of the burnt-sacrifice. The particulars in this and the three following verses are prescribed, in accordance with iii. 2–5, for the double purpose of completing the former account and connecting the present. 3–5. *All its fat,* as in the sacrifice of peace; indicating the satisfaction which completes propitiation. 6. The flesh is to be eaten by the priests, actual or prospective. This is a token of complete acceptance, as in the sin-sacrifice (vi. 19). 7–10. The dues of the priest in all the preceding offerings. The law of the trespass-offering is completed in the previous verse. Before proceeding to the peace-offering, the sacrifice in which the offerer partakes of the feast, the dues of the priests in the others are determined in a summary way. 7. *So is the trespass-offering.* This is the connecting link with the preceding passage. *They have one law,* regarding the disposal of the flesh. *That atoneth with it.* This points to the difference between the sin and the trespass-offering. With the former the priest expiates for sin (vi. 18); with the latter he atones for trespass, that is, for righteousness unfulfilled. The former represents the suffering of the penalty

atoneth with it shall have it. 8. And the priest that offereth any man's burnt-sacrifice, the skin of the burnt sacrifice which he hath offered he, the priest, shall have. 9. And every oblation that is baken in the oven and all that is made in the pot and on the pan, the priest that offereth it he shall have it. 10. And every oblation, mingled with oil or dry, shall all the sons of Aaron have, the one as the other. ¶

11. And this is the law of the sacrifice of peace, which he

incurred, the latter the performance of the duty neglected. 8. *The skin of the burnt-sacrifice.* From the perquisite of the priest in the trespass-offering and the sin-sacrifice the writer is led to mention the skin of the burnt-sacrifice as the only thing in it belonging to the priest. It is truly the whole-sacrifice, all the flesh being burned on the altar. According to Rabbi Levi the skins of the offerings for sin and trespass went also to the priest, while that of the peace-offering belonged to the offerer (see Mishnah, zeb. xii. 3). 9. All these oblations shall belong to the priest who officiates in receiving them and presenting the memorial of them on the altar. They were cooked, and therefore to be eaten immediately. The priest, whose perquisite they were, was no doubt at liberty to share his superfluity, if any, with other priests. 10. All other oblations of the people, after the memorial was placed on the altar, belonged to the priests in common (see chap. 2). *Mingled with oil or dry.* The former have already been mostly enumerated in chap. ii. The dry included the flour on which oil was merely poured (ii. 1), the sin-sacrifice of flour (v. 13), the sheaf of the first-fruits (xxiii. 10), the jealousy oblation (Num. v. 18), and the like. *The one as the other.* These oblations were not cooked, and were perhaps more abundant than the others. They form therefore a common store.

11–18. The law of the peace-offering. Of this there are three kinds, thanksgiving, the vow, and the free gift. 11. *Which he shall offer.* The phrase is indefinite, which one shall offer, or which may be offered. In the ordinance for this sacrifice the disposal of the blood and of the fat was very precisely and fully laid down in chap. iii., with a closing warning against the eating of fat or blood. But no intimation was

shall offer to the LORD. 12. If he offer it for a thanksgiving, then he shall offer with the sacrifice of thanksgiving sweet cakes mingled with oil, and sweet wafers anointed with oil, and cakes of toasted flour mingled with oil. 13. With cakes of leavened bread he shall make his offering, with his thank-sacrifice of peace. 14. And he shall offer of it one out of the whole offering, a heaving unto the LORD: the priest that sprinkleth the blood of the peace-offering shall have it. 15. And the

given of the use that was to be made of the flesh. This was in keeping with the end then in view, which was to mark that which effects atonement, and procured acceptance and all the blessings it involves. We are now to be made acquainted with a secondary or subsidiary part of the peace-offering of the deepest interest to the pious offerer. This is the sacrificial feast which was made of the flesh and accompanying oblation and libation (Num. xv.). This was the earnest and the foreshadow of all the blessings of peace with God through the atonement of the Mediator. 12. The thank-offering. Here we are informed that the sacrifice of peace is to be accompanied with sweet, that is unleavened, cakes, mingled with oil, sweet wafers spread with oil, and another kind of cakes toasted in a particular manner. 13. *With cakes of leavened bread.* These are not the proper offering, but an accompaniment of it. The offering is given in the previous verse. This was to be a communion feast, and an ample supply of bread was necessary, that it might be eaten with the flesh. But none of the leavened bread is to be placed on the altar (ii. 11). *With his thank-sacrifice of peace.* The sacrifice of peace now in question is the thanksgiving, with which is connected the oblation of cakes, laid on or presented with cakes of leavened bread for the accompanying feast. 14. *One out of the whole offering.* This one is an acknowledgment that the whole belongs to the Lord. It is not, however, a memorial to be burnt upon the altar, but a *heaving* or heave-offering to the Lord. The heaving is that which is heaved up in token of its being dedicated to the Lord, without being laid on the altar to be burned as a sweet smell (Num. v. 9). Instead of this, it shall be given to the priest who sprinkles the blood of the peace-offering on the altar. 15.

flesh of his thank-sacrifice of peace shall be eaten in the day of his offering: he shall not leave any of it till the morning. 16. And if the sacrifice of his offering be a vow or a free gift, it shall be eaten in the day that he offereth his sacrifice: and on the morrow that which is left of it shall be eaten. 17. And that which is left of the flesh of the sacrifice on the third day shall be burnt with fire. 18. And if any of the flesh of his sacrifice of peace be at all eaten on the third day, it shall not be accepted, it shall not be counted to him that offereth it; it shall be a foul thing; and the soul that eateth of it shall bear

In the day of his offering. The flesh of the thank-offering is to be eaten by the offerer on the day on which it is presented. None of it is to be left till the next day. This is the solemn and joyful act that imparts its peculiar character to the peace-offering. It is symbolic of the benefits and privileges of those who are reconciled to God, admitted to his home, and treated as his children and heirs. It stands at the end of all faith, the crowning solemnity and sole festival of the people of God, as the day of atonement stands at the beginning of all repentance, the solitary day of sorrow and self-humiliation throughout the year.

16. The vow or free gift. This may be eaten on the day of offering or the next day. The offering of gratitude is more worthy than that of the vow or the free gift. It is therefore to be exhausted by generosity to the poor on the day of offering (Corn. a Lap.). 17. The remainder on the third day is to be burned with fire in the clean place where the ashes of the altar are deposited, or in some place equally suitable. 18. If eaten on the third day, it will not be accepted. It will then be beginning to putrefy, and will be unfit for food, much less for being accepted as the representative of the unblemished victim. *It shall not be counted* to the offerer as a sacrifice of peace. To count or impute is to reckon to his account, so that he has the credit of it, and the full benefit accruing therefrom. This is a word of incalculable interest to him who is guilty and doomed to die. It indicates the possibility and the mode of deliverance from this doom, on two con-

his iniquity. 19. And the flesh that toucheth any unclean thing shall not be eaten; it shall be burnt with fire: but the flesh in itself every one that is clean shall eat. 20. And the soul that eateth flesh of the sacrifice of peace that belongeth to the LORD, while his uncleanness is on him, that soul shall even

ditions external to the sinner: first, that one be found willing and able to allow the sin to be counted to him, and so to do and to bear for the sinner all that justice demands; and second, that the Judge of all the earth be pleased to count the sin to the substitute, and his obedience and suffering to the guilty, and so to pardon and accept the sinner. One other condition in the sinner himself is necessary, in order that this merciful imputation may avail him. He must with becoming feelings come before his Maker, and lay his hand upon the substitute. *It shall be a foul thing*,[18] a fetid or corrupt thing, abhorrent to the pure taste or sense. *Bear his iniquity.* He shall incur blame by doing that which is forbidden; and, as his sacrifice ceases to have any propitiating power, all his guilt remains as it was before it was offered.

19-21. Uncleanness bars from communion. The nullifying effect of eating the flesh of the peace-offering on the third day naturally leads to the distinction of the clean and the unclean, and to the consequent determination that the former are admissible to the sacrificial feast, the latter not. The question is a practical one likely to arise, and needing an answer. This is the proper time to give it. 19. *The flesh that toucheth any unclean thing.* As contact with the flesh of the sin-sacrifice renders holy, so contact with anything unclean defiles the flesh of the peace-offering, and renders it ceremonially unfit for food. It is to be consumed by fire. Otherwise the *flesh in itself*, apart from such contact, may be partaken of by all that are clean. This precept applies to all flesh killed for food, as it was, in some respect, dedicated to the Lord (Lev. xvii.; Deut. xii. 6, 21-25). 20. *The soul that eateth flesh.* Ceremonial uncleanness unfits for sacrificial communion. The lesson here taught is of essential importance. We have seen above that the doctrine of imputation, in all its length and breadth, is the external condition of deliverance for a soul that has

be cut off from his people. 21. And the soul that toucheth anything unclean, the uncleanness of man or an unclean beast or any unclean loathsome thing, and eateth of the flesh of the sacrifice of peace which belongeth to the LORD, that soul shall even be cut off from his people.

22. And the LORD spake unto Moses, saying, 23. Speak

sinned against God. The internal condition requisite to salvation is not left in the background. Penitent faith, acknowledging, feeling, and accepting the mercy of God in the atonement, is the fruit of the new birth. This moral cleanness is represented by the ceremonial cleanness. He that draws nigh to God must be holy. His very drawing nigh is the consequence of a change of heart. For the penitent sinner the propitiation affords the legal qualification for acceptance; the penitence itself is the moral qualification for accepting the atonement and holding communion with God. *That belongeth to the Lord*, and hence is set apart to a holy use. *Cut off from his people.* This is to be excluded from the covenant of grace, and treated as a heathen or alien (Gen. xvii. 14). He that wittingly violates the sanctity of the law tramples under foot the blood of the covenant, and thereby makes himself an alien from the commonwealth of Israel and a stranger from the covenants of promise. This exclusion was sometimes attended with the sentence of death, as in Ex. xxxi. 14. But this was owing to the violation of some civil law, and not the necessary consequence of excommunication. 21. Ceremonial defilement arises from touching anything unclean (v. 2, 3). *Any unclean loathsome thing,*[21] either fish, fowl, or smaller animal. A loathsome thing is more comprehensive than a crawler, a word which some read here. The necessity of cleanness, and therefore of the holiness which it symbolizes, is enforced by the reiteration of the sentence of excommunication.

22–27. A communication is here made emphatically forbidding the eating of fat or blood. As the peace-offering is a sacrificial feast, in which alone the offerer and his company partake of the flesh of the victims, this is the appropriate place for reiterating this precept, and inserting a special communication on the subject. 23. *No fat of*

unto the sons of Israel, saying, Ye shall eat no fat of ox or sheep or goat. 24. And the fat of the dead and the fat of the torn may be put to any use; but ye shall in no wise eat of it. 25. For whosoever eateth the fat of the beast of which he may present a fire-offering unto the LORD, the soul that eateth shall be cut off from his people. 26. And ye shall eat no blood in all your dwellings of fowl or of cattle. 27. Every soul that eateth any blood, even that soul shall be cut off from his people. ¶

ox, or sheep, or goat. This refers to the fat pieces constantly enumerated (iii. 3, 4, 9, 10, 14, 15) and not to any fat intermixed with the flesh in other parts of the body. 24. *The dead,* that which has died of itself. *The torn,* is that which has been killed by a wild beast. All oxen, sheep, or goats slain, while the people were in the wilderness, were to be brought to the door of the tent of meeting, that the blood might be sprinkled on the altar and the fat burned for a sweet smell unto the Lord (Lev. xvii. 3–6). Among the changes required for a settled state in their own land, permission is given to slay cattle for consumption in their gates, with the sole condition that the blood be spilled on the ground (Deut. xii. 20–25). The fat is not mentioned in the passage quoted. 25. Hence it appears that the prohibition refers to the fat of those kinds of animals that may be used for sacrifice, and not to that of other kinds of clean animals that may be eaten, but not sacrificed. The penalty of violating this prohibition is excommunication. We have already seen that the fat burned on the altar represents the perfect obedience of the Mediator, which is the essential element of propitiation for sin. The fat being exclusively devoted to this sacred use is not to be applied to any profane or common use. 26, 27. The prohibition of blood is here added. *In all your dwellings.* These words extend the precept to the residence of the people in the land of promise. In this respect the law concerning blood is more comprehensive than that concerning fat. *Fowl and cattle.* The fat of fowl has not been previously noticed; but the blood is made as important as that of cattle. The penalty of excommunication is applied also to the neglect of this precept. This gives

28. And the LORD spake unto Moses, saying, 29. Speak unto the sons of Israel, saying, He that offereth his sacrifice of peace unto the LORD shall bring his offering to the LORD of his sacrifice of peace. 30. His hands shall bring the fire-offerings of the LORD; the fat with the breast he shall bring,

a unity to the three offences of eating the flesh of the peace-offering in a state of uncleanness, of eating the fat or the blood, inasmuch as they all cut off from the communion of the faithful, and therefore from the feast of peace, which is only open to the children of the covenant.

28–36. The priest's portion in the peace-offering. This is a special communication. It comes in here in its right place, as it completes the account of the peace-offering. This offering stands out by itself as that in which the flesh remains the property of the worshipper, whereas in all the others it was burnt on the altar, burnt in the place of ashes, or eaten by the priests. Hence, when the priest's rights in all the other sacrifices were enumerated, this was omitted, because the people here took the place of the priest in respect of the flesh. When the special nature of this offering in this respect has been made prominent, a new communication is made, addressed to the sons of Israel, and directing them, among other things, to assign certain portions of the victims to the priest. 29. *His offering to the Lord*, the part that is set apart to the Lord from the peace-offering. The Lord is present at this festival, partaking with his people. The beatitude of holiness is common to the Lord with all his intelligent and holy creatures. 30. *His hands shall bring.* It shall be a solemn act of the worshipper in person. The only apparent exceptions to this are the acts of the people by their representative head, and of the family by the father. *The fire-offerings*, those parts which are to be burned on the altar. These are described as the fat with the breast. This goes to prove that the use of any part as food by the priest is of the same import as the turning of it by fire into a sweet smell before the Lord. *With the breast*, or brisket. The breast is particularly relished as a dainty (Kalisch). It is also central in the body, and adjacent to the seat of life. It is therefore suitable for the Lord's part of the

the breast to make it a waving before the LORD. 31. And the priest shall burn the fat upon the altar; and Aaron and his sons shall have the breast. 32. And the right leg shall ye give as a heaving to the priest out of your sacrifices of peace. 33. He of the sons of Aaron that offereth the blood of the peace-offering and the fat shall have the right leg for his part. 34. For the wave-breast and the heave-leg have I taken of the sons of Israel from their sacrifices of peace, and I give them to Aaron the priest and to his sons as a statute forever from the

sacrifice of peace. This was to be waved before the Lord. *Waving*[30] is moving to and fro. It probably denotes communion among the worshippers, as heaving points to their relation to God; (see in Ex. xxix. 24). With the apparent exception of this and the corresponding passage Lev. viii. 27, it applies to that which is reserved from the altar to be assigned to the priest for his own use. The exception is only apparent; for the ram of consecration was a priest's offering, and therefore the right leg which would otherwise fall to the priest is consumed on the altar, as in the case of the priest's daily oblation. The communion of saints is founded on communion with God. Hence the waving is before the Lord. 31. The fat is burned as a sweet smell unto the Lord. The breast is handed over to the priests. 32. *And the right leg.*[32] The Sept. uniformly gives the fore-arm for this word in the present application. There is no decided reason against this rendering, as the word only applies in one other passage (1 Sam. ix. 24) to the limb of an animal. It appears to be used in a large sense here, to include the thigh as well as the leg properly so called, since the latter would yield very little flesh. *As a heaving.* This was a raising up in token of dedication to God, or communion with him. 33. *He . . . . . that offereth.* The priest that officiates receives it, as he is the representative of God. The blood is for expiation and the fat for propitiation, in which consists the proper function of the priest. 34. The wave-breast, which is the Lord's part in the sacrificial feast, is given to the priests in common; the heave-leg falls to him who officiates on the occasion. *From their sacrifices of peace.* There is a different arrangement provided for other animals that were

102   LAWS OF THE OFFERINGS.

sons of Israel. 35. This is the portion of Aaron and the portion of his sons out of the fire-offerings of the LORD in the day when he presented them to be priests unto the LORD ; 36. Which the LORD commanded to give to them in the day that he anointed them, from the sons of Israel, by a statute forever for their generations.

37. This is the law for the burnt-sacrifice, for the oblation, and for the sin-sacrifice, and for the trespass-offering, and for the consecration, and for the sacrifice of peace. 38. Which the LORD commanded Moses in mount Sinai, in the day that he commanded the sons of Israel to make their offerings unto the LORD in the wilderness of Sinai.   ¶

slain for food in their own land (Deut. xviii. 3). *The portion*,[35] the unction or perquisite connected with their consecration. The heave-leg of the ram of consecration was burned upon the altar, and belongs to the Lord for his priest thenceforward. *In the day when he presented them.* The verb is without a definite subject. The Lord by his minister, Moses, brings them nigh to be his attendants. *To be priests;* literally to do the part of a priest. 36. *In the day that he anointed them.* The same subject is to be supplied also in this sentence.

37, 38. These verses contain the summing up at the close of this section. This refers in the first instance to the last two chapters, as it begins with the burnt-sacrifice and goes on in nearly the same order to the peace-offering. But it is evident that it really covers the whole section, as the supplementary directions contained in these chapters for the guidance of the priests, presuppose the fundamental principles of these offerings addressed in the first five chapters to the people, without which they would be defective and unmeaning. It affords us the opportunity of recalling to mind the contents of these chapters in the order of the present recapitulation.

The burnt-sacrifice was a victim of which the blood was wholly sprinkled on the altar, and the fat with all the flesh was burned on the altar as a fire-offering of a sweet smell unto the Lord. It is to be observed that the blood sprinkled on the altar does not awaken any emotions of a pleasing kind in God. It is never said to be a sweet smell. And when we reflect that it is the blood that atones or expiates, because the blood shed is the life given, we do not wonder at this. We feel that it must call forth far different emotions in the breast of God as well as in the heart of man. The sense of justice constraining to exact death from the sinner himself or from the voluntary victim that has taken his place is very far from being agreeable. It is the dire, hard, and strange work of the Holy and the Just One to vindicate the law and lay iniquity on the sinner or the sinner's friend. And wrath, indignation, grief, pity, and other painful feelings akin to these, contend with one another when this has to be done, and cannot be avoided. And what shame, sadness, and solemn awe, what regret and self-reproach, what unutterable throes of repentance, it is fitted to excite in the sinner who sees the victim bleed and die in his stead. On the other hand, the fat and the flesh turned by the fire of the altar into a subtile fume that scents the gale is the meet emblem of that righteousness with which the Lord is well pleased. Hence it is invariably said of the fire-offering that it is a sweet smell unto the Lord. The Scripture is full of the delight which the Lord takes in holiness, justice, goodness, truth, obedience, love. Passive, suffering satisfaction is to him a painful necessity; active, victorious satisfaction is a source of the purest delight. The burnt-sacrifice is, moreover, a whole sacrifice, to indicate a complete propitiation. It stands at the head, and contains the sum and substance of all sacrifice. It was accordingly presented not only by the individual on private occasions, but by the whole nation on the common altar every morning and evening, and formed the chief and central sacrifice in all the annual solemnities of the chosen people.

The oblation was a vegetable offering, chiefly of grain, mostly in the form of flour, and occasionally accompanied with oil and frankincense. In most sacrifices it was also associated with the libation of wine, mentioned elsewhere, (Num. xv.), which was of the same nature and significance. Like the fat and the flesh of the animal sacrifice, it represents obedience or good works, and therefore it is made a fire-offering of a sweet smell unto the Lord. It presupposes the burnt-sacrifice of propitiation, on the ground of which the offerer has already been accepted (i. 4). He is now walking with God and all his well-meant endeavors are accepted, with himself, through the merits of the unblemished Redeemer. He offers his oblation in token of his obligation and his purpose to do the will of God. The oblation of the high-priest every morning and evening has a peculiar significance. He represents the Mediator, and therefore his oblation symbolizes the obedience or righteousness of the Mediator himself. Hence it is the fitting accompaniment of the morning and evening burnt-sacrifice.

The sin-sacrifice and *the trespass-offering* are properly classed together. Like the oblation they presume the offerer to have been already accepted in the burnt-offering of propitiation, and now to be a member of the commonwealth of Israel and a party in the covenant of grace. While his full purpose is to endeavor after new obedience, yet sins of inadvertence sometimes intervene to mar the beauty of his work and disturb the peace of his conscience. The sacrifices now in question serve to represent a fresh pleading of the blood of sprinkling and of the unblemished integrity of the substitute for the relief of conscience, the deepening of humility, the perfecting of repentance, and the recovery of the assurance of God's love. The sin-sacrifice refers mainly to the wrong done to the Author of our being, and therefore impressively to the blood of expiation, while it presupposes the obedience that propitiates. The trespass-offering looks to the right that ought to have been done, and lays emphasis on the positive satisfaction which magnifies and glorifies the law. They are the counterparts of one another, and together make up that which is signified by the burnt-sacrifice. Hence it is that the sinner is constantly said to be a trespasser, and the trespasser a sinner in the same offence; and hence these two offerings are often made at the same time for the one object.

The consecration is the filling of the hands of the priests with the things to be offered. This was the simple and primitive mode of appointing them to their office. Filling the hands was, however, a wider phrase, as it applied either to the worshipper providing himself with gifts to appear before the Lord, or to the consecrator putting the gifts to be offered into the hands of the priest in the act of consecration. This ordinance does not come within the cycle of offerings contained in these seven chapters, though it consists of a number of these, and especially of the peace-offering. The proper formulary for it is contained in Ex. xxix., and forms part of the communications made to Moses during the first forty days he was on the mount. This in itself affords one of the presumptions in favor of these seven chapters having been revealed to Moses in the period posterior to the idolatry of the people, and the pitching of the tent of meeting far from the camp, and prior to the consecration of the priests and the dedication of the tabernacle. The only allusion to this ordinance is in vi. 12–16, when the oblation of the high-priest to be presented on the occasion of his consecration and thenceforward every morning and evening is prescribed. It is placed here after the sin and trespass offerings, and before the peace-offering, because the ram of consecration, which gives character to the consecrating ordinance, is of a kindred nature with the peace-offering, and forms an act of communion.

The sacrifice of peace is distinguished by the feast upon the sacrifice which indicates participation in all the benefits of acceptance with God through the Redeemer. Hence in a wide sense it includes the passover and the consecration of priests, in both of which fellowship in the benefits of redemption through the blood of atonement is symbolized. It is, then, a step in advance of the burnt-sacrifice, as fellowship is beyond propitiation. It transcends also the oblation on the one hand, and the sin and trespass offerings on the other hand, as fellowship with God in the Mediator is something beyond the imperfect endeavors of the accepted soul after new obedience. Hence we perceive that this cycle of offerings has its ground in the history of redemption, and is a faithful reflection of the beginning, progress, and end of salvation from sin.

In these remarkable chapters we have a striking example of the mode of composition habitually pursued by Moses. As in the last chapter of Exodus he pursues his stately march through the process of the solemn erection of the tabernacle, without allowing himself or his reader to be embarrassed by preliminary, collateral, or consecutive details, which are reserved to be afterwards inserted at convenience in the two subsequent books, so here, in the first five chapters he lays down the fundamental principles of the several offerings for the instruction of the people, and reserves for the sixth and seventh chapters the collateral regulations for the further guidance of the priests. When we consider that there are nine separate communications of very variable lengths in these seven chapters, we cannot but acknowledge the good order with which they are combined into a whole.

38. *In mount Sinai.* This appears to refer to the tent of meeting, which Moses pitched without the camp on the slopes of Sinai. (See on i. 1.) Otherwise the last two chapters must have preceded the former five. *In the day.* On the occasion of the erection of the tabernacle, which, with the consecration of the priests, occupied seven preliminary days, and was consummated on the eighth day, which was the first day of the second year, on which the princes of the tribes of Israel came forward to make their offerings. This goes to prove that these chapters were made known by Moses to the people shortly before the formal setting up of the tabernacle. *In the wilderness of Sinai.* The present regulations apply in several of their details to the encampment in the wilderness, a state of things which might have terminated in the course of the second year. They will at all events have to undergo the requisite modifications when the camp and the wilderness pass away. Some of these modifications are expressly ordered in the subsequent books of the Pentateuch, for instance, in Deut. xii. 15. Some of them are not put on record, though they must have been introduced in practice. And others still would have been made, had the course of events in the future history of Israel been different from what it actually turned out to be. For instance, one central plan was no doubt necessary for the ark of God, containing the two tables of the testimony, to impress upon men's minds the unity of God and of his people. But this is not inconsistent with the erection of an altar and a sanctuary, it might be in every tribe for the convenience of mothers and children, who could not go far from home (Lev. xii.), and for the relief of the metropolitan sanctuary, which would otherwise be overcrowded with worshippers. And it is certainly quite in keeping with the worship of God on the weekly Sabbath in the meeting-place of every village or township in all the dwellings of the people (Lev. xxiii. 3). A remarkable intimation of the lawfulness and probability in certain circumstances of establishing local sanctuaries is found at the very close of the moral law, and at the threshold of the civil code (Ex. xx. 24) : "An altar of earth thou shalt make unto me, and shalt sacrifice thereon thy burnt-sacrifices

and thy peace-offerings, thy sheep and thy oxen; in every place where I record my name I will come unto thee and bless thee." This implies, it may be, successive places; but we have no reason whatever to exclude simultaneous places of sacrificial worship also to meet the exigencies of a wide-spreading population. The groundless hypothesis that subordinate details adapted to the circumstances of the desert are, or are intended to be, stereotyped for all future stages of the history of God's people, is a fertile source of stumbling to the inconsiderate, objection for the sciolist, and difficulty in the way of the easy and safe interpretation of the law.

NOTES.

13. *With cakes*, עַל־חַלֹּת, upon cakes of. These broad round cakes may have been placed under the properly sacrificial cakes of the previous verse.

18. *A foul thing*, פִּגּוּל, Sept. μίασμα. The word occurs elsewhere only in Lev. xix. 7, Isa. lxv. 4, and Ezek. iv. 14, and it is well to distinguish it in the rendering from terms of kindred meaning.

21. *Loathsome thing*, שֶׁקֶץ. This form occurs about ten times, of which eight are in Leviticus. *Crawler* or *creeper*, שֶׁרֶץ.

30. *Wave*, הֵנִיף. It is used of the van in winnowing, the sieve in sifting, the saw in cutting, the stick in beating, the hand in beckoning and threatening. *A waving*, תְּנוּפָה.

32. *Leg*, שׁוֹק, Sept. βραχίων, the fore-leg, including both the leg and the shoulder, always in the present connection. Onk., the Syr., and the Arab. retain the original word; and the Latin versions of these have generally *armus*, but occasionally *crus*. The word is used six times of the human leg, Deut. xxv. 35; Judg. xv. 8; Ps. cxlvii. 10; Prov. xxvi. 7; Cant. v. 15; Isa. xlvii. 2. Only in 1 Sam. ix. 24 is it rendered κωλέα, *the thigh-bone*. This, indeed, is the only other passage in which it is applied to an animal. *Arm*, זְרוֹעַ, is applied to the fore-leg of animals in Num. vi. 19; Deut. xviii. 3. This seems to be the same limb, only more precisely defined by a term borrowed from the human form, and so distinguished from the hind-leg, which corresponds strictly to the human leg. כְּרָעַיִם seems to apply to the two hind legs in particular.

35. *Portion*, מִשְׁחָה, ointment, gift; r. *spread over*, *lay on*, *anoint*. This noun is rendered in Onk. רְבוּת, *increase* or *gift*.

SECTION II.—CONSECRATION OF THE PRIESTS.

VIII. AARON AND HIS SONS CONSECRATED.

THE directions concerning the raiment and the consecration of the priests are given in Ex. xxviii. and xxix. The execution of the order concerning the raiment is recorded in Ex. xxxix. 1-31. The remainder of this chapter contains the announcement that the work of the tabernacle, having been completed, was presented to Moses. The present section of the Book of Leviticus contains the record of the consecration of the priests, and the solemn events that accompanied that ceremonial. It was strongly felt by the rabbis that the consecration of Aaron and his sons, which lasted seven days, must have preceded the formal inauguration of the national worship in the tabernacle. Hence Rabbi Salomo affirms that the consecration here narrated took place on the last seven days of the first year. There is much to be said in favor of this view. It would be preposterous to suppose all the offerings of the princes made and the passover celebrated in the first month before the consecration of the priests. And it would be a very cumbrous and embarrassing arrangement to have the offerings of the princes and the consecration of the priests going on with equal pace during the first seven or eight days of the first month. And the fire from the Lord consuming the sacrifices, which is the closing event of the eighth day (ix. 24), fits in very well with the glory of the Lord filling the tabernacle when the process of erecting it was completed (Ex. xl. 34). Moreover, the princes are said to come forward to offer on the day on which Moses finished setting up the tabernacle (Num. vii. 1), which implies that the setting up had occupied several days. Other coincidences will present themselves to the attentive reader; and we have now only to add that the narrative is not inconsistent with this arrangement. We may suppose that the command to have the tabernacle erected on the first day of the new year was given to

Moses at the time when the priestly attire and all the parts and properties of the tabernacle had been presented before him. This may have been eight or ten days before the end of the first year About the same time the order to consecrate the priests was issued, as the necessary preliminary to the opening of the tabernacle service. This order required a period of seven days for its due execution. On receiving it, therefore, Moses proceeds to convene the assembly at the door of the tent of meeting. The tent of meeting must have been so far constructed as to admit of this locality being fixed for the convocation. We are not to suppose, with some of the rabbis, that the tabernacle was set up and taken down every day of the seven during which the consecration of the priests was going on; though, as it was a tent designed to be moved from place to place, and therefore frequently taken down and set up again, the supposition is not absurd. In the absence of any record we cannot tell how the matter was actually arranged. But we see no reason why Bezalel might not present the tabernacle with all its parts put together in due form, or, what is no less probable, why Moses, with the assistance of the master and his craftsmen, might not once for all set it up as far as was necessary for the consecration of the priests. On the former supposition, we may conceive that Bezalel would take the tent to pieces that it might be formally erected again by Moses. The latter hypothesis is not inconsistent with the statement of Ex. xl. 17: "And it came to pass, in the first month, in the second year, on the first day of the month, that the tabernacle was set up." This implies that the solemn pitching of the tabernacle was completed on that day. And the following verses (18 sq.) then merely describe the process, which may have been commenced some days before. This view is also favored by the statement of Ex. xxix. 36, 37: "And thou shalt offer every day a bullock of sin-offering for atonement; and thou shalt purge the altar, when thou atonest for it, and shalt anoint it to hallow it. Seven days shalt thou atone for the altar, and hallow it." Hence it appears that the seven days of consecration were, at the same time, seven days of hallowment or dedication of the altar. This gives a new significance and comprehensiveness to these seven days; as they apply not only to the priests, but to the tabernacle and its sacred furniture. It also speaks very strongly for the consecration of the priests being prelim-

VIII. 1. And the LORD spake unto Moses, saying, 2. Take Aaron and his sons with him, and the garments, and the anointing oil, and the bullock of sin-sacrifice, and the two

inary to the inauguration of the tabernacle service. If the altar must be purged seven days before it is fit for the solemn worship of God, must not this have taken place before the formal opening of the daily service, and the long succession of inaugural offerings to be made by the princes of the tribes? It is befitting the grandeur and sacredness of the occasion that the successive steps in the formal erection of the tabernacle should not be crowded into a single day, but extended over the period of seven days, a number not only of suitable magnitude, but of hereditary sacredness. It may be added that this view goes to confirm the conclusion that the preceding seven chapters were communicated at a still earlier period.

The present section contains three chapters: the first recording the consecration of the priests and the sanctifying of the tabernacle, and especially the altar; the second, the inauguration of the national worship on the first day of the new year; and the third, the occurrence of a melancholy event on the occasion, and the remainder of the details that are necessary to complete the previous chapter.

The eighth chapter reports the consecration of Aaron and his two sons. It contains the arraying of the priests and the anointing of them and of the tabernacle (1–13), and the consecration of the priests (14–36). The latter may be subdivided into the sin-sacrifice (14–17), the burnt-sacrifice (18–21), and the ram of consecration (22–36).

1–13. The arraying of the priests and the anointing of the tabernacle, of the furniture, and of the high priest. This command is given to Moses after Bezalel had finished his work, and presented it all before him. 2. *Take Aaron.* He is thus called of God to be a priest. This divine appointment assures the people of acceptance through his mediation. *And his sons with him.* This secures the succession not of one line, but of the whole family, and provides the high-priest with duly qualified assistants in his work. *And the garments*, which Bezalel and his craftsmen have now prepared (Ex. xxxix.). *And the anointing oil.* The directions for the composition of this oil are given

LEVITICUS VIII. 1-7.   111

rams, and the basket of sweet bread. 3. And gather all the assembly unto the door of the tent of meeting. 4. And Moses did as the LORD commanded him: and the assembly was gathered unto the door of the tent of meeting. 5. And Moses said unto the assembly, This is the thing which the LORD hath commanded to do. 6. And Moses presented Aaron and his sons and washed them with water. 7. And he put

in Ex. xxx. 22–33, which is a part of the communication made to Moses on the mount. From this passage we learn that the tabernacle with its furniture, and Aaron and his sons were to be anointed with it. Moses, of course, had it prepared by the perfumer. *And the bullock.* This and the two rams and the basket of sweet bread are all prescribed in Ex. xxix. 3. *And gather all the assembly.* This consecration was to be public, that the whole congregation might be aware that the priests had been duly appointed to their office. The assembly consisted of the adult men of twenty years old and upward. It was the lawfully constituted convention of the nation. When regularly summoned, those who were present formed a lawful assembly. Those who were absent, including the women and minors, would learn the event from those who were present. *Unto the door of the tent of meeting*, where the altar stood, in the rear and by the sides of which the people would stand at a respectful distance. We cannot tell whether the hangings of the court were yet put up. But only the slaves of a narrow literalism can suppose the whole people to be present to a man at any public meeting. The tent of meeting was the place where God met with man. 4. Moses obeys, and convenes the meeting. 5. He explains what is about to be done, that the assembly may be intelligent witnesses. The obedience of man to God is a reasonable service. 6. *Presented.* This is the word usually rendered "offered." It means, literally, "brought near." *And washed them*, according to the directions in Ex. xxxix. 4. The washing with water is a symbol of internal cleansing or sanctification. This washing was performed at the laver, which stood between the altar and the door of the tabernacle. See on Ex. xxix. 4. 7. Moses now arrays Aaron with the robes of the high-priesthood. *The coat* and *girdle*

upon him the coat and girded him with the girdle, and clothed him with the robe, and put upon him the ephod, and girded him with the belt of the ephod, and bound it with it. 8. And he put upon him the breast-plate, and set in the breast-plate the Urim and the Tummim. 9. And he put the mitre on his head, and put upon the mitre on his forehead the golden plate,

are mentioned in Ex. xxviii. 40; xxxix. 27-29. The coat was the inner garment, worn over the shirt and reaching to the feet. The robe and the ephod, with its belt, are described in Ex. xxviii. 31-35, 6-12, and explained in the remarks on these passages. The robe is entirely of blue, and on the skirt of it were pomegranates of blue and purple and crimson, alternating with bells of gold. It reached to the knee. It was worn over the coat. The ephod with its belt covered the back down to the waist. On the shoulder-straps of it were attached two onyx stones, set in gold, and having each six of the names of the twelve tribes of Israel engraven on it. 8. *The breast-plate.* The robe, the ephod, and the breast-plate were the three pieces of dress peculiar to the high-priest. The breast-plate covered the breast, as the ephod did the back, and was fastened to it by laces. *The Urim and the Tummim*, the Lights and the Rights, or perfections, are the twelve precious stones, fitted in a case and placed in the breast-plate, having the names of the twelve tribes engraven on them. 9. *The mitre* and the golden plate, *the holy crown*, on which was engraven the words, HOLINESS TO THE LORD, are described in Ex. xxviii. 36-39. For the details of the explanation of the priestly attire, we refer to Ex. xxviii. Suffice it to say here that the coat shadowed forth the holiness, and the robe the righteousness, of the high-priest. The ephod bearing the onyx stones on the shoulder-straps, with the breast-plate containing the Urim and the Tummim, is symbolic of the priestly function. He bears the people on his shoulders as the propitiator, taking upon him their responsibilities, and on his breast as the intercessor pleading their cause. Each stone in the breast-plate is a light and a right, and all together are emblematic of the complete light and righteousness, or illuminating and propitiating virtue of the great High Priest. The holy crown, with its legible and intelligible motto,

LEVITICUS VIII. 8-13.   113

the holy crown; as the LORD commanded Moses. 10. And Moses took the anointing oil, and anointed the tabernacle and all that was therein, and sanctified them. 11. And he spattered thereof upon the altar seven times, and anointed the altar and all its vessels, and the laver and its stand, to sanctify them. 12. And he poured of the anointing oil upon Aaron's head, and anointed him, to sanctify him. 13. And Moses presented Aaron's sons, and clothed them with coats and girded them with a girdle, and bound bonnets upon them; as the LORD commanded Moses.

indicates the holiness and authority which appertain to the royal Priest. And in their correlation the stones on the shoulder specially denote the priestly, those on the breast-plate the prophetic, and the golden plate on the forehead the kingly, function of the Mediator.

10-12 The anointing (Ex. xxix. 7). The unction is typical of sanctification (1 John ii. 20). The tabernacle, the altar, the laver, and all their appurtenances were to be anointed (Ex. xxx. 26-29). *And sanctified them.* Sanctifying is here setting apart to a holy use. It is the symbol of internal or moral sanctification. It is here described as the effect of the anointing. 11. *And he spattered thereof.* The mode of anointing is here indicated. The seven times are significant of the perfection of holiness which is to belong to the altar. 12. *And he poured.* On Aaron's head the anointing oil is not spattered but poured, so that it trickled down his beard and reached to the skirt of his garment (Ps. cxxxiii.). This indicates the plenitude of holiness which is to be in the high-priest. *And anointed him to sanctify him.* This is the constant phrase to denote the effect of anointing. 13. The coats, girdles, and bonnets of the ordinary priests are then put on. Aaron's sons may, in Scripture phrase, include grandsons, if any of them were of the proper age. The silence of Scripture regarding them is not a proof to the contrary effect. *As the Lord commanded Moses.* The whole ceremonial is a divine institution and derives all its authority and all its significance from this fact. Hence the writer is careful to note this circumstance. Rites of human institution have no authority or valid significance.

AARON AND HIS SONS CONSECRATED.

14. And he brought nigh the bullock of the sin-sacrifice; and Aaron and his sons laid their hands on the head of the bullock of sin-sacrifice. 15. And he slew it; and Moses took the blood and put it on the horns of the altar around, and

14–36. The consecration. This begins with the sin-sacrifice 14–17. (See on Ex. xxix. 10–14). *And he brought nigh.* Some one did this on behalf of Aaron and his sons, who are the offerers in this case. *The bullock of sin-sacrifice.* When the children of God, already accepted through the one coming propitiation, appear before him on solemn occasions it is meet to present the sin-sacrifice for such sin of inadvertence as they may have contracted. Hence, on the consecration of the priestly family the sin-sacrifice is presented first to set them right in the view of the law for the coming solemnity. *Aaron and his sons,* as the offerers laid their hands on the head of the victim in due form. Moses is here the officiating priest, by the command of the Lord. 15. *And he slew it.* Some one of or for Aaron and his sons performed this part. *And Moses took.* The acts proper to the officiating priest are carefully distinguished from those which are performed by the worshipper or his assistant. *The blood* that expiates. *On the horns.* These are more elevated than the sides of the altar. The place of application is more solemn, in keeping with the pre-eminent solemnity of the occasion, though the significance of the blood is the same. The ritual here agrees with Ex. xxix. 12; and though it differs from Lev. iv. 6, 7, it agrees with Lev. iv. 25, 30. The actual fact of a known sin of inadvertence in the high-priest is more pregnant with evil consequences than in an ordinary member of the sacred community, or than the possibility of an inadvertent sin which is unknown and unproved. *And sanctified it to atone for it.*[15] We are to notice the distinction between this sentence and "anointed to sanctify." The latter points to sanctification as the end, the former to propitiation. Sanctification and propitiation, though perfectly distinct, go hand in hand. The application of the blood implies sanctification, because in this application the sinner lays his hand on the victim, which act involves a change of mind. The blood itself effects the atonement. The latter phrase

purged the altar, and poured the blood at the foot of the altar, and sanctified it, to atone for it. 16. And he took all the fat that was upon the inwards, and the caul of the liver, and the two kidneys, and their fat, and Moses burned it upon the altar. 17. But the bullock, and its hide, its flesh, and its dung, he burned with fire without the camp; as the LORD commanded Moses.

18. And he presented the ram of burnt-sacrifice; and Aaron and his sons laid their hands on the head of the ram. 19. And he slew it; and Moses sprinkled the blood on the altar around. 20. And the ram he cut into its pieces; and Moses burned the head and the pieces and the fat. 21. And the inwards and legs he washed with water: and Moses burned the whole ram upon the altar: it was a burnt-sacrifice for a sweet smell, a fire-offering unto the LORD; as the LORD commanded Moses.

here might be rendered "to atone upon it," and yield a good meaning. But the context favors the former rendering. 16. This is in accordance with the ritual of the sin-sacrifice (iv. 8–10). 17. This corresponds with iv. 11, 12. *He burned.* The worshipper or his attendant removed the carcass to the place of ashes, and there it was burned to ashes as an accursed thing. The burning here represents penal death.

18–21. The ram of burnt-sacrifice. (See on Ex. xxix. 15–18). *And he presented.* The offerer or one on his behalf. *The ram of burnt-sacrifice.* As the bullock has been offered for a sin-sacrifice, a ram is ordered for a burnt-sacrifice. As the former gave prominence to expiation, this brings out propitiation and shadows forth and here brings to remembrance the one great atonement on which salvation rests. It is here offered by Aaron and his sons for themselves, as sinful men needing an atonement, to obtain legal acceptance with God. Moses, it is still to be remembered, is now the officiating priest and mediator. *And he slew.* One of the offerers or of their attendants here acts (vs. 20, 21). The whole process is in accordance with the directions in chap. i.

22. And he presented the second ram, the ram of consecration: and Aaron and his sons laid their hands on the head of the ram. 23. And he slew it; and Moses took of its blood and put upon the tip of Aaron's right ear and upon the thumb of his right hand and upon the great toe of his right foot. 24. And he presented Aaron's sons, and Moses put of the blood upon the tip of their right ear and upon the thumb of their right hand and upon the great toe of their right foot; and Moses sprinkled the blood upon the altar around. 25. And he took the fat and the tail, and all the fat that was upon the inwards, and the caul of the liver, and the two kidneys and

22–36. *The ram of consecration.* (See on Ex. xxix. 19–37.) The place usually assigned to the sacrifice of peace is here given to the ram of consecration. This means the ram of fillings, because now for the first time the hands of Aaron and his sons are filled with that which is afterwards placed on the altar. It is therefore in all respects a sacrifice of fellowship and peace. For they not only now officiate as priests, but partake afterwards of the sacrificial flesh. 23. *Put upon the tip of Aaron's right ear.* The blood of consecration is now applied to Aaron. The right side is the seat of activity. The ear, the hand, and the foot are organs intimately connected with intelligence, will, and power. By the ear we hear and understand; by the hands and feet we obey the will. The application of blood to these organs denotes the expiation of guilt in thought, act, and movement, in order that the expiated person may consecrate all the faculties of mind and capacities of body to the service of God. 24. *And he presented Aaron's sons.* We are not informed who presented them. The Sept. supposes Moses. It may have been the minister of Moses, or one of the elders of the tribe of Levi. The blood of expiation is in like manner applied to them. It is then sprinkled on the altar, the place of expiation.

25–29. The filling of the hands, or consecration proper. In the order of directions given to Moses (Ex. xxix. 21) the spattering of the blood and the oil upon Aaron and his sons is set down before this

their fat, and the right leg. 26. And out of the basket of sweet bread that was before the Lord he took one sweet cake and one cake of oiled bread and one wafer, and put upon the fat and upon the right leg. 27. And he put the whole upon the hands of Aaron and on the hands of his sons, and made them a waving before the LORD. 28. And Moses took them from their hands, and burned them on the altar upon the burnt-sacrifice: they are a consecration for a sweet smell, a

act. In the order of narrative here it is placed after it. As there is no obvious reason for a transposition of the narrative we take the order here for that of actual occurrence. In Exodus the legislator, we may presume, speaking of the blood in the previous verse completes what he has to say about it before proceeding to another topic. But in practice, as the oil and the blood had been just before applied to the priests, it was natural that an intervening ceremony should take place before a second application of the same elements. Besides, as all the blood seems to have been sprinkled on the altar, some time must be allowed for it to drip into a vessel in which it might be gathered for this other purpose. And, moreover, a new meaning comes out for this second application of blood and fat as soon as the priests are installed in their office, but not before. 25. *And the right leg.* This is the priest's portion of the peace-offering (vii. 32), and hence we learn that this is, in fact, a sacrifice of peace. As the priest, however, is in this case the offerer, the right leg is burned upon the altar according to the principle of vi. 16. 26. One of each of the three sorts of cakes is placed upon the fat and the right leg. 27. *Put the whole upon the hands.* This is the solemn filling of the hands of Aaron and his sons, whereby they are instituted into their office. *And made them a waving.* The waving was accomplished by Moses placing his hands beneath those of the designated priests and waving them to and fro with that which was laid upon them. It denotes the communion of the priests with Moses in this solemn act, and of both parties with God. 28. *And Moses took them.* That which was waved usually went to the priests instead of being burnt upon the altar. But in this great act of initiation the memorial cakes, which always

AARON AND HIS SONS CONSECRATED.

fire-offering unto the Lord. 29. And Moses took the breast, and made it a waving before the Lord: of the ram of consecration it was the part of Moses; as the Lord commanded Moses.

30. And Moses took of the anointing oil and of the blood which was upon the altar, and spattered upon Aaron, upon his garments, and on his sons, and on the garments of his sons

go on the altar, are waved along with the right leg. And the latter, which was given to the priests, is on this occasion consumed on the altar, because the ram of consecration was a priest's offering according to vi. 16. *Upon the whole sacrifice.* This represented the one great real propitiation, on which is founded all just and true fellowship with God, of which the peace-offering was the emblem. This completes the filling of the hands by which the priests were inducted into their office. 29. *The breast.* This is the peculiar portion of the Lord in the peace-offering (vii. 30), which is given over to the priests. In the present instance it falls to Moses as the consecrating priest. *As the Lord commanded Moses.* We observe how carefully this is noted on every suitable occasion. In this case it has the additional effect of showing that he did not appropriate this part of his own accord.

30–36. The completion of the consecration. Now that the blood of expiation has been sprinkled and the fat of propitiation has been burned on the altar, between which the solemn act of filling the hands has intervened, Moses takes of the anointing oil and of the blood upon the altar, and spatters upon Aaron and his sons and their garments. This is a significant act. When they were merely designated to the priesthood the oil and the blood were applied that they might be morally and legally qualified for consecration. But now the blood has been sprinkled on the altar and trickled down into the receptacle prepared for it on this occasion. It has therefore now made the expiation. And Aaron and his sons have been formally introduced into the priestly office, and authorized to perform its functions. And hence the blood of expiation and the oil of sanctification are once more applied to them and to their garments in token of their complete

with him, and sanctified Aaron, his garments, and his sons and the garments of his sons with him. 31. And Moses said unto Aaron and to his sons, Boil the flesh at the door of the tent of meeting and there eat it, and the bread that is in the basket of consecration; as I have commanded, saying, Aaron and his sons shall eat it. 32. And that which remaineth of the flesh and of the bread shall ye burn with fire. 33. And

qualification as invested priests for their sacred and sublime part. This repeated application, while it expresses their typical fitness for the functions of a ceremonial service, indicates at the same time with equal emphasis their personal unfitness to accomplish the task of a real mediator. The true mediator must need no propitiation or sanctification for himself; in other words, he must need no mediator. He must be holy in nature and in life as the moral condition of his competence to make reconciliation for others. 31. *Boil the flesh.* After the solemn lustration comes the crowning privilege of full communion with God. The ram of consecration is truly a sacrifice of peace. Hence the flesh is to be prepared for the sacrificial meal. *At the door of the tent of meeting.* It is a holy meal to be partaken of in the holy place. *The basket of consecration,* in which the remaining cakes of consecration are contained. *As I have commanded, saying.* Moses here speaks in the name of the Lord according to Ex. xxix. 32. He himself has no part in that which belongs to the offerer; but he has the breast which falls to the consecrator. 32. *That which remaineth* is to be burnt with fire, as in the peace-offering (vii. 17); but on the next day after it is offered. 33. *Ye shall not go forth.* They were not to leave the court of the tabernacle day or night during seven days. It is manifest that shelter and other conveniences for refreshment and repose must have been provided in some part of the court, which was now manifestly marked out and enclosed. *Seven days shall he fill your hands.* Seven is the number of the covenant, of completeness and consecration. 34. *As he hath done this day.* "He" is used, without more exact definition, to denote the Lord, who by his servant Moses effects their consecration. This filling of hands, it appears from these statements, is to be repeated on each of the seven

120   AARON AND HIS SONS CONSECRATED.

from the door of the tent of meeting ye shall not go forth for seven days, until the end of the days of your consecration; for seven days shall he fill your hand. 34. As he hath done this day, the LORD hath commanded to do to atone for you. 35. And at the door of the tent of meeting ye shall abide day and night seven days, and keep the charge of the LORD, and ye shall not die: for so I am commanded. 36. And Aaron and his sons did all things which the LORD commanded by the hand of Moses.   26 § § §

days. This accords with Ex. xxix. 36, where a bullock of sin-sacrifice is prescribed for every day. If the sin-sacrifice and the consecration ram are to be repeated every day the same rule will also apply to the ram of burnt-sacrifice. All this imparts a profound solemnity to the occasion. 35. *At the door.* This fixes the place. *Day and night.* This is explicit as to the time of service. *Keep the charge,* discharge all the priestly functions necessary during this preliminary period. *And ye shall not die.* This means that these duties must be exactly fulfilled, lest death by the special visitation of God be the consequence. *For so I am commanded.* This sevenfold repetition of the inaugural service demands a divine warrant. At the same time it teaches most distinctly and emphatically the inherent imperfection of the Levitical priesthood. A sacrifice having atoning validity needs no reiteration; and the sevenfold repetition only serves the more clearly to point to a propitiation and a propitiator that will be perfect. 36. This verse puts on record the uniform diligence of Aaron and his sons.

NOTES.

15. *Atone for it,* כִּפֶּר עָלָיו. The latter word might be rendered "upon it," if it suited the context. But it does not suit here or in Ex. xxix. 36, 37.

IX. THE OPENING OF THE TABERNACLE SERVICE.

IX. 1. And it came to pass on the eighth day, that Moses called Aaron and his sons and the elders of Israel. 2. And he

On an attentive examination of the fortieth chapter of Exodus, with an endeavor to realize in imagination the actualities of the scene described, we shall come to the conclusion that both the order given in the first fifteen verses and the execution of it in the remainder of the chapter are of the nature of a summary of events that may occupy several days. In vs. 31, 32 the narrative even passes from the actual into the habitual. The order in Ex. xxix. 35–37 to fill the hand of Aaron and his sons seven days, and to atone for the altar and sanctify it during the same period, acts which are indicated in vs. 9–15 of the order given in Ex. xl., prepare us to expand the time occupied with its execution into at least eight days. For it is to be observed that Moses in the following part of the chapter makes no allusion whatever to the anointing of the tabernacle and its furniture and its priests, and yet goes on to record the manifestation of the divine glory in the erected tabernacle. The natural inference is, that the seven days anointing had already taken place, and that the concluding event took place on the formal erection of the already expiated and anointed tabernacle. The consecration of the priests and the dedication of the tabernacle recorded in Lev. viii. goes far to corroborate this inference. The chapter now to be considered will contribute in no small measure to its more general acceptance with thoughtful readers of the Bible.

In this chapter we have the inauguration of the national worship. It consists of the orders conveyed through Moses (1–7), the offerings for Aaron himself (8–14), the offerings for the people (15–21), and the glory of the Lord appearing after the benediction (22–24).

1–7. The orders conveyed by Moses. *And it came to pass on the eighth day.* This form of words indicates the introduction of a new and distinct course of events. The eighth day is, we conceive, the first day of the month Abib, with which the sacred year commenced. For this is manifestly the opening of the tabernacle worship. It therefore coincides with the close of the proceedings recorded in Ex.

said unto Aaron, Take thee a calf of the herd for a sin-sacrifice, and a ram for a burnt-sacrifice, both perfect, and offer them before the LORD. 3. And thou shalt speak to the sons of Israel, saying, Take ye a kid of the goats for a sin-sacrifice, and a calf and a lamb of the first year, all perfect, for a burnt-offering. 4. And a bullock and a ram for a peace-offering to sacrifice before the LORD, and an oblation mingled with oil:

xl. *Called Aaron and his sons and the elders of Israel:* the former to officiate, the latter to offer, for the people whom they represented on this national festival. 2. *Unto Aaron,* who is now the ordained high-priest about to enter upon the discharge of his functions. He is directed to take for himself a calf for expiation and a ram for propitiation. The typical high-priest is compassed with infirmity, like other men, and needs to begin with offering an atonement for himself. The acknowledgement of infirmity and the expiation for it come first. Then the great propitiatory sacrifice itself is foreshadowed by the burnt-sacrifice. 3. *And thou shalt speak.* Aaron is here initiated into the prophetic and kingly parts of his office. He is henceforth to instruct and direct the people as their spiritual guide. *To the sons of Israel,* many of them at hand, no doubt, but all of them represented by the elders already mentioned. The people are directed also to present a kid of the goats for a sin-sacrifice, and a calf and a lamb for a burnt-sacrifice. 4. But a peace-offering also is to be presented by the people, as this was a day of privilege, honor, and fellowship with God. *And an oblation.* This was the indispensable accompaniment of the peace-offering, the flesh of which was to be dressed and eaten with bread by the worshipper. But this oblation seems to be a special one, associated afterwards with the burnt-sacrifice (vs. 17). *For.* The reason is now to be assigned for the peace-offerings of the people. *To-day the Lord appeareth*[4] *unto you.* The cloud may have already covered the tent of meeting, and the glory of the Lord filled the tabernacle, as it is recorded in Ex. xl. 34. This was a new thing only in so far as the transition from the temporary to the permanent tent of meeting was concerned. But the present statement seems to refer to the same event as that in vs. 6. It is therefore really a new

for to-day the LORD appeareth unto you. 5. And they took that which Moses commanded before the tent of meeting: and all the assembly drew near and stood before the LORD. 6. And Moses said, This is the thing which the LORD hath commanded that ye do; and the glory of the LORD will appear unto you. 7. And Moses said unto Aaron, Draw near to the altar, and

appearance of the Lord. This is evidently the greatest of all days since the proclamation of the moral law on mount Sinai. The Lord is about to follow up the established service with a visible manifestation of his acceptance with his people and their worship. The peace-offering is the appropriate service for those who are accepted of God. This manifestation of the Lord also suits the day on which the setting up of the tabernacle was completed. 5. *And they took.* They willingly complied with the requirement. *Before the tent of meeting,* where the victims are to be slain (i. 11). *All the assembly,* the regularly constituted meeting of the people. *Drew near,* with solemn reverence as willing and unanimous worshippers. 6. *And Moses said.* He is still supreme under God over the people. *Hath commanded that ye do.* This is no human device or will-worship. God has appointed the way in which you may approach him with acceptance. *The glory of the Lord.* The visible sign of his presence will be miraculous and glorious. But the outward and sensible glory will only be a faint shadow of the inward and spiritual glory which it signifies. The glory of God is his spiritual nature, his power, wisdom, holiness, justice, goodness, and truth. But the glory that excelleth is his mercy. In keeping with this the glory of his justice is the propitiation for sin, foreshadowed in this ceremonial observance. The glory of his power is the regeneration of the soul by his word and Spirit. All this glory is to shine forth in the deep meaning of this day's service. *The Lord* is the God not merely of eternity and omnipotence, but of the promise and covenant of mercy. *Will appear unto you.* Whatever any think of the appearance mentioned in v. 4, it is evident that this refers to the manifestation of the Divine presence and acceptance of the sacrifice which is recorded at the end of this chapter. 7. *Draw near to the altar.* What a solemn moment for Aaron, the represent-

make thy sin-sacrifice and thy burnt-sacrifice, and atone for thyself and for the people; and make the offering of the people, and atone for them, as the LORD hath commanded.

8. And Aaron drew near to the altar; and slew the calf of the sin-sacrifice which was for himself. 9. And the sons of Aaron presented the blood to him; and he dipped his finger in the blood, and put it upon the horns of the altar; and he

ative mediator between God and man now about to enter upon his office. *Make³ thy sin-sacrifice and thy burnt-sacrifice.* After all the expiation and propitiation of the seven days of consecration he is to come with a sin and a burnt sacrifice for himself. He is but an imperfect, or only ceremonially perfect, shadow of the true High-priest. His multiplied and diversified sacrifices are only symbols of the one true, all-sufficient sacrifice that is hereafter to be made. *Atone for thyself and for the people.* In atoning for himself he was atoning virtually for the people. An accepted high-priest was necessary to make atonement for the people; so that in setting himself right at the court of heaven he was only qualifying himself for effectually undertaking the cause of the people. *And make the offering of the people,* when thou art thyself accepted through the expiatory and propitiatory sacrifices for thyself. *And atone for them.* The atonement for them demanded a perfect priest and a perfect victim. In the real propitiation these two are combined in one. *As the Lord hath commanded.* This one word gives hope and vitality to the broken and humbled heart of Aaron. With this voice of authority he is encouraged to gird up the loins of his mind to the sublime task laid upon him.

8-14. The offerings for Aaron. *Drew near to the altar,* with all the weight of his official responsibility pressing upon him. *Which was for himself.* The writer emphatically distinguishes for whom the offering is made. It is to be observed too, that Aaron, being himself the offerer, slays the victim as usual, either himself or by his assistants. 9. *And the sons of Aaron,* acting in this case as priests. *He dipped his finger.* As there is not a particular offence charged against Aaron, he himself officiates. *Put it upon the horns of the altar.* The sacrifice is not made for a known sin of inadvertence as

poured out the blood at the foot of the altar. 10. And the fat and the kidneys and the caul from the liver of the sin-sacrifice he burned upon the altar, as the LORD commanded Moses. 11. And the flesh and the hide he burned with fire without the camp. 12. And he slew the burnt-sacrifice: and Aaron's sons handed unto him the blood, and he sprinkled it on the altar around. 13. And they handed to him the burnt-sacrifice in its pieces and the head; and he burned them upon the altar. 14. And he washed the inwards and the legs, and burned them upon the burnt-sacrifice on the altar.

15. And he presented the offering of the people; and he took the goat of the sin-sacrifice which was for the people, and slew it, and he offered it for sin, as the first. 16. And he

in iv. 1–12, but to expiate the sinful infirmity of the official, and fit him for the proper discharge of his functions. Hence the blood is not spattered on the veil and applied to the horns of the altar of incense (iv. 6, 7), but simply put upon the horns of the altar of burnt-sacrifice, as in the offering of the prince or one of the people (iv. 25, 30). The mode varies according to the circumstances, but the meaning is the same. 10, 11. The sacrifice is made according to the rule laid down in chap. iv. *As the Lord commanded Moses.* This shows that the ritual canons of the first eight chapters were given before the proceedings of the day. 12. The burnt-sacrifice representing the great propitiation is now briefly noticed. *Handed,*[12] actually placed in his hands. 13, 14. It is treated according to the rule. The offerings on the part of the priests now cease. They are merely preliminary. The day is not the day of the priests, but of the people.

15–21. The offerings for the people. *And he presented.* The subject, not being expressed, is to be supplied according to the exigency of the occasion. In this case it may be some one acting for the people. The only case in which the priest is necessary as the subject is the last sentence, *and he offered it for sin,* as in vi. 19, made it an expiation for sin. 16. Here again the first sentence may have for its subject the representative of the people, the second must have the

presented the burnt-sacrifice, and he made it after the manner. 17. And he presented the oblation and filled his hand from it and burned it upon the altar, besides the burnt-sacrifice of the morning. 18. And he slew the bullock and the ram, the sacrifice of peace which was for the people : and Aaron's sons handed the blood to him, and he sprinkled it on the altar

priest. The burnt-sacrifice is offered according to the order prescribed in the ritual. It consisted (vs. 3) of a calf and a lamb. It is not stated whether the latter be the same as the lamb of the morning sacrifice. It is generally considered to be different. The offering is at all events made according to the usual canon. 17. *The oblation.* If this be the oblation mentioned in vs. 4 after the peace-offering, it is here transposed, and presented after the burnt-sacrifice. According to Num. xv. 3-11 such an oblation was invariably to accompany the burnt-sacrifice or peace-offering when the people were come into the land of their habitation. The same is to be done here in the wilderness on this extraordinary occasion. *Besides the burnt-sacrifice.*[17] This may be understood in two ways. If the lamb prescribed be not the morning sacrifice, then the burnt-sacrifice is additional to the standing one of the morning. But several considerations are in favor of their identity. First, Aaron was now manifestly to act for the first time as duly constituted high-priest, and it seems incongruous that he should have offered a morning sacrifice beforehand. Secondly, this was manifestly the commencement of the national worship; there cannot therefore have been a previous morning sacrifice distinct from this, as the latter would have been the real commencement. Thirdly, the erection of the tabernacle had to be completed on this morning, and this, though of trivial amount, would occupy some time. Fourthly, the manifest propriety of the initiatory sacrifice being kindled by the fire from God points the same way. And, lastly, the phrase "besides the burnt-sacrifice of the morning" is mostly simply explained to mean that the oblation already mentioned was in addition to the morning sacrifice on this special occasion, though it did not usually accompany it while the people were in the wilderness. 18. *The sacrifice of peace* is now presented. After propitiation comes fellowship. This is fol-

around. 19. And the fat of the bullock, and of the ram, the tail, and that which covereth, and the kidneys, and the caul of the liver: 20. And they put the fat upon the breasts, and he burned the fat upon the altar. 21. And the breasts and the right leg Aaron made a waving before the LORD; as Moses had commanded.

22. And Aaron lifted up his hands towards the people and blessed them; and came down from making the sin-sacrifice

lowed by a sacred feast upon the victim, and is therefore according to rule (vii. 12-14) accompanied with its oblation. *Which was for the people.* It is carefully noted that this is for the people, who are now in full and happy communion with their God. 19, 20. *The fat of the bullock.* This is first mentioned by itself in one word. *And of the ram.* Then follow the several parts which compose the fat of the ram. *That which covereth.* This is briefly put for the fat that lay as a lining over the inwards. *The caul of the liver*, usually the caul upon the liver. This whole verse is summed up by the single word 'fat' in the next verse. 21. *The breasts* of the bullock and the ram. These belong to the Lord as his special part. *And the right leg of each.* This belongs to the officiating priest (Lev. vii. 34), as the former is awarded to the whole order. These are accordingly waved, but not burnt on the altar. *As Moses had commanded.*[21] Moses is as God unto Aaron (Ex. iv. 16).

22-24. The blessing of the people and the acceptance of their offering. After the offering of the sacrifice of peace, at the close of the whole public sacrifice by which the tabernacle service was inaugurated, Aaron, while he was still on the landing at the altar, and therefore elevated above the people, lifted up his hands toward them and blessed them. The formula of benediction is first put on record in Num. vi. 22-27. It is there said to be delivered to Moses for the guidance of Aaron, and may have been communicated before the present very solemn occasion of using it. *And came down* from the landing on which he stood while ministering at the altar. (See i. 11.) The sacrifice of expiation, propitiation, and peace had been completed, and the blessing is pronounced as the natural consequence. As the

128   THE OPENING OF THE TABERNACLE SERVICE.

and the burnt-sacrifice and the peace-offering. 23. And Moses and Aaron went into the tent of meeting, and came forth and blessed the people: and the glory of the LORD appeared to all the people. 24. And fire went forth from before the LORD,

sacrifice lay on the altar unconsumed, this was a moment of intense emotion to the onlooking assembly who had been led to expect an extraordinary manifestation of the presence and glory of the Lord. 23. Moses and Aaron then went into the tent of meeting. The consecrator and the consecrated on this solemn occasion go together into the holy place. We are not here informed of the purpose for which they entered. But the general purpose is to be gathered from the design with which the tabernacle was constructed. "And I will meet with thee there, and speak with thee from above the mercy-seat (Ex. xxv. 22.) "When I will meet you to speak there unto thee. And there will I meet with the sons of Israel, and it shall be sanctified by my glory" (Ex. xxix. 42, 43). Meeting with God is holding communion with him. The interview of Moses with God is carried on by means of speech. "I will speak to thee of all that I command thee concerning the sons of Israel." And Moses speaks with God of all that he desires for the people (Ex. xxxiii. 7–23). This is no doubt the ground on which Moses and Aaron now enter the tabernacle. They go in to make intercession for the people on this great occasion. They ask for the acceptance of the people who have now approached the Lord their God for the first time under the new economy. Moreover if, as we conceive, the morning sacrifice has now been offered, Moses and Aaron go in to burn incense on the golden altar and trim the lamps on the golden candlestick (Ex. xxx. 7, 8). This could not be omitted on this great day, and Moses could not but accompany Aaron on the first occasion of his officiating regularly within the tabernacle. After making intercession they came forth, and once more blessed the people. When intercession has been made.for them at the throne of grace, the benediction is no less appropriate. It is then added that the glory of the Lord appeared to all the people. A sudden burst of light in and over the tabernacle now appeared. 24. *And fire went forth.* The manifestation of the divine glory is

LEVITICUS IX. 24.

and consumed upon the altar the burnt-sacrifice and the fat: and all the people saw, and they shouted, and fell upon their faces.

attended with an issue of fire from the presence of the Lord. This fire consumes the burnt-sacrifices and the fat of the other sacrifices and the handful of the oblation of flour and oil which had been all laid upon the altar. This is a conspicuous sign of acceptance, miraculously given by God himself. The people take cognizance of the presence and power and grace of the Lord, shout with joy and thanksgiving, and fall down on their faces in trembling adoration. They had been, deservedly as they felt, rejected on account of the worship of the golden calf, as the sacred writer very plainly calls it, or the worship of Apis, which they had witnessed in Egypt. The tent of meeting had consequently been removed and pitched far from their camp. Moses had no doubt interceded for them, and prevailed with the Lord to pardon them. But now the new tent of meeting has been erected in the midst of them once more, and the appointed sacrifices have been offered for the first time by the newly instituted priesthood. These sacrifices have now been manifestly accepted by a miraculous sign from the Lord; and they themselves are thus fully restored to the divine favor. This was a gracious and fitting reception of the people on the first day of the new year, and in all probability coincides with the statement in Ex. xl. 34, 35, near the close of the account of the rearing up of the tabernacle.

NOTES.

4. *Appeareth*, נִרְאָה, is shown, literally as it is pointed, *hath appeared*. If this were intended by the Masoretes to refer to an event already past, there must have been two appearings on this day, one at the rearing of the tabernacle, and another on the blessing of the people at the close of the sacrificial service. If it be meant to refer to an event yet to come, it must be literally rendered "will have appeared," which apart from ו copulative is not usual. נִרְאָה would in this case be the easier reading, though the other is in keeping with the Hebrew style. The Sept. and Vulg. give the future.

7. *Make,* עָשָׂה, including all the priestly functions connected with sacrifice.

12. *Handed,* יַמְצִיא, cause to find; more definite than יַקְרִיב, *cause to approach.*

17. The explanation, following in the text, of this sacrifice, as identical with the lamb of the prescribed burnt-sacrifice, simplifies the narrative and facilitates the conception of the possibilities of the scene. It also makes the appearance of the phrase in this place more natural. The statement that Aaron burned the various offerings on the altar (vs. 10, 13, 14, 17, 20), may simply mean that he laid them all on the altar as usual, when they were burned in due course of time by the fire kindled from heaven.

21. Some MSS. have here, as the Lord commanded Moses. The meaning is to the same effect. The variety of expression is in favor of the common reading.

X. OTHER EVENTS OF THE OPENING SERVICE.

The last chapter, according to the manner of Moses, is brought to a close worthy of the occasion. But in this case he was enabled to do so only by stopping short of circumstances of a very shocking and humiliating character. The proceedings, which up to the very culminating point were so auspicious, were suddenly overcast by the shade of a direful catastrophe. This was the offering of strange fire by two of the sons of Aaron, instantly followed by a terrific outbreak of divine judgment upon them (1–7). This leads to a solemn and significant injunction laid on the priests to refrain from wine or strong drink when about to officiate in the holy place (8–11). The remainder of the chapter is occupied with directions and inquiries concerning the parts of the sacrifices which were not burned on the altar (12–20). After the sublime event and the high-strung enthusiasm of the former chapter we here sink down far below the ordinary level of human infirmity. We find ourselves walking on earth, amid the manifestations of a heart that is deceitful above all things and desperately wicked. The lessons we learn are salutary indeed, but inexpressibly sad.

LEVITICUS X. 1, 2. 131

X. 1. And Nadab and Abihu, sons of Aaron, took each his censer, and put fire therein, and laid incense on it, and offered before the LORD strange fire, which he commanded them not. 2. And fire went forth from before the LORD and consumed

1–7. *The strange fire.* 1. *Nadab and Abihu.* These were the eldest sons of Aaron (Ex. vi. 23 ; Num. iii. 2). *Took each his censer.* We should be at a loss to imagine any shadow of a reason for this proceeding on the part of Nabab and Abihu, if it were not that the solemn sacrifice already described was the morning sacrifice enlarged in proportion to the occasion, after which Aaron, accompanied by Moses, went in with fire to kindle the incense on the golden altar. This solemn act of Moses and Aaron may have suggested to the two young men, who had taken a part in the sacrifices at the outer altar, the daring attempt to intrude into the holy place without any mandate or invitation. We cannot say what other influences contributed to their impious resolve, whether they took umbrage at being excluded from the tabernacle, or rashly imagined they were free to follow the steps of Moses and Aaron. *And put fire therein,* as they may have seen Moses and Aaron doing. *And offered before the Lord.* They were in the court on the way to the door of the tabernacle. They were therefore in the act of presenting the burning incense before the Lord. *Strange fire.* This is explained by the words following, " which he commanded them not." The fire is strange, because it differed from that prescribed by law, either in the men, the matter, the manner, or the time. It is therefore in one or more of these respects a thing not commanded, and consequently forbidden ; and the presenting of it is an act of will-worship. It was moreover presumptuous, when they knew that Moses and Aaron were called of God to regulate the whole service, while they themselves had received no such authority, and occupied only a subordinate place. What other unworthy motives were lurking in their mind, whether idolatrous or selfish, we are not informed, and it is bootless to conjecture. 2. *And fire went forth.* The very element of their sin is the element of their retributive punishment. *From before the Lord.* The presentation of the strange fire took place after Moses and Aaron came out of the

them; and they died before the LORD. 3. And Moses said unto Aaron, This is that which the LORD hath spoken, saying, I will be sanctified in those who come nigh me, and before

tabernacle and before the eating of the oblation and certain parts of the sin-sacrifice and the peace-offering that had been made. There is nothing to forbid the supposition that it happened precisely after they had blessed the people on coming out of the holy place. In that case the very flashing forth of fire that consumed the victims may have at the same time struck those self-willed intruders, as they were drawing nigh to the door of the tabernacle. At any rate the one event must have been quite close upon the other: for the very next step of the procedure would have been the holy communion of the priests and the representatives of the people with God in the sacrificial feast. Thus on the same occasion the act of divinely appointed worship is solemnly accepted and the act of presumptuous will-worship instantly and sternly punished. And fire is strangely seen doing its twofold work of accepting and of destroying. *And they died before the Lord.* Death is the inevitable doom of presumptuous sin. 3. *And Moses said unto Aaron.* This was an agonizing moment; yet Moses has presence of mind equal to the occasion. The whole past of his wonderful history prepared him for such a crisis. *This is that which the Lord hath spoken.* He feels that the eternal interests of the people of God are trembling in the balance. He will raise up his brother's mind above the concerns of his own heart to his transcendent relation to God and his people. The principle he announces is contained in the words of the Lord to himself, recorded in Ex. xix. 22. But it is here given by Moses as the Lord's present explanation of the judgment that had now been executed. *I will be sanctified in those who come nigh me.* I require exact compliance with my will in my attendants, and visit any wilful departure from it with prompt and condign punishment. The reasonableness of this is obvious. The ritual of worship which the Lord himself has instituted has an important and authoritative meaning, foreshadowing the divine purpose and plan of salvation. That which man devises is, in the nature of things, devoid of either significance or authority. Its inculcation is an arrogant

all the people I will be glorified. And Aaron was mute. 4. And Moses called Mishael and Elzaphan, sons of Uzziel, Aaron's uncle; and he said unto them, Draw nigh, take your brethren from before the sanctuary to the outside of the camp. 5. And they drew nigh, and took them in their coats to the outside of the camp. 6. And Moses said unto Aaron and to

assumption of the prerogative of God, and its practice a daring intrusion into his presence without leave. And either is calculated to deceive the on-looker to his eternal ruin. Hence it is added, *before all the people I will be glorified*. The further consideration that God is the Governor and Judge of all the world makes it an incumbent duty to execute retributive justice on the offender. There is moreover a peculiar importance in the phrase "those who come nigh me." Those who are in actual relation with God as confidential servants are vastly more blamable for acts of disobedience than those who do not hold such offices of trust, or those who stand in no close relation to him, when they commit similar acts of sin. But a still greater stress is to be laid on the gravity of their offence, when we pass from the type to that which is typified. The whole function of the priest was a figure of the real atonement for sin to be made by the great Highpriest on behalf of the fallen race of man. A violation of this function was therefore a crime of the deepest die, as it was an annulling of the atonement for man. This alone is sufficient to account for the instant vindication of the divine holiness. *And Aaron was mute.* He bowed in humble submission to the judgments of God, and entirely acquiesced in the explanation of Moses.

4. *Mishael and Elzaphan*[4] (Ex. vi. 22). *Your brethren*, taken in the wide sense of kinsmen: they were the sons of their cousin Aaron. *From before the sanctuary.* Hence they were struck down in the court on their way to the sanctuary. 5. *And took them in their coats.* From this we perceive that the fire by which they were killed was the lightning flash, which left their coats still comparatively uninjured. *To the outside of the camp.* The bodies and the priestly dress in which they were arrayed were desecrated by the presumptuous act of the deceased. Hence they are to be removed out of the sacred

Eleazar and Ithamar his sons, Bare not your heads, nor rend your garments, lest ye die, and wrath fall upon all the assembly: and your brethren, the whole house of Israel, shall bewail the burning which the LORD hath kindled. 7. And ye shall not go out from the door of the tent of meeting, lest ye die: for the anointing oil of the LORD is upon you. And they did according to the word of Moses. ¶

precinct. 6. *Eleazar and Ithamar*⁶ are now associated with their father. *Bare not your heads.* Baring the head so that the hair might flow unkempt was an ancient and natural sign of grief. Rending the garments was of similar import. The priests in their official capacity stood in higher and closer relation with God on the one hand, and with the whole people on the other, than with their own kindred. They are not therefore to disturb the complacence of God or the gratitude of the people by such outward displays of personal grief. The mitre or bonnet on their head and the coat on their body are sacred, and not to be violated: they are the outward symbols of their office, which is not to be interrupted by the minor concerns of private life. *Lest ye die.* The feeling of grief is not forbidden. But the frustrating of the vitally important functions they have to discharge by such outward acts is a grave offence that may be visited by instant death; for it severs the bond of peace between God and man, and brings " wrath upon all the assembly." *The whole house of Israel,* however, is allowed to show the outward signs of grief for the judgment of "burning," both in its cause and consequences. This high mark of respect and sympathy was well fitted to soothe the sad hearts of Aaron and his surviving sons. 7. *Ye shall not go out,* to take part in the burial of the deceased. The service of the sanctuary is of paramount importance; it is not to be interrupted by private occupations, and especially by the defiling concerns of the grave. The priests were not absolutely confined to the court of the tabernacle: they had to go out, for example, to burn the bodies of the sin-sacrifice, the blood of which was carried into the sanctuary, and doubtless on other necessary occasions. But no other occupation was to interfere with the functions of the sacred office. *For the anointing oil of the Lord is*

8. And the LORD spake unto Aaron, saying, 9. Drink not wine nor strong drink, thou nor thy sons with thee, when ye go into the tent of meeting, lest ye die: it is a statute forever unto your generations. 10. And to separate between the holy and the profane, and between the clean and the unclean. 11. And to teach the sons of Israel all the statutes which the LORD hath spoken to them by the hand of Moses. ¶

upon you. This is the symbol of the spirit of life, and has no relation with the pageantry of death. It is the emblem of purity and must be kept free from the contamination of evil. It proclaims you to belong to the Lord, and does not permit you to engage in anything that would interfere with his claim upon your service. *And they did.* There is an unreserved compliance with this solemn injunction.

8–11. Abstinence from stimulant drinks in the discharge of sacred functions enjoined. *Spake unto Aaron.* This is the first communication made directly to Aaron. It takes place after his induction into office. *Drink not wine,* the juice of the grape usually fermented. Strong drink was made from the date or sap of the palm, and sometimes also from a preparation of honey or barley. It was usually strengthened with spices (Hieron. Ep. ad Nepot.). These were intoxicating drinks. The propriety of the prohibition is obvious. The worship of God is an intelligent service (John iv. 24), and therefore requires a clear and collected mind; it is a holy exercise (xix. 2), and therefore demands a pure and undivided heart. This is therefore to be a perpetual statute for all generations. The occasion on which it is introduced leads to the surmise that Nadab and Abihu may have been under the influence of stimulants when they violated the sancties of the worship of God. 10. 11. This rule serves two purposes: (1) It separates between the holy and the profane; the clean and the unclean. The profane is the common, or that which is not devoted to the sanctuary. Uncleanness may befall either the holy or the profane. Abstinence during the worship of God from stimulating drinks, the use of which was allowed on ordinary occasions, made obvious the separation between the holy and the profane. (2) It teaches the people, deepens in their minds the memory and the meaning of the divine ordinances *By the hand of Moses.* By his agency.

12. And Moses spake unto Aaron, and unto Eleazar and Ithamar, his remaining sons, Take the oblation that remaineth of the fire-offerings of the LORD, and eat it sweet beside the altar; for it is most holy. 13. And ye shall eat it in the holy place, for it is thy due and the due of thy sons out of the fire-offerings of the LORD: for so I am commanded. 14. And the wave-breast and the heave-leg shall ye eat in a clean place, thou and thy sons and thy daughters with thee: for they are given as thy due and the due of thy sons out of the sacrifices of peace of the sons of Israel. 15. The heave-leg and the

12-20. *The public service concluded.* After this abrupt and awful interruption to the solemnity and exultation of the moment, Moses recalls the newly appointed priests to the completion of the sacrificial service. 12. *Take the oblation.* This is according to the rule vi. 9. *That remaineth*, after the memorial has been presented. *Sweet*, that is, without leaven. *Beside the altar*, in a covered space prepared for the purpose.[12] *It is most holy.* Everything that, if not eaten by the priests, would have been consumed on the altar as a fire-offering, is regarded as most holy. 13. *Thy due*,[13] thy portion, settled by statute. *So I am commanded.* Moses is careful to intimate on all suitable occasions that his directions have the authority of God. The reiteration of this statement shows that he considers it of essential importance. Nothing ceremonial is to be imposed or accepted that has not the stamp of heaven. 14. *The wave-breast and the heave-leg.* (See on vii. 28-36.) *In a clean place.* Here they are not limited to the court of the tabernacle, but only to a clean place. The whole family, male and female, are entitled to partake of these pieces. They are set apart for the priests from the sacrifice of peace, which includes the feast of fellowship wherein the worshippers participate. The Lord has the breast, the priests the right leg, including, of course, the shoulder, and the offerer and his friends the remainder. In this case the offerer is the assembly appearing by its representatives. This is therefore in reality a feast of communion between the Lord, the priesthood, and the people. 15. Upon the fat the two pieces already men-

wave-breast upon the fire-offerings of fat shall they bring, to make a waving before the LORD: and it shall belong to thee and to thy sons with thee by a statute forever; as the LORD hath commanded. 16. And the kid of the sin-sacrifice Moses sought diligently, and behold it was burnt: and he was wroth with Eleazar and Ithamar, Aaron's remaining sons, saying, 17. Why have ye not eaten the sin-sacrifice in the holy place, for it is most holy; and it he hath given you to bear the

tioned are to be waved before the Lord. Heaving therefore seems to be regarded as a species of waving. Waving accords with fellowship. The fat is then consumed as a fire-offering on the altar, while the breast and the leg are to be eaten by the priests. 16. The present sin-sacrifice (ix. 3) being offered not for any special sin of the people, but as a preparative for the presentation of the burnt-sacrifice and peace-offering, is not a bullock, as in the former case (iv. 14), but a kid. And its blood is not taken into the sanctuary, and hence its flesh is not to be burned in the place of ashes (iv. 21), but eaten by the officiating priest (vi. 19). *Moses sought* it diligently for this purpose, but found it was burned in the customary place, without the camp. *He was wroth*, he expressed his displeasure to the sons of Aaron, either because he felt for Aaron and did not like to rebuke him, or because the sons took part in officiating and should have looked to this duty. 17. *Why have ye not eaten.* The flesh of the victim for sin should have been eaten in the holy place by the priests officiating (vi. 17). *It hath he given you.* The reason why it is most holy and why it is to be eaten by the priests is here assigned. *To bear the iniquity* of the worshipper, in this case, the whole assembly. The victim is to bear the iniquity of the assembly, and so are the priests. It is to be remembered that priest and victim are not two things, that on the other hand, the true Mediator is in himself both priest and victim. Hence it is quite intelligible to say that the priest bears the iniquity of the sinner for whom he makes expiation (Ex. xxviii. 38). To bear iniquity for another is to expiate. *To atone for them before the Lord.* The sin-sacrifice primarily expiates sin. But wherever there is expiation, there cannot but be satisfaction as its inseparable

iniquity of the assembly, to atone for them before the LORD. 18. Behold its blood hath not been brought into the holy place within: ye should indeed have eaten it in the holy place, as I have commanded. 19. And Aaron spake unto Moses, Behold, to-day have they offered their sin-sacrifice and their burnt-

accompaniment, and therefore full atonement. This propitiation is that which is properly signified by the priest burning the fat upon the altar and eating the flesh before the Lord. 18. *Its blood has not been brought into the holy place within.*[18] Hence, according to vi. 19, 22, 23, it should have been eaten in the holy place. The law was clearly as Moses has stated. It was a matter of fact that the blood had not been spattered on the veil or put upon the horns of the golden altar; and the flesh of the victim it was in that case ordinary for the priest that expiated with it to eat. 19. The sons of Aaron were probably abashed by the rebuke of Moses. At all events, they reply not, and Aaron speaks for them. *To-day have they offered their sin-sacrifice and their burnt-sacrifice.* The state of things seems to have been this. The sin-sacrifice of the priests was to be burnt on the ash-heap. That for the people might have been eaten by the officiating priest in token of the full acceptance of the people. But meanwhile the presumptuous offering of strange fire by two of those who had that day joined in a common sin and burnt sacrifice brought out the fire of vengeance upon the reckless transgressors. In these circumstances it was felt by Aaron that expiation should be prominent, and propitiation in the background, as in the cases of the high-priest or the congregation sinning inadvertently (iv. 3, 13). Hence the kid was sent to be burnt without the camp as a type of the awful expiation required for sin. It is not to be supposed, however, that the eating of the sin-sacrifice was a feast of joy. Rather was it a meal of solemn awe in view of the absolute holiness of God. *Good in the eyes of the Lord.* This does not mean, would it have been accepted? Doubtless it would, seeing it was in strict accordance with the statute as understood by Moses. It rather means, would it have been in God's sight suitable under the circumstances? There were two ways of disposing of the flesh of the victim for sin, burning it in the clean place outside the camp, or eating it

sacrifice before the LORD, and such things befell me: and had I eaten the sin-sacrifice to-day, would it have been good in the eyes of the LORD? 20. And Moses heard, and it was good in his eyes. ¶

before the Lord in the holy place. As the blood was not brought within the sanctuary it was the right, and no doubt the first intention, of the officiating priests to eat the flesh. But a right to eat is not an obligation, if there be an alternative allowed. As in the peace-offering and the oblation accompanying it, that which was not eaten was to be burnt with fire (vii. 17; viii. 32), so Aaron might forego his right to eat, and burn the flesh in the usual manner. Meanwhile, therefore, when the avenging judgment of God came down upon his erring sons, his intention was altered. Deep sorrow and humiliation so unfitted his mind for the task, that he declined to exercise his right of eating the sin-victim, and hence he availed himself of the humbler alternative, and sent it away to be burnt without the camp. This course commended itself as proper to Moses also, when the whole circumstances were laid before him. This case is peculiarly interesting on this ground, that it shows a reasonable latitude in the application of ritual canons to unexpected circumstances. It exhibits a certain freedom in the arrangement of the minor details, while the substance of the rules is still kept inviolate. It is one of the examples we occasionally meet, of a distinction being judiciously and honestly made between the letter and the spirit of a law. It does not therefore stand alone. A notable instance has occurred to us in the consecration of the priests, where the spattering of them and their garments with the mingled oil and blood stands before the filling of hands in the specification (Ex. xxix. 21), and after it in the execution (Lev. viii. 30). Practice must, in fact, vary somewhat; principle only is invariable. Figures, forms, types may and must vary, while the archetype, body, or substance to which they refer is one and the same. This principle deserves the attention of the interpreter.

NOTES.

1. *Nadab and Abihu*, נָדָב וַאֲבִיהוּא, willing, and the Father himself. The former seems to express devotedness; the latter, all glory to

God. Significant names of children indicate the wishes and hopes of the parents.

4. *Mishael and Elzaphan,* מִישָׁאֵל וְאֶלְצָפָן, who is as God, and God protects. עֻזִּיאֵל, *God is might.*

6. אֶלְעָזָר וְאִיתָמָר, *God helps,* and *palm tree.*

12. Exedra (Hisc.).

13. *Due,* חֹק, statute, that which is determined by statute.

18. *Within,* פְּנִימָה, that which faces the entrant (Ges.), or that which is sequestered, secret, inmost (F.).

SECTION III.—CLEANSING AND ATONEMENT.

XI. CLEAN AND UNCLEAN ANIMALS.

THIS section of six chapters contains seven communications from the Lord: the first to Moses and Aaron for the people, concerning clean and unclean animals (chap. xi.); the second to Moses for the people, respecting birth (chap. xii.); the third to Moses and Aaron, about the discerning of leprosy, in chap. xiii.; the fourth to Moses, concerning the cleansing of the leper; the fifth to Moses and Aaron, about leprosy in a house, both in chap. xiv.; the sixth to Moses and Aaron for the people, concerning issues, in chap. xv.; and the seventh to Moses for Aaron, after the death of his two eldest sons, relating to the day of atonement, in chap. xvi. It is natural to suppose that the communications to Moses and Aaron in common were made after the consecration of Aaron. Of the three which were addressed to Moses alone, that concerning birth applied to married women, that on cleansing referred to the leper, and that concerning entrance into the holy of holies applied to Aaron the high-priest. As Aaron had his sacerdotal duties to perform, he was not present with Moses on all occasions when he had a communication from the Lord. The arrangements concerning cleansing naturally come after the consecration of the priests; and the ordinance for entering into the holy of holies on the day of atonement, in chap. xvi., is historically connected with the profane attempt of Nadab and Abihu to appear before the Lord with strange fire.

In a salvation which restores entire fellowship between the sinner and his Maker whom he has offended, there are three essential and co-ordinate elements, pardon of sin, propitiation for sin, and purification from sin. The first needs, and perhaps admits of, no figurative representation. It comes forth in its unadorned simplicity from the mercy of God, that eternal mystery of the divine breast, that prime attribute of revelation, that inexhaustible source of all the ways and means of salvation. The second, propitiation, is set forth in the manifold symbols of the sacrifice in the first seven chapters of this book. It is the nature of a reality to be one, constant, and self-consistent in all its evolutions; but it is characteristic of its symbols to be diverse, variant, and inconsistent with one another in some of their qualities. Hence we have the burnt-sacrifice, the oblation, the peace-offering, the sin-sacrifice, and the trespass-offering, variously representative each of some prominent feature of one and the same propitiation. These symbols are a kind of prophecy, and therefore follow its general law in foreshadowing by their variety the diverse aspects of the same great event, while it is yet in the womb of futurity. This wondrous event is the propitiation for sin, which these sacrifices forebode, but do not accomplish. The third great requisite of salvation is moral or spiritual purification, which David calls the creation of a new heart, the renewal of a right spirit. Propitiation is external; purification, internal. Propitiation tenders on behalf of the defaulter the full practice of all that the law demands; purification re-establishes in the heart of the transgressor the living principle of the law itself.

Propitiation and purification are in experience inseparably connected. The Mediator propitiates by a full obedience and a full suffering unto death for disobedience: the Spirit of God purifies by presenting this propitiation to the unclouded and unveiled heart of the sinner, which thereupon becomes disabused, confiding, consenting, penitent, grateful, loving. Thus it may be said, in a worthy sense, that the propitiation cleanses, because it is the instrument by which the Spirit begets repentance in the soul. The word is said to purify, because it tells of propitiation; it is the gospel of reconciliation. The blood is said to cleanse, because it expiates and, in conjunction with the moral perfection of the true victim, propitiates, and the conception and acceptance by the soul of this atonement stirs the very depths of the resuscitated affections. If the Spirit of God were to lift the veil from the human heart without presenting to view the gospel of pardon and propitiation, a far different tide of emotions would overwhelm the soul. From the immutably holy God and a guilty self the dark inference would be the doom of perpetual death. The indescribable horror of despair would brood over the conscience. But when the

Spirit not only removes the veil but at the same time holds out mercy, proffers pardon, and above all announces propitiation, the dawn of hope rises on the mind, the wonder of a nascent faith swells the breast and the rising emotions of repentance towards God indicate the new birth of the soul. This clearly shows that propitiation made for man is the instrument by which the Spirit begets the soul anew unto sanctification of life. We may conceive in the abstract propitiation apart from purification. But propitiation without application would be a mere play of the practical faculty without a purpose and without a heart. We cannot, however, conceive purification brought about without the glad tidings of propitiation, unless we will call the despair of self-condemnation by such a name. Thus, propitiation without purification as an effect is conceivable; but purification without propitiation as a cause or concause, is not conceivable.

The first seven chapters of this book set forth propitiation in type and shadow. The next three record the consecration of the propitiator in a like sense. The next five lay all animated nature under tribute to illustrate the distinction between the clean and the unclean, and evoke the notion of moral purification. And these are followed by a chapter which describes the grand crowning act of propitiation in its essential and effective bearing upon the cleansing of the soul. This chapter is therefore of transcendent importance, because it points to propitiation as the instrumental cause, in the hands of the Spirit, of sanctification, and thus determines the ground of the intimate relation subsisting between them. It thus forms the connecting link between the seven chapters of propitiation and the five chapters of purification, between which are naturally inserted the three chapters on the consecration of the priests. Hence these sixteen chapters form a compact, logical whole, and constitute the first part of the Book of Leviticus.

The eleventh chapter distinguishes the clean from the unclean among cattle (1–8); among fish (9–12); among fowl (13–25); among wild beast (26–28); and among creeping things (29–38). It declares unclean the carcass of an animal that has died a natural death, though it were clean when living, and eatable when slain (39, 40), and then returns to other classes of creeping things (41–43). It lays down the general principle that God's people should be holy, which lies at the ground of these formal distinctions (44, 45), and sums up the whole matter in two concluding verses (46, 47).

CLEAN AND UNCLEAN ANIMALS.

XI. 1. And the LORD spake unto Moses and Aaron, saying unto them, 2. Speak unto the sons of Israel, saying, This is the beast that ye shall eat of all the cattle which are upon the earth. 3. All that parteth the hoof and hath the cleft of the cloofs, that raiseth up the cud among the cattle, that shall ye

1-8. The cattle. 1. *Unto Moses and Aaron.* Aaron has now been consecrated. He has already received one communication directly from God (x. 8). And he is henceforth associated with Moses in the reception of some divine instructions. It is meet that he should understand the distinction between the clean and the unclean. 2. *Speak unto the sons of Israel.* It is necessary that the people also should be acquainted with these regulations which were to be carried out in their daily life. *The beast.* This is the generic term for animals. It is employed here in a collective sense, to denote the several kinds of cattle, or larger gentle animals, which are familiar to man. 3. *All that parteth the hoof,*[3] in which there is a visible division of the hoof into two parts. *And hath the cleft of the cloofs,*[3] in which the division is not merely on the surface, but beneath it, so that the hoof is severed into cloofs, as in the cow or sheep. *That raiseth,*[3] or bringeth up the cud. This is more general than what is now technically understood by ruminating or chewing the cud. The latter is restricted to animals called ruminants, which have a fourfold stomach, into one bag of which the imperfectly masticated food enters, passes into the second, where it takes the form of moist pellets, and then rises into the mouth to be perfectly masticated. This last process alone is regarded in the expression of the text; and this occurs partially with some animals that have not the fourfold stomach, as the hare and the kangaroo. *That shall ye eat.* The animals so distinguished are counted as clean and fit for food. The distinction here made is simply ceremonial. It may have some ground in nature which it is competent for the physiologist to investigate and ascertain. But it does not at all rest on the "vanity" and "corruption" into which the creation has sunk in consequence of the fall of man (Keil), inasmuch as this is universal, and therefore affords no ground of distinction among things into clean and unclean.

eat. 4. Only this ye shall not eat, of those that raise up the cud or part the hoof: the camel, because it raiseth up the cud but parteth not the hoof, it is unclean to you. 5. And the coney, because it raiseth up the cud but parteth not the hoof, it is unclean to you. 6. And the hare, because it raiseth the cud but parteth not the hoof, it is unclean to you. 7. And the hog, because it parteth the hoof and cleaveth the hoof, but raiseth not the cud, it is unclean to you. 8. Of their flesh shall ye not eat, and their carcass shall ye not touch: they are unclean to you.

9. This shall ye eat of all that is in the water, all that hath fin and scale in the water; in the seas and in the rivers, this shall ye eat. 10. And all that hath not fin nor scale in the seas and in the rivers, of all that move in the water, and of all living things which are in the water, they shall be loathsome to you. 11. They shall even be loathsome to you; of their

4–8. Certain animals having one of these qualities and wanting another are excluded from the class of the clean and the allowable for food. *The camel*,[4] because it does not part the hoof, though it chews the cud. 5. *The coney*.[5] This is another name for the rabbit. It is, however, believed by many to be the hyrax, a pachyderm intermediate between the rhinoceros and the tapir, resembling the rabbit, but smaller, and of a dull russet color (Dr. Thomson). The term "coney," being more familiar to us, is retained in the translation. 6. *The hare*[6] and the coney agree in bringing up the cud, but do rot part the hoof. They are not what are technically called ruminants, as they have not the fourth stomach, and hence the legislator excludes them. 7. *The hog*[7] has cloofs, but in strictness there are four of them, instead of two. It is not, therefore, of the normal class, and it does not chew the cud. It was avoided as food by many of the ancients, on account of its uncleanliness. 8. *Their carcass*. The dead body of any of them ye shall not touch. It conveys uncleanness.

9–12. The natives of the water. The fish that has fins and scales[8]

flesh shall ye not eat and their carcass ye shall loathe. 12. All that hath not fin nor scale in the water, that shall be loathsome to you.

13. And these of the fowl ye shall loathe; they shall not be eaten, they are loathsome: the eagle and the ospray and the sea-eagle; 14. And the vulture and the kite after its kind; 15. Every raven after its kind; 16. And the ostrich and the

may be eaten. Other aquatic animals, whether fish properly so called, or not, are to be an object of loathing. Hence all amphibious reptiles, molluscs, crustaceans, annelids, echinoderms, and acalephs are excluded. *In the seas and in the rivers.* The same test applies to fresh-water and to salt-water fish. Those without fins and scales have their uses; but they are to be loathsome to the taste or the touch.

13–25. Those that wing their way in the air. *These ..... ye shall loathe.* The exceptions are here set down. The rest are suitable or allowable for food. Twenty species are here forbidden. *The eagle*[13] is well known. It is the king of birds. It hunts and slays for itself, but occasionally preys upon fresh carrion. *The ospray.*[13] This is the ossifrage, or *gypatus barbatus*, the lammer-geier of the Swiss, the *aquila ossifraga* of the Romans. The name ospray or ossifragus is derived from the supposition that it let its prey fall from a great height on the rocks to break its bones (Plin. Nat. Hist. xxx. 7). *The sea eagle*,[13] *pandion haliaetus*, called also the fish-hawk. It subsists on fish, on which it pounces with incredible velocity. 14. *The vulture.*[14] The vulture has the head and part of the neck destitute of feathers, is weak in the talons and strong in the beak, is of a cowardly nature, and usually feeds upon carrion. The vultures are the scavengers of the land, and form a very numerous tribe. *The kite.*[14] This rapacious bird is placed by Linnaeus under the genus *falco*. It has a forked tail and long wings, a short and weak beak and leg, and hence it is the most cowardly of all birds of prey. It seizes upon small quadrupeds, birds, and chickens. 15. *Every raven.*[15] This is of the genus *corvus*. It flies high, scents carrion afar, and feeds not only on this, but on seeds, fruit, and small animals. Hence it is troublesome to the farmer. It is mentioned as early as Gen. viii. 7. 16. *The ostrich.*[16] This is

LEVITICUS XI. 16-18. 147

night-hawk and the gull and the hawk after its kind; 17. The owl and the cormorant and the ibis; 18. And the coot

literally the daughter of the ostrich, according to the custom in the East, of using the words "father," "mother," "son," "daughter," to denote analogous relations of the most general kind. It includes both sexes, though feminine in form. This is the largest of fowls, being four feet from the ground to the back, and seven or eight to the crown of the head. It exceeds in running the swiftness of the horse. It is negligent of its nest. It feeds on seeds and plants, and probably lizards, snakes, and young birds. It swallows indiscriminately almost anything, even stones or glass. It has a doleful howl. Hence its name has been rendered daughter of screeching. *The night-hawk.*[16] This is a bird of the night, common to Egypt and Syria. It feeds on insects, but has been called the goat-sucker, and accused of entering at an open window and sucking the blood of infants, without any warrant. *The gull.*[16] This is of the genus *larus*, frequents the shores in all latitudes, and is a great devourer of fish. It may include the tern. *The hawk.* This is of the genus *falco*. Most of the species are rapacious, feeding on birds and other small animals. It abounds in Western Asia and Egypt. 17. *The owl.* The genus *strix* flies chiefly in the night, and feeds on small mammalia, little birds, and insects. It is common to all countries, but chiefly abounds in cold climates. *The cormorant,*[17] the sea-raven, a large fowl of the pelican kind, feeds on fish, and is very voracious. It is found in the old and new hemispheres. *The ibis.* This is one of the *grallae*, or wading birds. Cuvier has proved that it is a kind of curlew. It feeds on shell-fish, and it is said on serpents. It frequents Egypt and Arabia. 18. *The coot.*[18] This bird is called the porphyrion, or purple bird, its color being that of indigo mingled with red. It frequents marshes, stands on one leg, and holds its prey in the claws of the other. It is found in the Levant and the islands of the Mediterranean. It was an object of idolatry, and kept tame in the vicinity of the temples. *The pelican* [18] is remarkable for an enormous bill, and in the under chap a pouch capable of holding many quarts. Here it deposits the fish it has caught, and with these feeds its young, of which it is very

and the pelican and the gier-eagle ; 19. And the stork, the heron after its kind, and the hoopoe and the bat.

20. All winged creepers, that go on all four, shall be loathsome to you. 21. Only this ye may eat of all winged creepers, that go on all four, that hath legs above its feet to hop withal upon the earth. 22. These of them ye may eat, the locust after

fond. It is found in all quarters of the globe. *The gier-eagle.*[18] This is the *vultur percnopterus*, commonly called Pharaoh's chicken. It visits Palestine in the summer, and feeds on carrion. 19. *The stork* [19] is of the heron tribe, feeds on fish, reptiles, worms, and insects, is found in Europe, Africa, and Western Asia, and on the New Continent. It is noted for its harmless disposition and its attachment to its young. It builds on the roofs of houses, and is familiar with man. *The heron.*[19] The genus *ardea* is a great devourer of fish, and is found all over the world. *The hoopoe* [19] is of the genus *upupa*, has a beautiful crest variously waving, feeds on insects, worms, and snails, and is found in Egypt and Palestine. *The bat* [19] belongs to the class *vespertilio*, has a membrane between the fingers or claws which enables it to fly, reposes during the day, and hibernates during the winter, and preys by night on insects. The vampire bat, which is found in Southern Asia, makes a small wound in the toe of the sleeper, out of which it sucks blood till it sometimes causes death. The smaller bat is found in Palestine. The bat is the natural transition from the fowl proper to the winged creeper.

20–25. The winged creepers. 20. *Winged creepers* or swarmers are so called from their minuteness and their multitude. *That go on all four.* They crawl on the ground with four feet. These are to be avoided as loathsome. 21. *That hath legs above its feet.* This describes an excepted class that may be eaten. With these legs they are able to hop on the ground. They are specified in the next verse. 22. The four classes of edible locusts are here enumerated. We cannot distinguish these classes otherwise than by the meaning of their names. *The locusts,*[22] see on Ex. x. 4, where the species is mentioned. It is named so from its multiplying or being gregarious. *The gulper.*[22] This is a mere translation of the name. *The hopper.*[23]

its kind, and the gulper after its kind, and the hopper after its kind, and the cricket after its kind. 23. And every winged creeper, which hath four feet, shall be loathsome unto you. 24. And for these ye shall be unclean; all that touch their carcass shall be unclean until the even. 25 And whosoever taketh up aught of their carcass shall wash his clothes and be unclean until the even.

26. All cattle that part the hoof and have not the cleft nor raise the cud, these are unclean to you; every one that toucheth them shall be unclean. 27. And whatsoever walketh upon its paws among all animals that walk on all four, they are unclean unto you; every one that toucheth their carcass shall be unclean until the even. 28. And he that taketh up their carcass shall wash his clothes and be unclean until the even: they are unclean to you. §

29. And this shall be unclean to you, among the creepers that creep on the earth, the weasel and the mouse and the

---

The same remark applies to this term. This is variously rendered cutter or leaper. *The cricket.*[22] These names denote, not certain stages of the one locust, but, according to the text, certain kinds of this large tribe. 23. *Winged creeper which hath four feet.* All of this class are unclean. He that touches them shall wash his clothes and be unclean until the evening.

26–28. Other larger land animals. 26. Gentle animals that part the hoof, but do not divide it into cloofs nor bring up the cud, are here for the first time enumerated. They are placed here because in the view of the legislator they are closely allied to those comprehended in the following verses. 27. *Whatsoever walketh upon its paws.* The paw is the sole of the foot unprotected by a hoof. Cats, dogs, and most of the wild or ferocious animals come under this head. *Toucheth the carcass.* To touch the living body of an animal of this kind did not necessarily produce defilement. But the dead body is defiling.

29–38. Creeping things. 29. *The weasel*[29] is common in Europe,

150 CLEAN AND UNCLEAN ANIMALS.

lizard after its kind. 30. And the gecko and the skink and the newt and the stellion and the chameleon. 31. These are unclean to you among all creepers; all that touch their carcass shall be unclean until the even. 32. And everything on which any of them when dead falls shall be unclean; every vessel of wood or raiment or skin or sack, whatever vessel it be wherein work is done, it shall be put into water and be unclean until the even, and then be clean. 33. And every earthen vessel whereinto any of them falleth, all that is in it shall be unclean, and it ye shall break. 34. All food which may be eaten upon

Asia, and America, feeds on mice, rats, moles, and small birds. *The mouse.*[29] This is not the jerboa (Boch.), but the field-mouse, which is very destructive to grain. *The lizard.*[29] This word occurs only here in this sense. The lizards are a very numerous class in the East. This is perhaps the dabb of the Arabs which bears the same name. 30. *The gecko*[30] is found in the East, is of a reddish-grey color, spotted with brown, feeds on insects, and utters a croak or groan somewhat like a frog. *The skink*[30] is the waran el-hard, the *varanus arenarius*, the land-lizard of Herodotus. It abounds in the deserts of Arabia. It sometimes reaches six feet in length. It feeds on insects. *The newt*[30] is a species of salamander. It is called the *triton cristatus*, and dwells in Europe and Western Asia. The salamanders border on the lizards and frogs. *The stellion*[30] is noted for bowing the head. Hence the Mahometans kill it, because it mimics their motion in prayer. It is common in Palestine, and infests the pyramids. *The chameleon.*[30] This is a kind of lizard, having four feet and on each five toes, arranged two against three. It is of a bluish-grey color in the shade, and of a tawny color in the sun. Its changes of color are ascribed by some to its capacious lungs and by others to a double layer of pigment. It lives on insects, and is a native of Asia and Africa. 31. Contact with these defiles. 32. That on which any part of their carcass falls shall pass through water and be unclean until the evening. 33. And the earthen vessel shall be broken, because being porous it is liable to absorb the defilement, so that it could

which water cometh shall be unclean; and all drink that may be drunk in any vessel shall be unclean. 35. And everything on which part of their carcass falleth shall be unclean; oven or pot, it shall be broken; they are unclean; and they shall be unclean to you. 36. Only a spring and a well, a gathering of water, shall be clean; and that which toucheth their carcass shall be unclean. 37. And when part of their carcass falleth on any sowing-seed which is to be sown it shall be clean. 38. And when water is put on the seed and part of their carcass falleth upon it it shall be unclean to you. §

39. And when any of the cattle, which ye may have for food, dieth, he that toucheth its carcass shall be unclean until the even. 40. And he that eateth of its carcass shall wash his clothes and be unclean until the even; and he that beareth its carcass shall wash his clothes and be unclean until the even. 41. And every creeper that creepeth on the earth is loath-

not be removed by washing. 34. The food on which it falls, if prepared with water, shall be unclean, and likewise the drink, because the impurity pervades the fluid, or that which is steeped in it. If dry, that part of the food may be removed which was in contact with the unclean thing. 35. The vessel on which it falls shall be unclean. *Oven or pot.* These are earthenware. The pot consists of two parts, a dish and a lid, and hence it is in the dual number. These shall be broken; for they are unclean, and you are so to regard and treat them. 36. A well or pool of water, which is continually purifying itself by overflowing or precipitation, is to be regarded as clean. But the portion that is in contact with the carcass is unclean. 37. Dry sowing-seed is not so defiled or rendered unfit for sowing. 38. But if it be soaked in water it is unclean.

39–45. Concluding regulations. 39. He that touches the carcass of a clean animal that has died a natural death shall be unclean until the evening. 40. He that eats of it or carries of it shall be unclean. It is to be presumed that the former partook of this defiling fare unwittingly. 41. All creepers are loathsome, and are not to be eaten.

CLEAN AND UNCLEAN ANIMALS.

some: it shall not be eaten. 42. All that goeth on the belly and all that goeth on all four, with all that hath many feet of all creepers that creep on the earth, ye shall not eat them, for they are loathsome. 43. Ye shall not make your souls loathsome with any creeper that creepeth, nor shall ye defile yourselves with them nor be defiled with them. 44. For I am the LORD your God, and ye shall sanctify yourselves, and

42. So are all that go on the belly, as serpents and worms, all that go on four feet among the small animals, as rats and mice, and all that have many feet, that is, more than four, including various kinds of insects. 43. *Your souls*, that is, your living bodies, your persons, yourselves. *Loathsome*, objects of religious abhorrence. *Defile yourselves . . . . . nor be defiled.* The repetition is emphatic. The former intimates some degree of activity in getting oneself defiled. 44. The transcendent reason for avoiding impurity is now assigned. *For I am the Lord your God.* I am holy. And ye who are to be in fellowship with me must be holy. This reason lifts us up above all ceremonial purity to that spiritual purity of which the former is merely the shadow. The aim of this laborious chapter now at length stands before the mind. It awakens and sharpens the sense of the distinction between the clean and the unclean in material things, and thus prepares for a keen and unerring sense of the difference between right and wrong, between moral good and evil. The distinction between animals as clean and unclean is mainly ceremonial. In their own line all things are pure; every creature of God is good in itself and for its proper end. Only in a typical sense and in a certain relation to man is there a distinction of things into clean and unclean. And only when we come to man do we meet with a moral nature, and, to our blame and shame, with moral defilement. The shunning of ceremonial impurity calls forth and exercises the sense of moral distinctions. But it is not merely the distinction of clean and unclean that is taught in this chapter. This might be a mere intellectual exercise of no moral significance. We now see the point of the word loathing or loathsome when it is so often repeated. Were it not that instinct awakens in us an abhorrence of most of the unclean animals mentioned,

ye shall be holy, for I am holy: and ye shall not defile your souls with any creeper that creepeth on the earth. 45. For I

and of the carcass of a dead animal, we might think it strange that we should be required not merely to avoid, but to loathe such objects. But when we rise to moral questions we find that right and wrong, good and evil, rest on self-evident principles. And hence when reason distinguishes between right and wrong, conscience inevitably approves of the right and abhors the wrong. This alone brings out the full force and point of the loathing which we are so frequently called upon to feel toward that which is unclean. This loathing becomes even more intensified by contrast. When the Lord reveals himself to the sinful soul as merciful and gracious, penitence and purity of heart come to the birth. This involves a peculiar loathing of sin on the one hand, and a growing love of holiness on the other. All this is summed up in that evangelical watchword, "I am the Lord your God," which has met us so often and cheered us so much in the reading of the Old Testament. It is the opening sentence of the ten words spoken from Sinai. He who addresses us is GOD, the only absolutely and eternally Almighty; THY GOD having come to thee with the invitation of mercy, and having made thee willing by his Spirit to accept the invitation, and become his as he has become yours; THE LORD THY GOD, the Self-existent, the Author of all that exists, the Keeper of covenant, and Performer of promise is thy God. Nothing can transcend this. *And ye shall sanctify yourselves.* The gospel contained in the above words will sanctify you so far as word or truth or deed can do it. If by this gospel, explicitly or implicitly, ye be not softened, shamed, drawn to God, sanctified, there is no instrument by which you can be sanctified. *Ye shall be holy, for I am holy.* Another fundamental principle. After the image of God man was made. After his image, if renewed at all, he must be renewed. This sentence finds its multiplied echo reverberating through the Old and the New Testament. *And ye shall not defile your souls with any creeping thing.* A descent, and yet not a descent, but a uniform carrying out of the one great principle into all the details of a moral life. 45. The great God of mercy and grace raises up the heart of the people once more to the principle of the gospel, and recalls to their mind the

am the LORD that brought you up from the land of Mizraim to be your God: and ye shall be holy, for I am holy.

46. This is the law of the cattle and of the fowl and of every living thing that moveth in the water, with every thing that creepeth on the earth. 47. To separate between the unclean and the clean; and between the beast that may be eaten and the beast that may not be eaten.   ¶ ¶ ¶

grandest practical illustration of it within their experience, namely, the deliverance from the land of bondage.

46, 47. The recapitulation. *This is the law,* the doctrine or discipline concerning every kind of living creature. *To separate* or distinguish between two things, first between the clean and the unclean, and next between that which may be eaten and that which may not. After the key we have received to the bearing and import of this chapter, it is impossible for us to rest in the mere natural or ceremonial significance of these words. They have undoubtedly also a moral meaning. In this their widest and truest meaning they divide all morality into two parts, our duty to others and our duty to ourselves. When we distinguish between the morally clean and unclean we learn what is right and good towards our God and towards our neighbors, and what is the contrary. When we distinguish between what is to be eaten and what is not, we learn by a striking example what is to be enjoyed and what is not to be enjoyed, what is allowable and what is not, what is the lawful gratification of the appetite and what the unlawful, even in things allowable. In a word, we have before us the two great branches of scriptural and rational morals — justice and temperance. The former has been more or less illustrated and enforced; the latter has been most culpably and ruinously neglected. They stand upon a par in Scripture. This is not the place to treat of them at length.

NOTES.

3. *Parting the hoof,* מַפְרֶסֶת פַּרְסָה. *Having the cleft of the cloofs,* שֹׁסַעַת שֶׁסַע פְּרָסֹת. The old word cloof serves to express the meaning of the plural noun here. *Raising the cud,* מַעֲלַת גֵּרָה. גֵּרָה is that which is sawn, crushed, chewed.

LEVITICUS XI. 155

4. *Camel,* גָּמָל, the strong, complete, or fully grown; r. *finish, ripen.* No animal is more obviously or completely fitted for its place. Its padded feet and its stomach having an arrangement for containing a store of water for many days are among its prominent adaptations for the desert. It is a native of Arabia and is a most serviceable help to the Bedawin.

5. *Coney,* שָׁפָן, burrowing (Ges.) gnawing (F.), δασύπους (Sept.); a quadruped living gregariously among rocks (Ps. civ. 18; Prov. xxx. 26), the hyrax, jerboa (Ges.), rabbit or the like. Elsewhere only in Deut. xiv. 7.

6. *Hare,* אַרְנֶבֶת=אַנֶּבֶת, leaper, runner, χοιρογρύλλιος; r. רנב or אנב, *go before, hasten.* Only here and in Deut. xiv. 7.

7. *Hog,* חֲזִיר, turning, or strong; r. *turn, wind, be strong,* ὓς. It occurs seven times in Scripture.

9. *Fin,* סְנַפִּיר; r. סָנַף, *move, wave, row. Scale,* קַשְׂקֶשֶׂת, קשׂשׂ, *peel, scale.*

13. *Eagle,* נֶשֶׁר, tearer, ἀετός. It pounces suddenly upon its prey (Hab. i. 8), moults its feathers annually (Isa. xl. 31; Ps. ciii. 5), makes its nest on the crag (Job xxxix. 27), takes great care of its young (Deut. xxxii. 11), and lives long (Ezek. i. 10). *Ospray,* פֶּרֶס, breaking, severing, γρύψ. Only here and in Deut. xiv. 12. *Sea-eagle,* עָזְנִיָּה, strong or keen-sighted, ἁλιαίετος.

14. *Vulture,* דָּאָה, rushing, rapid, γύψ. Only here. In Deut. רָאָה. *Kite,* אַיָּה, said to be so named from its cry, אַי, ἰκτῖνος. Also in Deut. xiv. 13 and Job xxviii. 7. It is keen-sighted. Here it is regarded as a genus.

15. *Raven,* עֹרֵב, dark-colored, κόραξ.

16. *Ostrich,* בַּת־הַיַּעֲנָה, daughter of screeching, moaning, στρουθός. *Night-hawk,* תַּחְמָס, bird of violence, γλαύξ. Also in Deut. xiv. 15. *Gull,* שַׁחַף, lean, λάρος. Also in Deut. xiv. 15. *Hawk,* נֵץ, swift in flight. Also in Deut. xiv. 15 and Job xxxix. 26.

17. *Owl,* כּוֹס, having a cup or pouch, νυκτικόραξ. Bochart takes it to be the pelican or cormorant. It is mentioned in Deut. xiv. 16 and Ps. cii. 7. *Cormorant,* שָׁלָךְ, casting itself down from high rocks to pounce upon fish, καταράκτης. Also in Deut. xiv. 17. *Ibis,* יַנְשׁוּף, blowing like a horn, ἴβις, the Egyptian heron, inhabiting marshy places (Deut. xiv. 16; Isa. xxxiv. 11).

18. *Coot*, תִּנְשֶׁמֶת, πορφυρίων. The same word occurs with a different meaning in vs. 30. Fuerst makes it a kind of owl. Also in Deut. xiv. 16. *Pelican*, קָאָת, vomiting, πελεκάν. It is variously rendered by the Sept. pelican, gannet, chameleon, and bird. Also in Deut. xiv. 17; Ps. cii. 7; Isa. xxxi. 11; Zeph. ii. 11. *Gier-eagle*, רָחָם, affectionate, κύκνος and ἔποψ. Also in Deut xiv. 17.

19. *Stork*, חֲסִידָה, affectionate to its young, ἐρωδιός, ἔποψ. Also in Deut. xiv. 18; Ps. civ. 17; Jer. viii. 7; Zech. v. 9. *Heron*, אֲנָפָה, irascible. The χαραδριός of the Sept. is supposed to be the plover, lapwing, or curlew. Also in Deut. xiv. 18. *Hoopoe*, דּוּכִיפַת, has been analyzed into הוּ כִיפָא or הוּךְ, *cock*, or *master of the rock*, ἔποψ. Also in Deut. xi. 18. *Bat*, עֲטַלֵּף, said to be compounded of עָטַל עֵף, *dark-flying*, νυκτερίς. Also in Deut. xiv. 18 and Isa. ii. 20.

22. *Locust*, אַרְבֶּה, multiplier, *gryllus gregarius*, browser (אָרַב F.). Βροῦχος is said to be a locust without wings. The present word occurs about twenty-four times in the Hebrew Scriptures. *Gulper*, סָלְעָם. Ἀττάκης is said to be a small kind of grasshopper without wings. Only here. *Hopper*, חַרְגֹּל, leaper, ὀφιομάχης. Only here. *Cricket*, חָגָב, cutter (F.), coverer (Ges.), leaper. It occurs five times.

29. *Weasel*, חֹלֶד, gliding, digging, γαλῆ. Only here. *Mouse*, עַכְבָּר, nimble, μῦς. It occurs five times elsewhere, 1 Sam. vi.; Isa. lxvi. 17. *Lizard*, צָב, slow, κροκόδειλος χερσαῖος, the land-lizard. The dabb is eighteen inches long, and is frequent in the desert.

30. *Gecko*, אֲנָקָה, groaning, μυγάλη, shrew-mouse. Only here in this sense. *Skink*, כֹּחַ, strength, χαμαιλέων. Only here in this sense. *Newt*, לְטָאָה, hiding, ἀσκαλαβώτης, wall-climber. Only here. *Stellion*, חֹמֶט, bowing down, σαύρα. *Chameleon*, תִּנְשֶׁמֶת, breathing. Ἀσπάλαξ of the Sept. means a mole. Some pronounce it a salamander.

XII. PURIFICATION OF WOMEN.

This chapter contains a regulation concerning mothers. It is addressed to Moses, by him to be communicated to the sons of Israel. It may therefore have been revealed before the erection of the tabernacle or the consecration of the priests. It is now arranged in its proper place under the head of purification. The chapter contains

XII. 1. And the LORD spake unto Moses, saying, 2. Speak unto the sons of Israel, saying, when a woman conceiveth and beareth a male, then she shall be unclean seven days, as in the days of the separation of her infirmity shall she be unclean. 3. And in the eighth day the flesh of his foreskin shall be cir-

two parts: the first determining the time of seclusion on account of child-birth 1–5; the second prescribing the sacrifices to be offered when purification is completed 6–8.

1–5. The period of seclusion after child-bearing. 2. *When a woman conceiveth*,[2] is fruitful, yields seed. *Beareth a male.* This defines the sex of her seed. *She shall be unclean seven days.* Impurity is here connected with child-bearing. There can be no ground for this but the fall of man, in consequence of which the child is born in sin. The seven days are here a complete period. *As in the days of the separation of her infirmity.* Her infirmity is her monthly sickness. The separation is the state of seclusion in which she is kept in consequence of her uncleanness. This uncleanness also lasts seven days, as we learn from Lev. xv. 19. This is only another instance of the moral defilement connected with descent from fallen parents. 3. *And in the eighth day.* The infant is reckoned with the mother until the eighth day. As the mother and the father are members of the community of Israel, the child is in this respect also counted with them. On these grounds he receives the sign of circumcision. The origin and meaning of this rite we have in Gen. xvii. It is the symbol of moral renewal. It therefore implies the existence of depravity. But the mother in Israel having passed through her ceremonial defilement is now clean, and her child is clean with her. As the descendant of fallen man, he has the inheritance of original sin and must lie under the condemnation of the race. As the descendant of a circumcised father he has the inheritance of circumcision, the outward token of the covenant of grace. This involves the principle that in the right order of things the offspring of pious parents will be pious. It cannot mean that circumcision is itself regeneration. This would be to make a rite a charm, instead of a symbol of precious truth. As the mother, so the child becomes ceremonially clean, after the seven days have

cumcised. 4. And thirty and three days shall she sit in her blood of purifying; she shall not touch any holy thing, nor come into the sanctuary, until the days of her purifying be fulfilled. 5. And if she bear a female, then she shall be unclean two weeks as in her separation; and sixty and six days shall she sit in her blood of purifying.

elapsed; and, therefore, on the eighth day the rite of circumcision is performed. 4. *Thirty and three days.* These, with the previous seven, make the period of forty days, which is one of the perfect numbers in Scripture, and indicates a thorough purification. *Shall she sit,* abide in her house, being indeed clean and associating with her family, but not taking part in any public duties of religion. *In her blood of purifying.* This is the discharge of blood by which nature is relieved, the system purified, and the health restored. Hence it is called the blood of purifying. While it flows she is regarded as in some respect unclean, and after it ceases she is clean. The seven days and the thirty-three days have some relation to the *lochia rubra,* which may continue about a week, and the *lochia alba* which may continue a considerable time after. But the numbers mainly refer to the formal and typical character of this uncleanness, which points to the moral depravity connected with and conveyed by birth in a fallen race. *Not touch any holy thing.* This indicates the typical nature of this uncleanness; since only moral defilement can occasion real impurity or exclude from the communion of God. *Nor come into the sanctuary.* This shows that females were admitted into the sanctuary as worshippers on the same footing with males. 5. *If she bear a female.* This case is treated distinctly from the former. The period of uncleanness is double, and so is that of seclusion. Though the ancients, as we learn from Aristotle (Hist. an. 6, 22; 7. 3) and Hippocrates were of opinion that the flux continued longer after the birth of a girl than of a boy, yet the difference of time, if any, must be quite inconsiderable, and cannot account for these double numbers. The only ground that can be assigned for this difference is the historical fact of the woman being first in the transgression. This difference between male and female, as well as some others, is done away in the

LEVITICUS XII. 5, 6.   159

6. And when the days of her purifying are fulfilled for a son or for a daughter, she shall bring a lamb of the first year for a burnt-sacrifice and a pigeon or a dove for a sin-sacrifice

Messiah, who is born of a virgin. In all births, however, purity and communion are recovered at the end of a short period, and so mercy mingles faith and hope with the remnant of corruption in all those who have entered into willing covenant with the God of all grace.

6–8. The sacrifices after purification. There is nothing said here of washing, as that is treated of in chap. xv. *When the days of her purifying are fulfilled.* The purification is quite distinct from the propitiation. It is accomplished before the sacrifice that denotes propitiation is presented. *For a son or for a daughter*, that is, on account of the birth of either. The mother is unclean, and with her the helpless child, until the week or fortnight is completed. Then both are clean, and on the eighth day the son is circumcised. After the period of seclusion has elapsed the mother comes forth to present herself and child before the Lord. *A lamb.* This is the burnt sacrifice. As the ceremonial defilement indicates sin as the inheritance of a fallen race, the burnt-sacrifice represents the propitiation for sin which avails for every penitent, confiding child of God. The sin-sacrifice speaks of expiation for any inadvertent sin of which the mother may have been guilty. Hence these sacrifices express on the part of the offerer confession of sin, appeal for mercy, reliance on the Mediator, and thankfulness for the goodness of God to the mother and the child in temporal, but above all in spiritual, things. The message of mercy and mediation, which these divinely appointed sacrifices convey, transcends all mere earthly deliverance. It would be an occasion of insufferable distress to a mother to bring forth a child with the tendency and under the doom of sin. Hence to her there is a new and unspeakably precious significance and blessing in the burnt-sacrifice and the sin-sacrifice that tell of propitiation and of expiation, not only for herself but for her offspring. She enters with all the earnestness and cheerfulness of hope upon the task of training up her child for God, believing with all confidence that as there is an atonement, so there will be a new birth by which her child will

unto the door of the tent of meeting to the priest; 7. And he shall offer it before the LORD and atone for her, and she shall be cleansed from the fountain of her blood. This is the law of her that beareth a male or a female. 8. And if her hand find not enough for a lamb, then she shall take two

become a child of God and an heir of life. The purification now becomes doubly interesting to her, as the earnest as well as the emblem of the spiritual purification of her child, when faith in God and repentance towards him will indicate that out of the death of sin has sprung the new life of a heart cleansed by the Spirit. 7. *And atone for her.* Being a mother, she has a new life given to her. This is of a sinful nature. But there is a propitiation for sin and a great High Priest. She humbly accepts the glad tidings and lays hold of the Saviour. Her heart that was bowed down under the burden of sin is lifted up again. *And shall be cleansed.* She is now declared or pronounced clean. The process of purification has come to an end, betokening the coming of the sinner with the whole heart's consent to the God of salvation. The act of propitiation, represented by the sacrifice offered, is now made available for the acceptance of the believing mother and her child. *This is the law*, the instruction or regulation suitable to the mother who has brought into being another individual of the fallen race of man. 8. *And if her hand find not.* Yet merciful consideration for the poor adds as an appendix, that a dove or a pigeon may be substituted for the lamb as a burnt-sacrifice. This met the case of Mary the mother of the Messiah himself (Luke ii. 24).

No event is more interesting to the parent or to the race than the birth of a child. In a state of innocence it would have been a source of unmingled and unutterable gladness. On the part of the parents it was the nearest approach possible to a new creation; and in regard to the race it was another unit added to the fellowship of holiness and happiness. And the whole outward scene of diversified activity and enjoyment was made for man, not man for the outward scene. Hence the birth of man transcends in importance the whole growth and development of animate and inanimate nature. But above all, man is

doves or two pigeons, one for a burnt-sacrifice and one for a sin-sacrifice; and the priest shall atone for her and she shall be clean. ¶

made after the image and in the likeness and for the fellowship of his Maker, and on this ground he has dominion over the earth and all that it contains. Another child of such a race is another source of good to man and glory to God. But the fall casts a shade of impenetrable darkness over the birth of a child of man. All that reason can say is, that this is another child of sin and heir of death. The thoughtful husband and wife may well hesitate to become the parents of an offspring having such a bent and such a doom. This single consideration justifies the insertion of this short and reassuring chapter in the book of propitiation. The mother in Israel is here taught that while there is impurity and guilt connected with the bearer and the born of the fallen race, yet there is a propitiation on which she may rely for herself and for her offspring, and a purification which she has for herself and may ask and confidently expect for her child, while she trains him up in the way he should go. This lifts the believing parents out of the gulf of despair, and encourages them to enter upon the hopeful task of training up their child for glory, honor, and immortality. As the mother and her child emerge out of the impurity, she learns to hope for the day when both will emerge out of the bondage and corruption of sin; as the child is circumcised on the eighth day the confiding parents pray and wait and watch and work for the circumcision of the heart, which is hopefully foreshadowed by the outward rite: as the mother offers her burnt-sacrifice and sin-sacrifice she rejoices in the knowledge that there is a propitiation that is sufficient for her and for her children and for her children's children to all generations. This chapter could not be wanting in the book of atonement; and assuredly it has not been written in vain.

NOTE.

2. תַזְרִיעַ, *yieldeth seed*, as in Gen. i. 11.

XIII. THE LEPROSY DISCERNED.

This is the third communication in this section. It is made to Moses and Aaron in common, and was therefore, no doubt, given after the consecration of the priests. It concerns the priests, whose duty it was to examine and pronounce upon cases of leprosy. Two kinds of leprosy are described in this chapter; that of the human body (1-46), and that of a garment (47-59). A third kind is brought forward in the next chapter (33-48), that of a house. This is a notable instance of the wider and more popular meaning of many Hebrew terms than that of any representatives they have in our modern tongues. With us the leprosy is a disease peculiar to man, and having nothing corresponding to it in any other department of nature. But the Hebrew word which we render leprosy designates also according to native usage an unhealthy state of a garment or of the surface of a wall. The leprosy seems to be a native of Egypt, but is found in Syria, Palestine, and Arabia, and rarely in other countries. It was reported by Manetho, and repeated by Strabo, Tacitus, Justin, and other ancient writers, that the Israelites brought this disease into Egypt. But the fact is precisely the reverse. Israel came into Egypt as a family consisting of seventy souls, and when they left it, two hundred and ten years after, some of them were probably infected with it, and carried it with them out of that country. It is not a merely cutaneous disease. It penetrates the whole system, and often lurks a long time unseen before it comes to the surface. It is a disease of the most virulent kind, and nearly, if not altogether incurable. It is moreover infectious in the highest degree. It appears in several forms, as the black leprosy, the white leprosy, and the non-contagious leprosy. "The black had dark brown spots. The white is characterized by blanched skin, white hair, the drying up of the juices of the body, and the decay of one member after another" (Duns, Bib. Nat. Sci. p. 98). This is the kind of leprosy to which reference is here made. It is still prevalent in the East. Descriptions of it may be found in Robinson and other travellers in the East. Four cases are here described.

1-8. First case. 2. *In the skin of his flesh.* The disease is only noticed when it comes to the surface or becomes cutaneous. *A rising,*[2]

XIII. 1. And the LORD spake unto Moses and Aaron, saying, 2. When a man hath in the skin of his flesh a rising, scab, or blotch, and it is in the skin of his flesh a plague of leprosy, then he shall be brought unto Aaron the priest, or unto one of his sons the priests; 3. And the priest shall look on the plague in the skin of the flesh, and the hair in the plague is turned white, and the look of the plague is deeper than the skin of his flesh, it is a plague of leprosy; and the priest shall look on him and pronounce him unclean. 4. And if the blotch be white in the skin of his flesh, and its look not deeper than the skin, and its hair not turned white, then the priest

a raised spot. *Scab*,[2] scurf or tetter breaking out. *Blotch*,[2] a bleached or whitish spot. *A plague.* This is to be taken as a stroke, attack, or touch of the disease. In this sense we have no term more suitable. *Leprosy.*[2] This is usually explained as a stroke or scourge; but it probably means a breaking out or rough swelling. This tallies with the Greek term adopted into our language, the scaly disease. *Unto Aaron, or unto one of his sons.* The ordinary priest was thus competent to make the diagnosis. 3. The two obvious signs of leprosy are the hair turned white and the plague being deeper than the skin. The hair is usually dark in the East. This is therefore a striking mark. The second sign means either that the surface of the spot affected is lower than the rest of the skin, or that the disease is deeper than the skin. Observers inform us that the patch of skin diseased is raised above the rest, though hollow in the middle, while the border around is reddish or inflamed. The second meaning therefore seems the more probable. *Pronounce him unclean.*[3] When these decisive marks appear the priest is to pronounce him unclean. The declaration does not make him unclean: the existing uncleanness gives occasion for the declaration. 4–6. *The blotch.* The peculiarity of the blotch is its white or bright color. This excites attention. But if on examination the characteristic symptoms of the hair turned white and the appearance deeper than the skin are absent, the priest is directed to shut him up for seven days. *Shut up the plague.* Some

shall shut up the plague seven days. 5. And the priest shall look upon it the seventh day, and behold the plague is at a stay in his sight and spreadeth not in the skin, then the priest shall shut him up seven days again. 6. And the priest shall look on it the seventh day again, and behold the plague fadeth and spreadeth not in the skin, then the priest shall pronounce him clean; it is a scab, and he shall wash his clothes and be clean. 7. But if the scab do spread in the skin, after he hath been seen by the priest for his cleansing, then he shall be seen again by the priest. 8. And the priest shall see, and behold the scab hath spread in the skin; then the priest shall pronounce him unclean; it is leprosy. ¶

have suggested that to shut up the plague is merely to bind it up, as in Gen. ii. 21. But the passage referred to is not a case of binding with a bandage, but of closing up an opening. And in vs. 26 the pronoun "him" refers not to the blotch, which in the original is feminine, but to the person affected with it. Hence to shut up the plague simply means to shut up him who has the plague. 5. If on re-examination the plague has not spread, but is at a stay, the priest is to shut him up other seven days. The period of seven days is nearly that in which the process of nature completes itself. A second seven days will usually afford time for signs of improvement to appear, if the process of healing have commenced. 6. If at the end of a fortnight the affection is manifestly giving way, and not spreading, it is but a scab[6] or scurf, and the captive is pronounced clean, and released. He is to wash his clothes, and be clean. 7, 8. But if after he has been inspected in order to be pronounced clean, the scab begin to spread, he is to be inspected again. The presumption is the charitable one, that the patient is free from the contaminating malady. He is therefore inspected in order, if possible, to be pronounced clean. If, however, even after he has past the priest's inspection, symptoms of an unfavorable kind appear, he is to be inspected again. If the signs of the disease are palpable he is to be pronounced unclean and leprous.

9. When a plague of leprosy is in a man, then he shall be brought to the priest. 10. And the priest shall look, and behold a white rising in the skin, and it hath turned the hair white, and quick flesh liveth in the rising. 11. It is an old leprosy in the skin of his flesh, and the priest shall pronounce him unclean; he shall not shut him up, because he is unclean. 12. But if the leprosy do burst forth in the skin, and cover the whole skin of the plague from his head to his feet, in all the sight of the priest's eyes, 13. Then the priest shall look, and behold the leprosy hath covered all his flesh, and he shall pronounce the plague clean: he is turned all white; he is clean. 14. But when quick flesh appeareth in him, he shall be unclean. 15. And the priest shall see the quick flesh and pronounce him unclean; the quick flesh is unclean; it is

9–17. The second case. The reappearance of an old leprosy. 9. *When a plague of leprosy is in a man.* This assumes the existence of the disease. He is to be brought to the priest, as usual, for inspection. 10. *A white rising.* This is accompanied with two other marks. *The hair white.* This indicates the depth of the disease. *Quick flesh liveth in the rising.* This is literally a quickening of the flesh which liveth in the rising. It denotes flesh that pushes forth without any skin over it. 11. This is a bad symptom. It indicates *an old leprosy*, a sleeping, latent, lingering form of the malady breaking forth with fresh violence. The patient does not require to be remanded for future examination. He is unclean. 12. *Do burst forth*, as a bud or blossom from the stem. *And cover the whole skin of the plague*, from head to foot, so that no quick flesh can be discovered by the closest inspection of the priest. The skin of the plague means the skin that has the plague, and the skin implies the man that has the plague. 13. In this alternative the scurf of disease has covered the whole body and is ready to dry up and fall off, leaving a whole skin behind. The man is really healed. He is to be pronounced clean. *He is turned all white*, and is clean. 14, 15. But if any quick flesh appear he is still under the influence of the disease. The quick flesh is a decisive leprosy. 16. Or if the quick flesh return and change into white, then he shall come to the priest; 17. And the priest shall see him, and behold the plague is turned white; and the priest shall pronounce the plague clean; he is clean. ¶

18. And when there is in the skin of the flesh a boil, and it is healed, 19. And there is in the place of the boil a white rising or a reddish-white blotch; and it is shown to the priest; 20. And the priest shall see, and behold its look is lower than the skin and its hair is turned white, and the priest shall pronounce him unclean; it is a plague of leprosy; it hath burst forth in the boil. 21. But if the priest see it, and behold the hair in it is not white, and it is not lower than the skin, and it fadeth away, then the priest shall shut him up seven days. 22. And if it do spread in the skin, then the priest shall pronounce him unclean; it is a plague. 23. But if the blotch

symptom, and he must be pronounced unclean. 16, 17. If, however, the quick flesh turn from red to white, and thus become a dry scab or scale, as before, the priest shall pronounce him clean.

18–23. *The third case. The scar of a boil.* 18. *In the skin of the flesh a boil.*[18] A boil or blotch such as was inflicted on the Egyptians in the sixth plague (Ex. ix. 9). *And it is healed.* The process of healing has begun. 19. *In the place of the boil,* which is still tender and susceptible of canker. *A reddish-white blotch.* A white rising has been already noticed. The blotch is called reddish-white because the redness of inflammation appears on the margin of the white. 20. The symptoms of disease are the same as before: it looks deeper than the skin and the hair is turned white. *It hath burst forth in the boil.* It effloresces from the seat of the boil. The part that is already weakened by disease is more exposed to the attack of the contagious virus. 21. If the symptoms, however, do not make their appearance, and the irritation is fading away, the patient is to be secluded seven days for after examination. 22. If on further examination it is found to be spreading, it is a leprous attack. 23. But if not, *it is the scar*[23] *of the boil.* He is to be pronounced clean.

stay in its place and spread not, it is the scar of the boil; and the priest shall pronounce him clean. §

24. Or when there is in the skin of his flesh a burn from fire, and the healing of the burn hath become a blotch, reddish-white or white; 25. And the priest shall see it, and behold the hair is turned white in the blotch, and its look is deeper than the skin; it is leprosy, it hath burst forth in the burn: the priest shall pronounce him unclean; it is a plague of leprosy. 26. But if the priest see it, and behold the hair is not white in the blotch, and it is not lower than the skin, and it fades away, then the priest shall shut him up seven days. 27. And the priest shall see him the seventh day; if it do spread in the skin, then the priest shall pronounce him unclean; it is a plague of leprosy. 28. But if the blotch stay in its place, spread not in the skin, and fade away, it is the rising of a burn; and the priest shall pronounce him clean; for it is the scar of a burn. ¶

29. When there is a plague in a man or a woman, in the

24–28. *The fourth case. The scar of a burn.* This bears a considerable resemblance to the preceding case. 24. *A burn*[24] *from fire*, a wound caused by fire. *The healing of the burn*, literally, the revival or recovery of the burn. *Reddish-white or white.* The scar of the burn has become white with or without the redness of inflammation. 25. When the usual signs of the disease are present, the priest has no other course but to pronounce him unclean. 26. If not, he is to be remanded, as usual, for further examination. 27. If on the seventh day it appears to have spread in the skin, it is leprosy. 28. But if it have not spread, but is manifestly fading, it is merely the residue of the burn, and he is to be pronounced clean.

29–37. *The head or chin.* These parts require a special regulation, because they are liable to other failings which may be mistaken for leprosy. 29. *In a man or a woman.* This shows that the skin and not the hair is intended in either case, inasmuch as the chin of the

THE LEPROSY DISCERNED.

head or the chin, 30. And the priest shall see the plague, and behold its look is deeper than the skin, and in it is yellow thin hair, then the priest shall pronounce him unclean; it is a scall, it is a leprosy of the head or the chin. 31. And when the priest seeth the plague of the scall, and behold its look is not deeper than the skin, and the hair is not yellow in it, then the priest shall shut up the plague of the scall seven days. 32. And the priest shall see the plague on the seventh day, and behold the scall hath not spread and there is no yellow hair in it, and the look of the scall is not deeper than the skin, 33. Then he shall be shaven, but the scall shall he not shave; and the priest shall shut up the scall seven days again. 34. And the priest shall see the scall on the seventh day, and behold the scall hath not spread in the skin, and its look is not deeper than the skin; then the priest shall pronounce him clean, and he shall wash his clothes and be clean. 35. But if

female is not usually covered with hair. 30. The marks in this case correspond with former cases, except in the color of the hair. The yellowness and thinness of the hair is a new specialty. The yellow is a golden-red, or fox color. The thinness is an index of disease. *A scall*[30] or scurf is the special name of this form of disease. *A leprosy* This form of disease seems distinct from the specific malady to which we attach the name. It is another instance of the generic application of the Hebrew original. 31. If the symptoms of leprous disease be wanting, the person affected is to be shut up for seven days. *Yellow.*[31] The word usually rendered "dark" stands here in the original. But the Sept. gives what must, from the context, be the correct reading. Compare the thirty-second and thirty-seventh verses. 32. *Hath not spread.* This is always an important criterion, and decisive even in the absence of the change of color in the hair. 33. The head is then to be shaven, with the exception of the scall itself. 34. After seven days more, if, on examination, there be no spreading nor deepening, then the patient shall wash his clothes and be clean. 35. *After his*

LEVITICUS XIII. 35–40. 169

the scall do spread in the skin after his cleansing, 36. And the priest see him and behold the scall hath spread in the skin, the priest shall not seek for yellow hair: he is unclean. 37. But if in his sight the scall be at a stay, and black hair groweth in it, the scall is healed, he is clean; and the priest shall pronounce him clean. §

38. And if a man or woman have in the skin of their flesh blotches, white blotches. 39. And the priest see, and behold in the skin of their flesh are blotches fading white; it is alphos, it hath burst out in the skin; he is clean. §

40. And when a man's head is peeled, he is hind-bald; he

---

cleansing. The priest's sentence is merely declarative. It has no effect on the physical state of the body. Neither is it final. New symptons demand a new diagnosis. 36. If, even after his purification, the eruption begins to spread, no other symptoms need be looked for by the priest. It is manifest that in this case the spreading or not spreading is the sole criterion. 37. The appearance of black hair growing in a scall that does not spread is a sign of health; and the patient is to be pronounced clean.

38, 39. The non-contagious leprosy. *Blotches.* This is mentioned in vs. 2 as a matter for examination. *White.* This shows that there is no very decided indication of color in the previous word. 39. *Fading.* A dim or wan white, ready to vanish away, appears to be designated by this term. *It is alphos.*[39] This is a convenient word instead of the phrase, "non-contagious leprosy." It is also called *leuce* from its white color. It is still known among the Arabs by a name slightly varied from the Hebrew *bahak*. It is a roughness on the skin with pale spots, causes little inconvenience, and disappears usually in the course of a year or two. In medical science it is called *lepra*, a scaliness, though quite distinct from the ordinary leprosy of the East. It is not a cause of uncleanness.

40–46. Leprosy in the bald head. *When a man's head is peeled,* stript of the hair by natural decay. *Hind-bald.*[40] This is used in contradistinction to the baldness mentioned in the next verse. Bald-

is clean. 41. And if his head be peeled toward his face, he is fore-bald; he is clean. 42. But when there is in the hind or fore baldness a reddish-white plague, it is leprosy bursting forth in his hind or fore baldness. 43. And the priest shall see him, and behold the rising of a reddish-white plague in his hind or fore baldness, like the look of leprosy in the skin of the flesh. 44. He is a leprous man, he is unclean: the priest shall surely pronounce him unclean; his plague is in his head. 45. And the leper in whom is the plague shall have his clothes rent and his head bare, and shall cover his beard, and shall cry, Unclean, unclean. 46. All the days that the

ness does not defile. 41. *Peeled toward his face*, from the border or margin of the face. *Fore-bald*, or front-bald, having lost the hair of the forehead. Neither does this of itself cause uncleanness. 42. *A reddish-white plague.* This has been described before in vs. 19. A plague here means as usual a spot smitten. 43. *Like the look of leprosy*, resembling some of the forms of leprosy in other parts of the body. 44. On examination this is pronounced to be leprosy. The turning of the hair white is not noticed, because the hair is gone. 45. The leper being unclean communicates not only uncleanness, but a highly infectious and incurable disease. He is therefore bound by law to make his state known by signs that cannot be mistaken. *His clothes rent.* This was usually done by rending the outer garment from the neck to the girdle. *His head bare.* See on x. 6. The turban was either removed or, at all events, the hair allowed to hang in loose disorder. *Cover his beard.* The beard was considered an ornament to a man, and to violate it was one of the greatest insults. To cover the beard is among the signs of mourning (Ezek. xxiv. 17). These three signs do not distinguish the leper from the ordinary mourner. But he is moreover to cry, "Unclean, unclean," so that all may be warned not to approach him. 46. The leper, as unclean, is to be completely isolated. He is to dwell alone outside the camp. This arrangement has reference to the desert life. A settled mode of life in the land of promise required a change in this regulation. At a still

plague on him shall be unclean, he is unclean; he shall dwell alone; without the camp shall be his dwelling.

47. And when the plague of leprosy is in a garment, either

later period lazarettos were erected outside the cities for the separate, residence of lepers. This dreadful disease is hereditary; it is also communicated by contact, and even by dwelling together; and in its proper forms is incapable of cure. After lurking in the system it appears at length in the skin, goes through its inevitable process, causes fingers and toes and other limbs to fall off, while the mutilated part heals without any application, and, if congenital, terminates life in about fifty years. If acquired by infection it usually causes death in about twenty years. The sufferer may not endure much pain; but he is a wretched and loathsome object. And the parent leaves the child an equally miserable abject from society. Even on sanitary grounds these regulations of Moses were excellent and indispensable. But this is a mere collateral result. It is manifest that these provisions are in no sense medical. They do not contemplate the cure, though they certainly check the spread of this fell and fatal malady. They do not in any way interfere with medical practice or science. They are at bottom purely ceremonial in their aim. While subserving the purpose of guarding bodily health from external danger in a wise and efficient manner, they are directly intended to determine the conditions of ceremonial purity, and to sequester the clean from all contact with that which is unclean. This is the main ground on which the subsequent directions in this chapter rest.

47–59. This second part of the present chapter relates to the leprosy of a garment. 47. *A woollen garment or a linen garment.* In this verse we have only woollen and linen garments mentioned. These were the materials for ordinary wear, the one from the animal, the other from the vegetable world. In the Old World wool was the chief material of clothing in Palestine, Syria, Asia Minor, Greece, Italy, and Spain; hemp in the northern countries of Europe, and flax in Egypt. The Israelites having come out of Egypt were familiar with flax. Cotton was a native of India, and silk of China. Cotton, if imported into Egypt at this early period, was a rare commodity. As

in a woollen garment or a linen garment; 48. Either in warp or woof of linen or wool; or in skin or in anything made of skin; 49. And the plague is greenish or reddish in the garment or in the skin, or in the warp or in the woof, or in any article of skin, it is a plague of leprosy; and it shall be shown

a vegetable product it would be popularly classed under linen. Sackcloth and tent-cloth were made of the hair of the goat and the camel. 48. *Warp or woof.* This may refer to the yarns designed for the warping reel or the shuttle before or after the process of weaving. In the latter case the cause of the decay in the garment, whether it arise from defect in the stuff or the ravages of the moth, may have had its seat in either the warp or the woof before they were interwoven. *Or in skin.* This was applied to the purposes of dress, either as a whole or as the material of some work of art. Sandals and girdles were among the parts of dress made of leather. 49. *Greenish or reddish.* The sources of discoloration or decay in woven or leather fabrics may be animal, vegetable, or mineral, of which the moth, the mildew, and the rust, may be regarded as the familiar forms. They attack animal as well as vegetable products. It is well known how much injury is done to wheat, fruit trees, and other plants, by the spores of various parasitical fungi that come under the general head of mildew, and there is no reason why they should not attack the manufactured article as well as the growing plant. "Minute fungi appear as spots in garments. These soon spread and infect the intervening parts. They vary in color from white to yellow, green, blue, red, and black" (Duns, Bib. Nat. Hist. 107). The moth is no less destructive. Five species of this are described by Linnaeus, called *Tinea Vestionella, T. tapetzella, T. pellionella, Laverna sarcitilla,* and *Galleria mellonella,* engaged respectively in preying upon garments, tapestry, skins, wool, and bees' wax. The *dermestidae* are so called from devouring skins. Beetles attack wool, fur, and old shoes. Ironmould is a familiar example of a stain caused by a chemical process. It is obvious that linen is not only bleached, but may be dyed, discolored, deteriorated, and destroyed by the chemical action of various minerals. Besides all this there are natural forms of decay

to the priest. 50. And the priest shall see the plague, and shall shut up the plague seven days. 51. And he shall see the plague on the seventh day; that the plague hath spread in the garment either in the warp or in the woof, or in the skin, in whatever may be made of the skin for use, the plague is a fretting leprosy; it is unclean. 52. And he shall burn the garment or the warp or woof in wool or in linen, or any article of skin in which the plague may be; because it is a fretting leprosy, it shall be burned in the fire. 53. And if the priest look, and behold the plague is not spread in the garment, either in the warp or in the woof, or in any article of skin; 54. Then the priest shall command, and they shall wash that in which the plague is; and he shall shut it up seven days again. 55. And the priest shall look, after the plague hath been washed, and behold the plague hath not changed its look and the plague is not spread, it is unclean: thou shalt burn it in the fire; it is a fray in its back or in its front. 56. And if the priest look, and behold the plague has faded, after being washed, then he shall tear it from the garment or from the skin, or from the warp or from the woof. 57. And if it appear

by which all organic matter is finally decomposed and reduced to the elements out of which it was formed. 50, 51. The spreading of the plague is the chief sign of the garment leprosy. *A fretting*[51] *leprosy*, raw, sore, not healing, but corroding, and hence permanent or persevering, as in the Sept. and the Vulg. This is the effect of the mildew or the moth. 52. Such a piece of dress is to be burned. 53–55. If the plague have not spread, and yet after being washed and shut up seven days have not changed its appearance, it is unclean. *A fray*[55] *in its back or its front*. A pit or hollow in the wrong or the right side, caused by the eating away of the nap or thread. This causes what is here called by an obvious figure, hind or front baldness, that is, a fray in the back or front. 56. If the plague appear to fade, the part affected is to be torn off and burned. 57. *An outbreak*,[57] a reappear-

still in the garment or in the warp or in the woof or in any article of skin, it is an outbreak; in the fire thou shalt burn that wherein the plague is. 58. And the garment or warp or woof or any article of skin, which thou shalt wash, and the plague depart from it, then it shall be washed again and be clean. 59. This is the law of the plague of leprosy in a gar-

ance of the disease. Such a garment is to be burned. 58. But if on washing the plague disappear, the garment is to be washed again and be clean.

59. This is the recapitulation. *This is the law.* This chapter is complete in itself. It contains the diagnosis of the leprosy in the human subject, and in that which is very near to him, his raiment, simply in reference to the determination of cleanness or uncleanness. This recapitulation, indeed, is limited to the latter part of the chapter which refers to garments. This part is in fact finished, as we have in every case the final decision concerning the garment. We are directed how to dispose of it, and that ends the matter. But the previous part of the chapter is strictly confined to the question of cleanness and uncleanness. But in the case of the human subject there is the ulterior question regarding the mode of re-establishing proper relations between the convalescent and the community of God. The matter is therefore not entirely settled in this communication, but is taken up in the next chapter. The effect of this is to keep the two questions of purity and atonement perfectly distinct. This is of the first importance in a work that is intended to be both instructive and practical. *To pronounce it clean or unclean.* The priest, we perceive, does not profess to purify in the sense of removing disease, and thereby impurity, and restoring health, and thereby purity. He merely pronounces or declares him or it clean or unclean. His declaration does not create or alter, but simply attests the state of the object in question. This applies equally to the man and to the garment. There is, however, a marked difference between the mode in which he deals with the garment and with the human subject. The leprous garment is to be burned, as noxious and incurable. The leprous man is to be shut out of the camp. Exclusion from the

ment of wool or linen, or in the warp or woof, or in any article of skin to pronounce it clean or unclean, 28 ¶ ¶ ¶

camp is a formal excommunication. The only ground of excommunication from the people of God is unholiness manifesting itself in unbelief and impenitence. Hence we gather that exclusion from the camp is a symbol of alienation from the commonwealth of Israel, or the family of heaven, on account of sin. And it is not difficult to see that leprosy is a most striking and awful emblem of sin. It is contagious, it is unclean, and it was incurable by any human means in the time of Moses. In all these it has a parallel in sin. Sin in the disposition and habitude of the mind is eminently contagious; it is essentially a moral defilement of the soul; and it is incurable by any appliance of human philosophy. As leprosy is a most loathsome disease of the body, so is sin the unseemly canker of the mind. As all proper disease is the consequence of sin, so this malady is well chosen as a type of the whole class to symbolize the moral disease. In this chapter, then, we are making progress in the discrimination of the clean and the unclean, and approaching step by step toward the higher discrimination of the right and the wrong, the holy and the unholy, the morally good and evil.

NOTES.

2. *Rising*, שְׂאֵת, οὐλή, scar; r. take up, raise up. *Scab*, סַפַּחַת, σημασία, mark; r. stick, spread, pour. *Blotch*, בַּהֶרֶת, τηλαυγής, far-shining; r. be bright. *Leprosy*, צָרַעַת, λέπρα; r. strike, sting, waste, roughen.

3. *Pronounce unclean*, טִמֵּא, one of the notable meanings of the piel or intensive form of the verb.

6. *Scab*, מִסְפַּחַת, a variation of סַפַּחַת, vs. 2.

10. *Quick flesh*, מִחְיַת בָּשָׂר, quickness, or a quick place of the flesh; ἀπό τοῦ ὑγιοῦς τῆς σαρκός τῆς ζώσης.

18. *Boil*, שְׁחִין, an enflamed sore, ἕλκος; r. un. be hot.

23. *Scar*, צָרֶבֶת, οὐλή.

24. *Burn*, מִכְוָה, κατακαῦμα. From the same root as כִּי (Isa. iii. 24).

30. *Scall*, נֶתֶק, θραῦσμα, breaking; r. tear.

31. שָׁחֹר, black. But Sept. ξανθίζουσα.

39. *Alphos*, בֹּהַק, ἄλφος, *vitiligo alba;* a kind of white tetter.
40. *Hind-bald*, קֵרֵחַ, φαλακρός; r. *shear, cut, make bald.*
41. *Fore-bald*, גִּבֵּחַ, ἀναφάλαντος; r. *be high.*
51. *Fretting*, מַמְאֶרֶת, ἔμμονος, *perseverans;* r. *sting, smart, embitter.*
55. *Fray*, פַּחֶתֶת, a pit or hollow; ἐστήρικται, *made firm, fixed;* r. *dig, deepen.*
57. *Outbreak*, פֹּרַחַת, a budding forth; λέπρα ἐξανθοῦσα.

XIV. THE LAW OF THE LEPER.

This chapter contains two distinct communications from the Lord; the former made to Moses alone, the latter to Moses and Aaron conjointly. The former refers to the sacrificial means by which the leper when cleansed is to be restored to the full communion of the faithful (1–32). This, of course, was applicable to present circumstances in the wilderness. The latter communication refers to the case of a house affected with leprosy (33–57). This, on the contrary, was designed for a future state of things, when the people would be settled in their own land. Hence we see the propriety of its forming a distinct communication. It is obvious that Moses, having received these three distinct instructions concerning leprosy, has arranged them in the natural order. That which regulates the discerning of leprosy in the human subject and in a garment is rightly placed first; that which prescribes the mode of re-instating the healed leper in the privileges of the people of God naturally follows; and that which refers to a future condition of the people is evidently in its right place at the close of the other two. It is equally manifest that Moses was not at liberty to take these communications asunder, and re-arrange them according to his own fancy.

1–20. The rite to be observed in formally pronouncing the leper to be clean. 2. *In the day of his cleansing.* When he became a leper there was a formal process by which he was uncleansed, or judicially pronounced unclean. So when he is healed of his leprosy, there is a solemn rite by which he is cleansed, that is, pronounced to be clean. No such formulary or ceremony could make him clean. It could only legally attest his cleanness. *Brought unto the priest.*

XIV. 1. And the LORD spake unto Moses, saying, 2. This shall be the law of the leper in the day of his cleansing; and he shall be brought unto the priest. 3. And the priest shall go forth out of the camp: and the priest shall look, and behold the plague of leprosy is healed in the leper. 4. And the priest shall command to take for him that is to be cleansed two live

Brought to a place in the outskirts of the camp, where the priest might meet him. 3. *The priest shall go forth out of the camp*, because the leper is not at liberty to enter the camp, until he is declared clean in a formal manner. The Mediator goes from heaven to earth to meet the sinner in his estrangement. *Is healed.* The function of the priest is altogether distinct from that of the physician. The latter applies his art to heal the diseased; the former simply ascertains that he is healed, in order that he may proceed to pronounce him clean, and re-instate him in the fellowship of the redeemed. *In the leper*, literally, from the leper, that is, in a pregnant sense healed and removed from him. 4. *The priest shall command.* He gives the authoritative order to take the steps necessary for the restoration of the excommunicated one. *To take*, or fetch. This is literally rendered thus, "and he shall take." But it is clear, from the issuing of the command, that the person who takes is different from the priest. The leper, or rather his friend for him, takes the things mentioned. *Two live, clean birds.*[4] The special meaning of the word bird here is sparrow. But the general signification, any small bird, including the sparrow of course, is obviously intended, as the epithet clean would have been superfluous in the case of the sparrow. The field-bird is chosen, because the scene of this curious transaction lies without the camp, in the field of the world. *Live.* Some understand by this, healthy birds. But it appears simply to mean living, because one of them is to be slain, and the other is to be sent away alive, and neither could be done, if the birds were not alive. *Clean.* This limits the kind of bird. But there is an obvious allusion to the sort of victim which is proper to stand for one who had been unclean. *And cedar wood.* Chips of cedar wood, or a rod of this wood, according to tradition, a cubit long. Some have suggested the juniper as the cedar

birds and cedar wood and crimson wool and hyssop. 5. And the priest shall command to slay the one bird in an earthen

of this passage, because the cedar grows not in Arabia Petraea, but on the Lebanon. But the wood of the cedar, however, was well-known in Egypt, where it was used for ornaments, coffins, doors, and boxes. There is also the cedar of Algeria and of the Himalayas, as well as of Lebanon. This is the first time the tree is mentioned in the Pentateuch. The cedar of Lebanon is a species of fir, or, as others say, of pine, at all events of the coniferae, and was the most magnificent tree with which the Israelite was familiar. Hence it is contrasted as an extreme with the hyssop (1 Kings iv. 33), and with the thistle or thorn (1 Kings xiv. 9). Its wood is fine, solid, free from knots, odoriferous, antiseptic. Chosen for its resistance to decay, it expresses perpetuity, the perpetuity of the covenant of peace. *Crimson wool.* The original means a material dyed with the kermes worm. The kermes is the coccus, formerly supposed to be a berry, but now known to be, as the scriptural name indicates, an insect living on the ilex or holm-oak. It is at first white, then green, and finally and permanently crimson. Scarlet was the name of the color in the time of our English translators. The color here doubtless belongs to a woollen thread or cloth. Red is the fastest color, or the most difficult to be disengaged from the material dyed with it. It is the color of blood, and therefore points to expiation. *Hyssop.* As the European hyssop (*hyssopus officinalis*) does not belong to Asia, this is generally supposed to be organy or marjoram, a plant of the order *labiatae*, or mint tribe. Sweet marjoram is peculiarly aromatic and fragrant, and much used in cookery. Its fragrance fits it to express faith in a propitiation, or in the acceptance of God. The conjecture that some stalks of this hyssop were bound to the rod of cedar wood by the crimson thread, forming the brush or aspergillus with which the sprinkling was performed, is plausible, and may be founded on vs. 51; though this is not here asserted, and these articles in themselves signify reliance on the propitiation, without being combined for the purpose of sprinkling, as we learn from vs. 52, where they are classed with the live birds, and are symbols of faith in the atonement, and from Num. xix. 6, where they are cast into the midst of the burning

vessel over fresh water. 6. And the live bird he shall take, and the cedar wood and the crimson wool and the hyssop; and shall dip them and the live bird in the blood of the bird that was slain over the fresh water: 7. And he shall

of the red heifer. These three emblems of incorruptibility, expiation, and renovation combine among themselves to indicate faith in an eternal redemption that never fails to make way for pardon and acceptance. 5. *The priest shall command,* order another to perform a certain part. *To slay the one bird.* Some have doubted whether this be a proper sacrifice, as the altar is absent, and therefore no sprinkling or burning on it takes place. But this is a narrow view. An altar is merely a convenient instrument. A piece of earthenware or wood will serve the same purpose. The priest is here, and that is all that is essential. Hence in vs. 53, the process here described is said to atone or propitiate. *In an earthen vessel over fresh water.* Water fresh from the running brook or overflowing fountain is to be received in an earthen vessel, like its native bed, over which the sparrow or little bird is to be slain, that its blood may mingle with the crystal stream. Here the emblems of expiation and purification are blended together, as they always concur in the experience of the saved. See John xix. 34; 1 John v. 6. The connection would be the same, even if the vessel receiving the blood were merely held over the fresh water flowing in its natural channel. 6. *And the live bird.* The reason for the double symbol is that we may have the emblem of life, as well as of death. The Mediator is one; but he must not only die, but live again, if he is to succeed in his mediation. He must not only bear death, but win life for the guilty. Hence the two birds. *And dip them in the blood.* The symbolic whole is one. This is represented by dipping the live bird in the water mingled with the blood of the slain bird. This significantly connects the two birds, and shows them to be symbolically one. The Mediator has died, and yet he lives. The blood indicates that he has died. The fresh water intimates that he is himself holy, and has the principle and the right of life in himself. He is gone through death to life. This involves the wonder of a resurrection, as we shall see. The cedar wood, crimson wool, and hyssop are also dipped in the water and blood. They are sym-

spatter upon him that is to be cleansed from the leprosy seven times; and he shall cleanse him, and shall send the live bird into the open field. 8. And he that is to be cleansed shall

bolic and instrumental — symbolic of the instrument by which the eternal redemption is applied; instrumental, when actually used in its application by sprinkling; symbolic always, whether actually used as an instrument for sprinkling, or thrown upon the fire by which the red heifer is consumed; instrumental, apparently, in the present case (Heb. ix. 19). The instrument which they represent is faith, which in the Spirit's hand applies the benefits of the redemption to the soul. 7. *And he shall spatter.* This method of application is used instead of sprinkling, when the quantity to be employed is small (See on iv. 6). The priest applies the blood and water to the unclean; the blood which expiates, the water which cleanses. Both are necessary. Without atonement he has no right or hope of cleansing; without cleansing of heart he is not inclined to accept the atonement. Without the good tidings of pardon, acceptance, ransom, propitiation, and invitation he will not be moved to repentance; without the principle of new life, he will not understand, believe, repent, or return to God. *Seven times.* The number of perfection, holiness, and communion. *Cleanse him,* formally, declare him clean by a symbolic act, in which is included the application of the water, the symbol of purification. As the priest uncleanses, that is, pronounces unclean, the leper, so he cleanses or pronounces him clean when healed of his leprosy. In both cases, his word or act constitutes ceremonial, but not actual, uncleanness or cleanness. In a moral sense the former is caused by some malign influence in the will of man; the latter, by the Spirit of God in the same spiritual sphere. The symbol of cleansing, in the foregoing ceremony, is water. The symbol of atonement, the properly mediative act, is the blood. *Send the live bird into the open field,* let him loose into his native element of life, of happiness. The Mediator, having yielded to death, rises again to the glory, honor, and immortality which are the reward of his perfect holiness. As this sacrifice has been offered by the leper, he avails himself of the good offices of the mediator. He has, therefore, by and with him died unto sin, and he is quickened and raised up together with him to a new enjoyment

wash his clothes and shave off all his hair, and wash in water and be clean, and afterwards come into the camp: and he shall tarry outside his tent seven days. 9. And it shall be on the seventh day, he shall shave all his hair off his head and his chin and his eyebrows, and all his hair he shall shave off; and he shall wash his clothes, and wash his flesh in water and be clean. 10. And on the eighth day he shall take two perfect he-lambs and one perfect ewe of the first year, and three tenth deals of flour for an oblation, mingled with oil, and one log of oil. 11. And the priest that cleanseth shall present the man

of all the blessings of life. By this highly significant process the leper who has recovered is prepared for re-admission into the camp of the holy nation. 8. The utmost precaution is to be taken to remove any remaining trace of the disease. He shall wash his clothes, shave off all his hair, wash his body in water, and be clean. He is then admissible into the camp. But as he was sprinkled seven times, so seven times are to pass over him before he is permitted to enter into his home. 9. On the seventh day a similar thorough purification of the person is to take place.

10–20. On the eighth day a special sacrifice is prescribed. 10. *On the eighth day*, after the seven days have been completed. As the young is to be seven days with the dam before it is fit to be offered, as the new-born infant is seven days with the mother and then circumcised on the eighth, as the high-priest was consecrated for seven days and on the eighth entered on his office, so the leper after being seven days healed is on the eighth day restored with all due formality to the right and duty and fellowship of the children of God. *Three tenth deals.* The tenth deal is the omer, the tenth part of an ephah (Ex. xvi. 36). The ephah contains about 4 gal. 1 quart, 1.4 pints, and the omer, therefore, about 1 quart, 1.54 pints. One tenth deal is appointed for each of the three lambs according to Num. xv. 4. *One log of oil.* According to Rabbinical authority the log contained six eggs, or about half a pint. It was the twelfth part of a hin. 11. *The priest that cleanseth*, that performs the ceremony by which he is declared clean. *Present the man to be cleansed.* Having been for-

to be cleansed and those things before the LORD at the door of the tent of meeting. 12. And the priest shall take the one lamb and offer it for a trespass-offering, and the log of oil, and make them a waving before the LORD. 13. And he shall slay the lamb in the place where he slayeth the sin-sacrifice and the burnt-sacrifice in the holy place; for as the sin-sacrifice, so the trespass-offering is the priest's; it is most holy; 14. And the priest shall take of the blood of the trespass-offering, and the priest shall put it on the tip of the right ear of him that is to be cleansed, and upon the thumb of his right hand and upon

mally admitted into the camp as clean, he may appear before the Lord with a sacrifice. 12. *Offer it for a trespass-offering.* The trespass-offering represents amends or satisfaction for positive duty unfulfilled, a righteousness in the stead of the righteousness left undone, giving a title not merely to release from death but to restoration to life. Now the leper, being healed of an incurable disease, was in a pre-eminent sense rescued from a state of death and restored to a state of life. But life is the reward of active obedience, and therefore it is befitting that the offering that represented active righteousness should in his case take the front place. Besides it is better fitted to shadow forth complete restoration to the privileges of adoption than either the sin-sacrifice or the burnt-sacrifice. *And the log of oil.* The oil is offered, but does not go upon the altar, as it has a special purpose and meaning of its own. This comes out in the sequel. *Make them a waving.* Waving denotes the communion of saints, which was a peculiarly appropriate symbol, when the recovered leper was to be restored to the companionship of his home. A waving was an offering of which not more than a part was laid on the altar, and the whole or main part handed over to the priests. 13. *And he shall slay the lamb.* The trespass-offering is to be slain in the usual place, and dealt with in the usual way. 14. *Put it on the tip.* This reminds us of the consecration of the priests; and the analogy is just. The leper who was ceremonially excommunicated is now restored to the kingdom of priests, as well as the holy nation (Ex. xix. 6). Hence the two rites must have their points of correspond-

the great toe of his right foot. 15. And the priest shall take of the log of oil, and pour it on the left palm of the priest. 16. And the priest shall dip his right finger in the oil that is in his palm; and shall spatter of the oil with his finger seven times before the LORD. 17. And of the rest of the oil that is on his palm shall the priest put upon the tip of the right ear of him that is to be cleansed, and upon the thumb of his right hand and upon the great toe of his right foot, upon the blood of the trepass-offering. 18. And the remnant of the oil that is on the priest's palm he shall put upon the head of him that is to be cleansed; and the priest shall atone for him before the

ence. 15–17. *Take of the log of oil.* This is not the anointing oil (Ex. xxx. 24; Lev. viii. 10), but mere olive oil. The blood denotes expiation; the oil sanctification. *Spatter.* This is usually done with the finger (iv. 6) *Seven times before the Lord.* Seven times in token of perfection. The spattering of the oil before the Lord at the altar of burnt-sacrifice is a dedication of the oil to its sacred use, and an acknowledgment that he is holy and the Author of holiness, and that all his people ought to be holy. 17. *Upon the blood of the trespass-offering.* This is an emphatic testimony that sanctification comes through atonement, and that both are equally requisite for the returning sinner. 18. *Upon the head.* This completes his priestly consecration to be a member of the holy nation. It is remarkable how closely the restoration of the leper here resembles the consecration of the priest. It is to be observed, however, that the characteristic ceremony of the filling of the hands, which is the essence of the official consecration, is wanting here. *Of him that is to be cleansed.* The old English phrase, "of him that is a cleansing," would be more exact here. Every part of the process, from the first command issued by the priest to the offering of the oblation, was included in the formal act of cleansing or declaring him clean. But the water and the oil symbolize the Spirit of holiness, the agent of cleansing or sanctification, and the sevenfold application of each is the formal cleansing of the leper. *And the priest shall atone for him.* This shows that the sacrifices now offered on the occasion of the leper

LORD. 19. And the priest shall offer the sin-sacrifice, and shall atone for him that is to be cleansed from his uncleanness; and afterward he shall slay the burnt-sacrifice. 20. And the priest shall offer the burnt-sacrifice and the oblation on the altar; and the priest shall atone for him and he shall be clean. §

being pronounced clean have a different function from that of cleansing. They atone. The leper was already clean, when the priest inspected and passed him. He had only to be ceremonially cleansed, or solemnly pronounced clean by the application of the water and the oil. This was necessarily accompanied with appropriate sacrifices, by which the priest atones for him, that is, makes him *rectum in curia*, right in heaven's court. 19. *The sin-sacrifice.* This is the ewe-lamb, which is equivalent to the she-kid of the goats, which was appointed as a sin-sacrifice for one of the people (iv. 28). Here we see the trespass-offering and the sin-sacrifice for the worshipper in one and the same condition of sin. This proves that they refer to different aspects of the same offence. The former respects the righteousness that ought to have been rendered, but was not; the latter, the wrong that was done, and must be undone by the endurance of an equivalent pain. As the leper is restored to life, it is natural that the offering that represents amends or righteousness should take the prominent place. *The burnt-sacrifice.* After being discharged from the guilt of the occasional sin of an inadvertent nature connected with his malady, he is prepared for offering the burnt-sacrifice, by which is at the same time commemorated and foreshadowed the great propitiation for sin, as the fallen condition of each member of the human race. Then it was strictly a foreshadowing; but after the first institution of the typical sacrifice, it was also a commemorating for the strengthening of faith and the revival of the sense of peace with God. 20. *The burnt-sacrifice and the oblation on the altar.* The burnt-sacrifice was wholly burned on the altar, as an emblem of the all-sufficient propitiation. The oblation, which was proportionate to the three offerings presented, appears on this occasion to have been also wholly consumed on the fire of the altar. As the life of the leper was restored, after

21. And if he be poor and his hand find not, then he shall take one lamb for a trespass-offering to be waved to atone for him, and one tenth deal of flour mingled with oil for an oblation, and a log of oil. 22. And two doves or two pigeons, as his hand may find: and the one shall be for a sin-sacrifice and the other for a burnt-sacrifice. 23. And he shall bring them on the eighth day for his cleansing unto the priest, to the door of the tent of meeting before the LORD. 24. And the priest shall take the lamb of the trespass-offering and the log of oil; and the priest shall make them a waving before the LORD. 25. And he shall slay the lamb of the trespass-offering, and the priest shall take of the blood of the trespass-offering and put it upon the tip of the right ear of him that is to be cleansed, and upon the thumb of his right hand, and upon the great toe of his right foot. 26. And the priest shall pour of the oil upon

having given way to the death that followed an incurable malady, it is natural that propitiation in contrast with expiation should have the foreground. And the oblation represents the righteousness which on the part of the substitute propitiates. Accordingly, it is added once more: "And the priest shall atone for him." The great propitiatory sacrifice is once more brought in remembrance before God on his behalf.

21–32. *The poor leper's offering.* The poor man is allowed to substitute two doves or pigeons for the lambs to be offered for a sin-sacrifice and a burnt-sacrifice. No exchange, however, is allowed for the trespass-offering. This intimates that the amends must be an exact equivalent, and admits of no abatement (v. 15). The process, which is otherwise the same, is, however, very minutely described, after the manner of Scripture. 21. *Poor*,[21] leaning or dependent on another, because unable to stand alone. *His hand findeth not;* his ability does not reach to two or three lambs. *One tenth deal,* corresponding to the one lamb which he brings. 22–31. The ritual observance is here the same as before. 23. *On the eighth day for his cleansing,* for the rite in which he declares him clean, and makes

the left palm of the priest. 27. And the priest shall spatter with his right finger of the oil that is on his left palm seven times before the LORD. 28. And the priest shall put of the oil that is on his palm upon the tip of the right ear of him that is to be cleansed, and upon the thumb of his right hand and upon the great toe of his right foot, upon the place of the blood of the trespass-offering. 29. And the remnant of the oil that is on the priest's palm he shall put upon the head of him that is to be cleansed to atone for him before the LORD. 30. And he shall offer the one of the doves or of the pigeons, as his hand findeth. 31. Whatever his hand findeth, the one a sin-sacrifice and the other a burnt-sacrifice, with the oblation: and the priest shall atone for him that is to be cleansed before the LORD. 32. This is the law of him in whom is a plague of leprosy, whose hand cannot find for his cleansing. ¶

atonement for him. 28. *Upon the place of the blood of the trespass-offering.* The expression is even more precise and pointed than in vs. 17. The place is the very spot on which the blood was applied. 29. *To atone for him.* The application of the oil is here made to have part in the atonement. This arises from the log of oil being waved before the Lord with the lamb of the trespass-offering. The atoning thus refers back to the lamb that was slain. And the lesson we have to learn is, that without faith in the Mediator the atonement will not avail for us. 31. *With*[31] *the oblation.* This is a mere variation for "and the oblation" (vs. 20). *Shall atone.* The atoning is mentioned a second time, as before. 32. *This is the law.* This verse recapitulates the last paragraph relating to the poor man. *For his cleansing*, for the offerings to be made and the symbols of cleansing to be applied on the occasion of his recovery. This closes the law of the leper. Uncleanness of the deepest degree attaches to the leper. Ceremonial uncleanness involves ceremonial guilt, and demands an atonement. So moral impurity involves moral guilt, which requires a propitiation. The uncleanness and the guilt mutually imply each

33. And the LORD spake unto Moses and unto Aaron, saying, 34. When ye go into the land of Kenaan, which I give you for a possession, and I put a plague of leprosy in a house of

other; yet they are totally distinct, and must be removed by totally different means. The Spirit of God by the truth of revelation removes moral impurity; the Mediator by his undertaking for the guilty relieves him from the consequences of his guilt. When the Spirit displaces impurity, he at the same time replaces purity in the soul; so when the Mediator by his dying releases the guilty from penal death, he at the same time by his doing restores him to rightful life. The symbols of purification and propitiation come together in the ceremonial connected with the leper's re-entrance into communion with God. The water and the blood meet in the initial sacrifice; the oil and the blood are associated in the final one. If the water and the oil are to be distinguished, the oil lays the emphasis on the enlightening of the understanding; the water, on the rectifying of the will. The blood and the fat of the victim invariably belong to the altar. The blood is sprinkled on its sides, or applied to its horns; the fat is burned upon its hearth. The blood expiates; the fat propitiates. They correspond to the passive and active obedience of the Mediator. The death and then the life are strikingly represented by the two birds. As these are two parts of the experience of the one Mediator, they really involve and shadow forth the doctrine of the resurrection. This is singularly appropriate to the case of the leper, who has in a physical sense passed from death unto life. The trespass-offering, which represents the active obedience of the Mediator, by which he becomes entitled to life, is justly conspicuous in the case of the leper who has been unexpectedly blessed with a renewal of life.

33–53. House leprosy. This forms a distinct communication addressed to Moses and Aaron. 34. *When ye go into the land.* This provision is not for the present, as the preceding paragraphs show themselves to be by the reference to the camp. It is a prospective arrangement for the future condition of the people, when they should dwell in houses in the land of promise. *Which I give you.* More

the land of your possession; 35. Then he that owneth the house shall go and tell the priest, saying, There seemeth to me as it were a plague in the house. 36. And the priest shall command, and they shall clear the house, before the priest goes in to see the plague, that all that is in the house be not

than four centuries ago the land was promised to the seed of Abraham. But it is only now to be given, for two reasons: first, because the iniquity of the Amorites is only now full, and they are to be judicially swept away; and secondly, because the seed has now become a nation large enough to occupy the land from which they were to be instrumental in expelling the doomed race (Gen. xv.). *And I put a plague.* God is the Governor and Administrator, as well as the Creator of the world; and, whatever man might say, from whose mind God is often more remote than the laws of nature, regards and speaks of the whole process of things ordinary and extraordinary as under the control of his providence. The pestilence which infests the walls of a house is designated by the general term leprosy, simply because it has, not an identity, but an analogy with the human disease called by that name. 35. *He that owneth the house* is bound to give notice to the priest. Even self-interest moves him to do so, as disease, as well as dirt and decay in a house, is an obvious cause of disease to its inhabitant. *As it were a plague.* The suspicion of a pestilential disease has been awakened in his mind by the appearance of the house. The priest only is competent to pronounce it clean or unclean. 36. *The priest shall command.* This phrase is used when something is to be done by others, and in this case by the inhabitants of the house. The thing commanded is contained in the following clause. *Clear the house*, prepare it for inspection by removing the furniture and the inhabitants. This was no great trouble in the mild climate and simple habits of the country. Tent life was not unfamiliar. The reason for this is that the things in the house may not partake in its uncleanness, in the event of the leprosy being found in it. There is a wonderful considerateness in the divine ordinances. This precaution is sufficient to show that the uncleanness spoken of in the text is ceremonial, and not arising from infection. The noxious

defiled; and after this the priest shall go in to see the house. 37. And he shall see the plague, and behold the plague in the walls of the house consists of greenish or reddish strakes; and their look is lower than the wall. 38. And the priest shall come out of the house to the door of the house, and shut up the house seven days. 39. And the priest shall return on the seventh day, and see, and behold the plague hath spread in the walls of the house. 40. Then the priest shall command,

growth on the walls was no doubt injurious to health, and might even conduce to leprosy; but there was no disease in the walls which could be communicated by contagion to the human subject. 37. *Greenish or reddish strakes.*[37] These streaks are the indications of the dry rot, a disease affecting timber. "When produced by the attacks of fungi, the first stage of it consists in the appearance of small white points, from which a filamentous substance radiates, parallel with the surface of the timber. This is the first stage of growth of the seeds of the fungus, and the filamentous matter is their thallus or spawn. This insinuates itself into the crevices of the wood, forces its parts asunder, and causes in the end the total ruin of the timber. The fructification and growth of *Merulius lachrymans*, *Polyporus destructor*, and other fungi exercise their destructive power on timber. This disease spreads from the wood-work to the walls of a house, especially in damp situations and amid heaps of refuse, and eventually succeeds in crumbling them to pieces. The greenish and reddish colors observed in the patches of fungous matter arise from the vegetative and chemical influences which are at work."[37] *And their look is lower than the wall.* The consumptive influence of these fungous plants has penetrated beneath the surface of the wall. It is not a mere discoloring moisture, flowing down the surface. It has sent its roots and filaments into the material of the wall. 39. The usual process of inspection takes place, and the plague is found to be spreading. 40. *Pull out the stones.* The priest now commands that the material affected by the plague be removed. If the fungous excrescence be entirely removed, the disease may be eradicated.

and they shall pull out the stones in which the plague is, and cast them outside the city in an unclean place. 41. And he shall have the house scraped within around, and they shall pour out the dust that they scrape off outside the city in an unclean place. 42. And they shall take other stones, and put them in the place of those stones; and other dust he shall take and plaster the house. 43. And if the plague return and break out in the house after pulling out the stones and after scraping the house and after it is plastered; 44. Then the priest shall go in and see, and behold the plague has spread in the house; it is a fretting leprosy in the house; it is unclean. 45. And he shall pull down the house, its stones and its

Cast them outside the city. This implies that the house is in a town, where the plague is more likely to arise, on account of the density of the population and the absence of any sufficient arrangements for ventilation or cleanliness. *In an unclean place,* that no clean place may be defiled with the rubbish. If there were no such place, some uncultivated or unprofitable spot would be chosen, which would become ceremonially unclean by the very presence of the infected material. 41. *Scraped within around,* the outer coating of mortar or clay removed from the whole inner side of the wall all around. Want of air and light favors the wall rot. Hence it appears, usually, in the inside of damp, unventilated rooms, especially cellars. *The dust,* the crumbled material out of which the plaster was made, by means of water, and into which it now when scraped off returns. This indicates a wall of clay or stone, covered with some kind of plaster. This was obviously the ordinary style of architecture in Palestine at the date of the enactment. 42. *Other stones* are to replace those taken away. *Other dust* is to be made into plaster, with which the whole wall is to be plastered anew. The dust was probably mere clay. 43, 44. If after this thorough repair the plague reappear and spread in the house, it proves itself to be too deep-seated for any partial remedy, and the house is condemned. *It is a fretting leprosy,* similar to that in a garment (xiii. 51), a noxious and incurable

timber and all the dust of the house, and carry them outside the city into an unclean place. 46. And he that goeth into the house all the while he hath shut it up shall be unclean until the even. 47. And he that lieth in the house shall wash his clothes; and he that eateth in the house shall wash his clothes. 48. And if the priest do go in and see, and behold the plague hath not spread in the house, after the house is plastered, then the priest shall pronounce the house clean, because the plague is healed. 49. And he shall take to purge the house two birds and cedar wood and crimson wool and

plague. 45. *And he shall pull down.* As the garment with the fretting leprosy is to be burned, so the house is to be pulled down. The house is, as it were, the outer garment of the man. Its materials are mostly incombustible; but it can be pulled down. This is done by the order of the priest. All the materials are to be removed from the town. Houses in the East, in those early times, were not of great value, and could be replaced at a moderate cost. 46, 47. *He that goeth into the house.* The needful or accidental occasion of going into the house is not indicated. The consequence only is noted. He that entered it during the period of its being closed for probation was unclean until the evening. He that slept or ate in it must further wash his clothes. 48. If the disease do not spread, or make its appearance in the new plaster, the house is to be pronounced clean. 49. *To purge*[49] *the house,* to release it from the guilt, and at the same time from the defilement of sin. The house is regarded as a part or property of the man, and hence is treated as involved in his guilt. It is hereby intimated that sin has tainted the human race, and this moral evil has caused that to be a source of defilement which otherwise would not. All things work together for good to the right-minded. But the self-same concatenation of events work together for evil to the wrong-minded. These are but the two sides of the one principle of things proceeding from the inscrutable wisdom of God. To purge the healed house, then, is virtually to make expiation for, and also to cleanse from, the sin of the inhabitant or owner of the house. The

hyssop. 50. And he shall slay the one bird in an earthen vessel over fresh water. 51. And he shall take the cedar wood and the hyssop and the crimson wool and the live bird, and dip them in the blood of the slain bird and in the fresh water; and he shall spatter on the house seven times. 52. And he shall purge the house with the blood of the bird and with the fresh water and with the live bird and with the cedar wood

word "purge" is here designedly adopted to allow of expiation and purification being both included. *Two birds*, sparrows, or the like, as in the case of the leper himself. There was, then, a very close parallel between the two cases. The disease of leprosy affected the body. But the body is not the man, and is not in itself capable of any moral activity or accountability. Yet it is the house of a soul capable of intelligent volition, and therefore of moral conduct and responsibility. When this body is affected with a mortal disease, it is suffering the consequences of the sin of the soul that inhabits it. The stone and mortar house is but an outer and wider habitation, which the rational creature, susceptible of heat and cold, constructs for himself to shelter him from the inclemencies of the weather. If the malady of the inner house is an index of guilt in the inhabitant affecting the habitation, the distemper of the outer house is to be regarded as a similar sign of guilt in the inmate. Hence each of them is purged by the same sacred rite. *Cedar wood and crimson wool and hyssop* are therefore associated with the two birds. 50–53. Hence the process of making expiation for the healed house is merely a reiteration of the interesting preliminary ceremony employed on the occasion of declaring the man who was healed of the leprosy to be clean. *In the blood of the slain bird and in the fresh water.* Here it is made more plain than in vs. 6 that these were dipped in the water, as well as in the blood, or in the blood diffused in the water. *Spatter on the house*, as he before spattered on the healed body (vs. 7). In this spattering of the commingled blood and water, the symbolic acts of expiation and cleansing are combined. 52. *And he shall purge.* It is remarkable that this word does not occur in the corresponding ceremony for the leper. Yet the meaning must be the same, as the same

LEVITICUS XIV. 52-57.   193

and with the hyssop and with the crimson wool. 53. And he shall send the live bird out of the city into the open field; and he shall atone for the house, and it shall be clean.

54. This is the law for every plague of leprosy and for the scall. 55. And for the leprosy of a garment and for the house. 56. And for the rising and for the scab and for the blotch.

elements are employed in precisely the same way. This is therefore a new instance of one account supplementing and explaining another. *With the blood of the bird and with the fresh water and with.* Here are three things with which this purging is accomplished — with the blood of the bird, which expiates; with the fresh water, which cleanses; and with the cedar wood and hyssop and crimson wool, which express the faith which flows from a cleansed heart, and relies on the shed blood of atonement. Hence we see that purging from sin is a pregnant word when it is accompanied with the symbol of sanctification, as well as that of justification, and denotes both expiation and cleansing. *And he shall atone,* that is, propitiate. This is employed, as before, to express making satisfaction for sin in contradistinction to expelling it from the heart by a new and holy disposition.

54–57. A formal recapitulation of this and the preceding chapter. 54. The leprosy proper is discussed in xiii. 1–28, the scall in xiii. 29–37. 55. The leprosy of a garment is regulated in xiii. 47–59, that of a house in xiv. 33–53. 56. The rising scab and blotch are mentioned in xiii. 2, and discussed under the head of leprosy. It is evident from this enumeration of topics that the sacred writer has before him three divine communications, which he does not feel himself at liberty to alter in matter or arrangement. In his enumeration, however, he touches upon the principal points in the order of thought. Under the head of leprosy proper he includes xiii. 1–28 and xiv. 1–32. Passing over minor topics, he distinguishes the scall, in xiii. 29–37, from the leprosy. He then brings together leprosy of a garment and of a house. He then notices the rising, scab, and blotch, which may in certain cases be distinct from real leprosy. 57. Lastly, he indicates the precise design with which these chapters were given. *To teach,* to give plain instructions for discerning the

57. To teach when he is unclean and when he is clean: this is the law of leprosy. ¶

leprosy. *When he is unclean,*[57] when the person examined is affected with the disease, and therefore unclean. *And when he is clean,* when he is free from disease, and must therefore be pronounced clean. It is remarkable that in this summary the priest is simply said to be taught to discern the disease and to pronounce unclean or clean, according to its presence or absence. To heal is no part of his official duty. From first to last this is a religious ceremonial, though it has an important bearing on health.

NOTES.

4. *Bird,* צִפּוֹר, small bird, sparrow, ὀρνίθιον; r. chirp, twitter. *Cedar,* אֶרֶז, κέδρος, cedar, but supposed to denote the juniper in Homer and in Theophrastus. *crimson,* שְׁנִי תוֹלַעַת, shining, or dyed with the worm. The worm is the coccus insect: κεκλωσμένον κόκκινον, *crimson yarn.* *Hyssop,* אֵזוֹב, ὕσσωπος. These words are evidently the same, the plant and name having come from the East.

21. *Poor,* דַּל, hanging, dependent.

31. *With,* עַל, upon. As the burnt-sacrifice in this case is a dove or pigeon, it may be placed on the flour. But the preposition may denote mere concomitancy.

37. *Strakes,* שְׁקַעֲרוּרֹת, sinkings; r. קָעַר (F.) or שָׁקַע (Ges.), *sink, be hollow.* "At work." See Penny Cyc., art. Dry-rot; Duns, Bib. Nat. Sci. p. 109; Brit. and For. Evang. Review XLVII. Bib. Bot.

49. *Purge,* חִטֵּא. This verb may have different objects. When the victim is its object it means to offer for sin (vi. 19). When the party for whom the victim is offered is its object it strictly means to expiate sin in or for. When the symbol of purification as well as that of expiation is expressed or implied, as in the present case, it may be rendered purge or deliver from the bondage as well as the guilt of sin.

57. When he is unclean and when he is clean; literally, in the day of the unclean and in the day of the clean.

XV. THE LAW OF ISSUES.

XV. 1. And the LORD spake unto Moses and unto Aaron, saying, 2. Speak unto the sons of Israel, and say unto them, When any man hath an issue from his flesh, in his issue he is unclean. 3. And this is his uncleanness in his issue: whether his flesh run with his issue or his flesh stop from his issue, it is his uncleanness. 4. Every bed on which he that hath the issue lieth is unclean, and every seat on which he sitteth is unclean. 5. And he that toucheth his bed shall wash his clothes and wash himself with water, and be unclean until the even. 6. And he that sitteth on the seat on which he that hath the issue sat shall wash his clothes and wash himself with water,

This chapter contains one communication, which is made to Moses and Aaron together, by whom it is to be conveyed to the people. It is on the subject of issues which involve uncleanness. It gives directions concerning an issue to which men are liable (1–15), the seed of cohabitation (16–18), the monthly secretion of women (19–24), and a bloody flux in women (25–30), followed by a conclusion (31–33).

1–15. An issue of the flesh. 2. *Hath an issue*, literally, is flowing or discharging, denoting a continuous flux. *From his flesh*, that is, from his body. This does not define the nature of the issue, nor the source of it, but leaves it in its generality, where we ought also to leave it. Even the distinction of sex is not here to be pressed. There are many diseases common to both sexes, which are characterised by a discharge of some kind. *In his issue he is unclean*. This is the point in question. The malady is not otherwise regarded than as an occasion of uncleanness. 3. *Whether his flesh run*. This is descriptive of some complaint in which the flux is intermittent, and may stop for a time, though the disease remains unhealed. This may include blind piles and other diseases of an analogous kind. While the malady remains, without or with a discharge, the uncleanness continues. 4. *Every bed*. Every bed or seat used by him is unclean. 5–8. He that touches his bed or his seat or his flesh or his spittle

and be unclean until the even. 7. And he that toucheth the flesh of him that hath the issue shall wash his clothes and wash himself with water, and be unclean until the even. 8. And when he that hath the issue spitteth on him that is clean, then he shall wash his clothes and wash himself with water, and be unclean until the even. 9. And every saddle on which he that hath the issue rideth shall be unclean. 10. And all that toucheth anything which was under him shall be unclean until the even; and he that carrieth them shall wash his clothes and wash in water, and be unclean until the even. 11. And all, that he that hath the issue toucheth and hath not rinsed his hands in water, shall wash their clothes and wash in water, and be unclean until the even. 12. And the earthen vessel which he that hath the issue toucheth shall be broken; and every wooden vessel shall be rinsed in water. 13. And when he that hath the issue is cleansed of his issue, then he shall count for him seven days for his cleansing, and wash his clothes and wash his flesh in fresh water, and be clean. 14. And on the eighth day he shall take for him two

shall wash his clothes, wash himself with water, and be unclean until the evening. *Wash himself.*[5] This word is used to avoid the employment of the word bathe, which implies immersion, a meaning which does not belong to the original word. 9. *The saddle*[9] or litter or carriage cushion on which he rides is unclean. 10. All that touch or carry anything that was under him shall be unclean until the evening. 11. This verse implies that if he rinsed his hands in water his touch would not defile. 12. The earthen vessel which he touches must be broken, and the wooden vessel rinsed in water. 13. When he is restored to health he is to count seven days, as usual, for his cleansing; he is then to wash his clothes, wash himself with fresh water, and be clean. It is to be observed that the priest is not required to determine whether he be unclean, as in the case of leprosy. The very fact of having an issue renders him unclean. 14. On the eighth day he is

doves or two pigeons, and come before the LORD to the door of the tent of meeting, and give them to the priest. 15. And the priest shall offer them, the one for a sin-sacrifice and the other for a burnt-sacrifice; and the priest shall atone for him before the LORD for his issue. §

16. And when a man's seed of copulation goeth from him then he shall wash all his flesh in water, and be unclean until

to bring an offering prescribed for the occasion. This was to be two doves or pigeons; the one for a sin and the other for a burnt sacrifice. From this we learn that the issue was merely a cause of uncleanness, but did not exclude from the society of the church or the home. It did not occasion excommunication like the leprosy, and therefore the subject of it was not regarded as dead and restored to life again on account of his disease and recovery. Hence he had not to offer the *asham* or trespass-offering, as the ground of restoration to new life. This shows that the leprosy was regarded as the exactest type of sin, the wages of which is death, as recovery from it was the most striking emblem of the new birth and life everlasting. 15. *Shall atone for him before the Lord.* Bodily disease was the consequence of sin, and the outward uncleanness, therefore, symbolizes the inward or moral uncleanness. Hence the healed patient comes in humble faith and penitence to present his sin-sacrifice for inadvertent sin, and his burnt-sacrifice for that sin of his fallen nature and practice which has been brought to his knowledge, and through the gospel of mercy has awakened in him repentance and reliance on his God. The appointed priest of God meets him and mediates for him. His atonement is made, and he is once more visited with the peace and joy of salvation.

16–18. Issue of seed of copulation. 16. *Seed of copulation*, literally, lying of seed. This Luther interprets to be the discharge of seed in sleep. But there is no such limit in the text. Neither is it determined whether the discharge be involuntary or induced by impure volitions. The ceremonial consequence, merely, is stated. As the human race is corrupted by the fall, its propagation is inseparably connected with sin. Over and above this, all unchaste thoughts, words, and deeds are in themselves sinful. But these do not appear

the even. 17. And every garment and every skin on which the seed of copulation is shall be washed with water, and be unclean until the even. 18. And when a man lieth with a woman with seed of copulation, then shall they wash with water, and be unclean until the even. ¶

19. And when a woman hath an issue, and her issue in her flesh is blood, seven days shall she be in her separation, and all that touch her shall be unclean until the even. 20. And

to be intended in the present passage. The bare fact of a discharge of seed is all that is supposed. This is manifest from the intimation that the party concerned shall merely wash with water and be unclean until the evening. 17. The garment on which such discharge may come is unclean, and is made clean in the usual manner. 18. Natural and lawful cohabitation is attended with this temporary uncleanness. The cohabiting of the sexes in wedlock was not thereby rendered unlawful; as we know there were other lawful acts, such as performing the offices due to the dead, burning the red heifer (Num. xix.), which incurred such uncleanness. This is, however, the most striking indication in this chapter that there is a taint in the human race, originating with the fall of our first parents, and transmitting itself by descent from parent to child. Were it not for the promises of mercy, a thoughtful man would shrink from an act which would tend to perpetuate a degenerate race, with all its disastrous consequences. But the humble, penitent, earnest father and mother, who endeavor to train their child for God, may confidently expect the blessing of a new heart and a heavenly hope for their offspring. May God of his mercy give pious and faithful parents!

19-24. The monthly secretions of women. 19. *Seven days*. The healthy secretion of blood may not last so long. But since the purpose here is religious, as throughout all these regulations, the number of sacredness and perfection is chosen as usual. *In her separation*.[19] This is by some rendered uncleanness. But this is only to confound it with other words, and the meaning separation, seclusion, or secretion is best suited to all the places in which it is found. 20-23. Not only all that touch her, but everything on which

LEVITICUS XV. 20-26.   199

everything on which she lieth in her separation is unclean, and everything on which she sitteth is unclean. 21. And whosoever toucheth her bed shall wash his clothes and wash in water and be unclean until the even. 22. And whosoever toucheth anything on which she sitteth shall wash his clothes and wash in water, and be unclean until the even. 23. And if he touch that which is on the bed or on anything on which she sitteth, he shall be unclean until the even. 24. And if a man do lie with her, and her secretion be upon him, then he shall be unclean seven days, and every bed on which he lieth shall be unclean.   §

25. And when a woman hath an issue of her blood many days not in the time of her separation, or when it floweth after her separation, all the days of the issue of her uncleanness shall be as the days of her separation; she shall be unclean. 26. Every bed on which she lieth all the days of her issue shall be to her as the bed of her separation; and everything on which she sitteth shall be unclean, as the uncleanness of her separation. 27. And every one that toucheth them shall be

she lies or sits, and every one that touches her bed or seat or anything on either is unclean. 24. Cohabiting with a woman in her flowers was a crime to be punished with excommunication (Lev. xx. 18). If unintentional or accidental, however, the extreme penalty may not have been inflicted. The present passage, however, has to do not with the criminality, be the same more or less, but with the ceremonial defilement consequent upon the act. It involves uncleanness which lasts for seven days, and extends to the bed on which he lies.

25–31. Morbid secretions of women. 25. *Many days.* Two indications of disease are noticed here. First, the issue is not at the usual time of the monthlies; and next, it lasts longer than the usual period of these. The same rule applies here as in the case of the natural secretion. The morbid issue renders unclean. 26, 27. Every

unclean, and shall wash his clothes and wash in water, and be unclean until the even. 28. And if she be cleansed of her issue, then she shall count for her seven days, and afterwards she shall be clean. 29. And on the eighth she shall take for her two doves or two pigeons, and bring them unto the priest to the door of the tent of meeting. 30. And the priest shall offer the one for a sin-sacrifice and the other for a burnt-sacrifice; and the priest shall atone for her before the LORD for the issue of her uncleanness. 31. And ye shall separate the sons of Israel from their uncleanness; and they shall not die in their uncleanness, by defiling my habitation that is among them.

32. This is the law of him that hath an issue, and of him whose seed cometh from him to defile him with it. 33. And

bed or seat that she uses is unclean, and whatsoever touches them shall be unclean. 28. Seven days after her issue is healed, she shall be clean as before. 29. On the eighth day she is to offer the usual sacrifice. 30. And the priest shall make atonement for her. 31. *Ye shall separate*,[31] induce them to avoid all possible sources of uncleanness and all occasions that lead to it. *And they shall not die in their uncleanness.* Death is the wages of sin, the moral uncleanness by which the soul is tainted. And the neglect of the divinely-appointed ordinances for the removal of ceremonial uncleanness was an offence involving the penalty of sin. *By defiling my habitation that is among them.* While they remain in their uncleanness, they cannot approach the holy dwelling of the Lord without defiling it, and constraining him to destroy them for their sins, or depart from the midst of them.

32, 33. The recapitulation. The former of these verses refers to the first two cases of which the chapter treats. 33. The second has three clauses, of which the first refers to the third case, the ordinary monthly affection of adult females; the second generalizes the unhealthy secretions, applying them to males, as well as to females, and thus referring to the first part of the chapter (1–15) and to the fourth

of her that is sick in her flowers; and of one that hath an issue for the male or the female; and for the man who lieth with the unclean. 29 ¶ ¶ ¶

case (25–27); and the third alludes to the case of a man lying with a woman in her sickness. The design of the generalization appears to be to intimate that the unhealthy secretions in the two sexes are parallel to one another, and hence its place in the summary.

At the close of these three chapters it may be observed that those forms of disease are noticed which come to the surface, and therefore may cause defilement. These are divided into the dry or scabby, and the moist or running sores. The former include the leprosy and its kindred maladies; the latter comprehend all running issues. Of these leprosy is the most virulent and deadly, and involves not merely uncleanness, but excommunication. The others occasion only uncleanness, and do not break up the social connection. In the five preceding chapters we have the various forms of natural uncleanness. They proceed in an orderly manner to the various animals, then to human birth, then to dry, cutaneous eruptions, and lastly to running sores. We shall meet with other sources of uncleanness; but they are rather external than internal, accidental than natural. The distinction of animals and of men into clean and unclean rests ultimately not on physical, but on moral relations. All things in their right place and time and application are clean. Sin only has put things out of the proper time and place and use, and so given rise to the distinction into clean and unclean. As it has its seat in the fallen race of man, this race is the only earthly subject of moral impurity. And one essential element of human salvation must be to restore moral purity to the heart, and root out the impurity that has grown up in its place. These chapters present to our view the primeval elements of sanctification in a form suited to the then existing stage of human progress. We cannot read the history of God's ancient people without perceiving that in the hand of the Spirit of holiness they were capable of effecting a holy change in the heart, and calling forth the most sublime and affecting displays of enthusiasm in the cause of truth and charity, of good will towards men and piety towards God. And from the history of divine revelation we learn that they embody the germs which are sure to be expanded with the expanding mind of man into the great immutable principles of a spiritual regeneration, of a new creation after the image of God. The most powerful and adventurous minds have gone astray in the evolution of these principles, whenever they have forgotten or forsaken the light of revealed truth and of the promised Spirit. And weaker minds have come equally short of their full and true development. But the humble learner, who searches the Scriptures and gives heed to the Spirit speaking in the heart, is born of God and walks in the light of salvation.

NOTES.

2. *Having an issue*, זָב, literally, flowing with the stream of disease.

4. *Seat*, כְּלִי, a very general word, denoting anything made for a purpose, a utensil, article, vessel, instrument, and here, that which is used for sitting on, a divan, stool, block, or stone.

5. *Wash*, רָחַץ, wash oneself, wash a chariot (1 Kings xxii. 38), wash thereout (Ex. xl. 31). כִּבֵּס is the word generally applied to the washing of clothes.

9. *Saddle*, מֶרְכָּב. The Sept. here has ἐπίσαγμα. The word occurs also in 1 Kings v. 6 and Cant. iii. 10.

19. *Separation*, נִדָּה; r. נָדַד, *flee into seclusion*.

31. *Separate*, הִזַּרְתֶּם; εὐλαβεῖς ποιήσετε, *docebitis*, as if the word had been הִזְהַרְתֶּם.

XVI. THE DAY OF ATONEMENT.

This most remarkable chapter puts the crown of completeness upon the preceding fifteen chapters. The first seven relates to propitiation in all its aspects. The next three narrate the consecration of the priest, the ordinance for which had been already put on record in Ex. xxix. We have thus the sacrifice and the priest, which rise into the higher unity of the Mediator who is both priest and sacrifice. The next five chapters refer to purification, both in its highest form of life from the dead, which is symbolized in the law of the leper, and in its lower forms of recovery from spiritual declension and progress in vital power, which are shadowed forth in the regulations concerning

XVI. 1. And the LORD spake unto Moses after the death of the two sons of Aaron, when they offered before the LORD and died. 2. And the LORD said unto Moses, Speak unto Aaron thy brother, and let him not go at all times into the holy place within the veil, before the mercy-seat which is upon the ark, that he die not; for in the cloud will I appear upon

issues of various kinds. The chapter now before us combines the propitiation and the purification, which are the two great elements of salvation that flow from mercy, the fountain of all. It proceeds in three stages: the first containing the preparatory arrangements (1-10); the second furnishing the details of the sacrifice (11-28), which falls into two parts, relating to the bullock for himself and the first goat for the people (11-19), and the second goat for the people (20-18); and the third stage recording some particulars concerning the day (29-34). It is addressed to Moses after the death of the two sons of Aaron, and therefore after the consecration of the priests. It is to be communicated by him to Aaron, whom it concerns.

1-10. The preparatory arrangements of the day of atonement. 1. The date of this communication is here given. It is after the inauguration of the tabernacle service on the first day of the second year. 2. *Speak unto Aaron.* This ancient document is very exact in detailing every historical circumstance of that which it is important to authenticate. Aaron is here to be the agent, and hence the instructions are to be conveyed to him. *Let him not come at all times*, at any time he may think fit. *Within the veil.* He comes into the holy place every day to trim the lamps on the golden candlestick. He draws nigh to the veil on the outside whenever he comes in with the blood of the sin-sacrifice (iv.). But he does not on these occasions go within the veil. *Before the mercy-seat.*[2] This is called in the original the propitiatory, the seat or throne where the Lord is propitious to his people, the place of ultimate atonement in the very presence of the Lord. *That he die not.* Aaron, though consecrated high-priest, is still a fallible son of the fallen Adam. Hence he is in himself sinful and unfit to mediate between God and man. Nay, disobedience is as invariably connected with death as obedience with

the mercy-seat. 3. With this shall Aaron go into the holy place: with a bullock of the herd for a sin-sacrifice and a ram for a burnt-sacrifice. 4. The holy linen coat he shall put on, and linen breeches shall be on his flesh, with a linen girdle shall he be girt, and be bound with a linen mitre: these are holy garments, and he shall wash his flesh in water and put them on. 5. And from the assembly of the sons of Israel he shall take two kids of the goats for a sin-sacrifice and one ram

life. Sinful Aaron cannot come by himself into the immediate presence of the holy God. He must appear before him only at the appointed time and in the appointed way. *In the cloud*, the well-known cloud of the presence of the Lord, that went before the sons of Israel in their march from Egypt, appeared to them on the smoking mount, and, last of all, filled the holy place and consumed with fire the sacrifice on the altar. The unholy may not approach into the manifested presence of the Holy One, except at the call of mercy and in the path of atonement and regeneration. 3. *With this shall Aaron go*. He must enter with a sin-sacrifice and a burnt-sacrifice for himself, the former for inadvertent sin, and giving prominence to expiation; the latter for the whole guilt of a past sinful character and conduct, and setting forth the plenitude of propitiation. 4. The holy linen garments and the washing with water are expressive of the righteousness and holiness that belong to the high-priest. At the same time it is to be observed that on this occasion the high-priest is formally to lay aside his glorious and golden attire, and put on the simple linen coat, girdle, and mitre. The linen breeches he is not said to put on, because they were always worn by the priest. There is a special significance in this change of raiment. The high-priest is here to be unadorned, as the emblem of the sin-victim which he is about to offer on this day of humiliation. He cannot be stripped of his integrity; but as a sin-bearer he is divested of all his hereditary glory, and humbled to the grade of one doomed to attainder and death. 5. *And from the assembly*. On this solemn day of national confession the victims for the people are of the same import as those for himself

for a burnt-sacrifice. 6. And Aaron shall offer the bullock of the sin-sacrifice which is his own, and atone for himself and for his house. 7. And he shall take the two kids and place them before the LORD at the door of the tent of meeting. 8. And Aaron shall cast lots upon the two goats; one lot for the LORD and one lot for the scape-goat. 9. And Aaron shall

— two kids of the goats for a sin-sacrifice, and a ram for a burnt-offering. 6–10. The order of the sacrifice is now laid down in general, to be afterwards carried out in detail. *Which is his own.* He is first to present the bullock of the sin-sacrifice for himself and his house. The priestly family are on this occasion to stand over against the people, as one great party in this transaction with God. They must be themselves at peace with God, in order to mediate between him and the people. *And atone,* make propitiation for himself and his house. Nothing can more clearly show that there is a higher Mediator, whose intervention both he and the people need, in order to appear with acceptance before God. He is only a shadow of the substance to come. 7. Then follow the two kids of the sin-sacrifice for the people. These constitute one sin-sacrifice; but two goats are required to indicate all that is implied in this sacrifice. *Place them before the Lord.* This is preparatory to a simple distinction to be made between them for the ends of this peculiar sin-sacrifice. 8. *Aaron shall cast lots.* This shows the perfect equality of the two goats as representatives, and intimates the unity of that which is represented. *One lot for the Lord.* The goat on which this lot fell was to be offered in sacrifice unto the Lord. *And one lot for the scape-goat.*[8] This is simply the goat that is to go away, escaping from death into the wilderness; a meaning which is suggested and sustained by the text. As the question to be determined by the lot is, who is to have the life, the scape-goat is naturally opposed to the Lord, inasmuch as he has the one life, while it has the other. And, as we have already seen, the victim, here merely shadowed forth by the goat, must be a divine person, and therefore not unsuitably matched with the Lord. This simple explanation has the superlative advantage of being level to the capacity of the common mind, while it is perfectly suitable to

offer the goat on which fell the lot for the LORD and make it a sin-sacrifice. 10. And the goat on which fell the lot for the scape-goat shall be placed alive before the LORD to atone upon it, to send it for a scape-goat into the wilderness.

11. And Aaron shall offer the bullock of the sin-sacrifice which is his own, and atone for himself and for his house; and he shall slay the bullock of the sin-sacrifice which is his own. 12. And he shall take a censerful of coals of fire from

the context. 9. The goat on which the Lord's lot falls is to be offered for sin. 10. The other is to be set before the Lord to bear its part in this peculiar sin-sacrifice. *To atone upon it.*[10] This phrase is parallel to that in Ex. xxx. 10, and is explained by the process described in vs. 21. The goat is an instrument or a sufferer in the work of making atonement. *To send it for a scape-goat.* This explains the part it has in accomplishing the atonement. The shedding of blood has already taken place. The sending away of the sin-bearer is now effected. This will receive its full explanation in vs. 21, 22. *Into the wilderness,* beyond the camp, the dwelling-place of the saints who are in communion with God. This makes more clear the condition and destiny of the scape-goat. With the sin of the people upon it, it is dismissed from the region of blessedness, that those for whom it suffers may escape the penalty of disobedience.

11–28. The sacrifices for sin. The solemnity of the occasion is indicated by the measured stateliness of the narrative, which now takes a new start to describe with fitting minuteness the transactions of this unique day. 11. *And Aaron shall offer.* He is now actually to proceed with the offering of the sin-sacrifice for himself. *Which is his own,* as distinct from that of the people. *And atone for himself and for his house.* The reiteration of this statement makes the conviction still more emphatic that Aaron himself needs a higher and a better Mediator, who needeth not to offer up sacrifice first for his own sins. *And he shall slay.* As he is in this case the offerer, it is his part, by himself or his minister, to slay the victim. 12. The process now described is peculiar to the day. *Take a censerful.* The censer

the altar before the LORD, and his handsful of incense of spices beaten small, and bring within the veil. 13. And he shall put the incense on the fire before the LORD; and the cloud of incense shall cover the mercy-seat that is over the testimony, that he die not. 14. And he shall take of the blood of the bullock, and spatter with his finger upon the mercy-seat

was employed on other occasions; but at no other time was it to be taken within the veil. It was a very sacred act to offer incense, and proper only to the priest in the appointed way (See Ex. xxx. 9; Lev. x. 1). *Fire from the altar*, from the consecrated hearth of God. *And his handsful*,[12] the full of the palms spread out and curved for the purpose of holding. *Incense of spices*[12] *beaten small.* Spices of a pleasant smell are beaten into small parts, in order to burn the better and give forth their scent more freely. *Bring within the veil.* The peculiarity here is that on this occasion only, throughout the whole year, the high-priest is permitted to go within the veil into the immediate presence of God. 13. *The incense.* This is the very highest and purest symbol of that part of propitiation which is called intercession, and therefore of prayer. *On the fire.* As the high-priest alone went in, he must have taken in the censer of live coals and the spices himself. By putting his handsful of spices into a tray or basket, it was possible for him to take in all at once. He then put the incense on the fire. It is not really inconsistent with the directions, however, that he should have put the incense on the coals even before passing within the veil. The putting on of the incense is then noticed in this verse simply to bring it into immediate connection with its intended effect. *The cloud of incense shall cover the mercy-seat.* This is the effect. The covering of the mercy-seat with the cloud of incense is at the same time the covering of Aaron himself by the propitiation made and pleaded. *Over the testimony*, the two tables of the law which were deposited in the ark (Ex. xxv. 16). *That he die not*, being sheltered and saved by the propitiation which stands between him and the doom of death. 14. *He shall take of the blood.* The blood alone truly expiates. For it is the life of one given for another. *And spatter with his finger.* This is the actual

eastward, and before the mercy-seat shall he spatter seven times of the blood with his finger. 15. And he shall slay the goat of the sin-sacrifice which is the people's, and bring its blood within the veil; and he shall do with its blood as he did with the blood of the bullock, and spatter it on the mercy-seat and before the mercy-seat. 16. And he shall atone for the holy place from the uncleanness of the sons of Israel, and from

offering of the blood to the Lord and application of it to the penitent. The Lord accepts the death of the substitute, and remits the death of the sinner for whom he has died. *On the mercy-seat eastward*, that is, on the front of it. This appears to indicate the front of the ark and of the mercy-seat over it; the two constituting one whole. The blood is then spattered seven times before, that is on the ground in front of, the mercy-seat. The mercy-seat is here the altar of ultimate resort. See on iv. 6. The seven times denote a perfect application, as usual. This finishes the priest's offering for his own sin within the veil. The further application of the blood will be subsequently mentioned.

15–19. The first goat of the sin-sacrifice for the people. 15. *And he shall slay.* On this solemn anniversary the high-priest or his minister may have slain the victim for the sin of the congregation; though the text does not make this interpretation necessary. Experience of the style of this book teaches us that we may supply the suitable subject where none is expressed, even though the following verb require a different one. *And bring its blood within the veil*, to be applied in precisely the same way as that of the bullock. 16. *And he shall atone.* A peculiar turn is now given to the mode of description, quite distinct from all that has gone before, and only intelligible after the preceding chapters on the clean and the unclean. The atonement now made is for the people, because the goat that has been slain is part of their sin-sacrifice. But in another aspect of it another effect is produced. *For the holy place.* The holy place is in this verse distinguished from the tent of meeting. Hence we learn that in this context it means the holy of holies, or most holy place within the veil. In the solemn rite performed within the veil with the blood of the bullock and of the goat atonement has been made for

their transgressions in all their sins; and so shall he do to the tent of meeting that dwelleth with them amidst their uncleanness. 17. And no man shall be in the tent of meeting

the most holy place. This has been actually desecrated by the imperfect priesthood and people among whom it has been placed, and needs an atonement. *From the uncleanness of the sons of Israel*, the uncleanness which they convey to that which abides among them. *And from their transgressions in all their sins.* The uncleanness was the taint of sin. "Their transgressions" points to the guilt of sin. The transgressions occasion the uncleanness, and the uncleanness betrays the transgression. Where sin has spread its demerit and defilement an atonement is needed. There was imperfection and impurity in the whole body of the people, by which the sanctuary was defiled. And hence it appears that the offering of the blood of bulls and of lambs would have been a labor in vain, had it not been a shadow of a really perfect sacrifice and an all-sufficient propitiation that was to come. To atone, then, for the holy place, purging it by the blood of a sin-sacrifice from the uncleanness and iniquity of the whole people, is simply another way of expressing an atonement for the high-priest and his house and the whole congregation by the same sin-sacrifice and the self-same rite. This plainly appears from a comparison of vs. 11, 14, 15, and 16. It is also to be noted in this pregnant sentence that the contaminating and condemning effects of sin are brought together. This is in keeping with a day of repentance, as well as expiation, and with a chapter that knits together the treatises on propitiation and purification. *And so shall he do to the tent of meeting.* This we conceive must mean, as the rabbis understand it, that the same spattering of blood was to be made on the horns of the golden altar and before the veil, as described in iv. 6, 7, which had been made on and before the mercy-seat. The tent of meeting, as distinguished from the holy of holies, must mean the apartment without the veil, where were the golden candlestick, the table of show-bread, and the altar of incense. If the most holy place needed atonement, much more the holy place or tent of meeting, into which the priest entered every day. *That dwelleth* [16] *with them amidst their uncleanness.* The moral unclean-

when he goeth in to atone in the holy place, until he come out; and he shall atone for himself and for his house and for all the congregation of Israel. 18. And he shall come out unto the altar that is before the LORD and atone for it; and shall take of the blood of the bullock and of the blood of the goat, and put on the horns of the altar around. 19. And he shall spatter upon it of the blood with his finger seven times,

ness is sin in its nature and contaminating power, which has been so strikingly illustrated in the preceding chapters. Atonement for the contamination which it conveys to all around, and so to the tent of meeting, as well as the holy place. 17. *And no man shall be in the tent.* No man was competent to take part in making atonement. For all had sinned and come short of the glory of God; and even if not, all were creatures, and therefore dependent, and owing all to their Creator. Only the Holy One, of whom the high-priest is in all respects the divinely-appointed type, can make a propitiation for sin. *When he goeth in to atone in the holy place.* The high-priest alone, of course, enters the holy place within the veil. But from the preceding words it appears that no one is to be in the tent of meeting without the veil during the time of making atonement within the veil. *Until he come out.* The whole period is very carefully marked off, as the whole work is to be completed by the high-priest alone. 18, 19. *He shall come out unto the altar that is before the Lord.* This is the third application of the atoning blood. The court of the tabernacle is in still closer contact with the great body of the people, who enter it for the purpose of sacrificial worship. The altar here spoken of is the altar of burnt-sacrifice, as is plainly indicated by his coming out to it. It is before the Lord, as it is before the door of the tabernacle, where he dwells. *And atone for it.* Here, for the third time, expiation is to be made by putting of the blood of the bullock and the goat on all the horns of the altar, and by spattering on it seven times. By this means the court which has its centre in the outermost altar is expiated. In this way there was a threefold sprinkling in a twofold mode on the day of atonement — at the mercy-seat within the veil, at the altar of incense without the veil, and on the altar of sacrifice without the

and he shall cleanse it and hallow it from the uncleanness of the sons of Israel.

20. And he shall make an end of atoning for the holy place and for the tent of meeting and for the altar, and he shall present the live goat. 21. And Aaron shall lay his two hands upon the head of the live goat, and shall confess over it all the iniquities of the sons of Israel, and all their transgressions in

curtain at the door of the tent of meeting. The last is the place of sacrifice; the intermediate, the place of intercession; and the first the place of fellowship. The twofold mode of applying the blood points to a twofold need of expiation; the spattering of the blood seven times, like the sprinkling of it round the altar, refers to atonement directly for the worshipper; the spattering of it once, like the putting of it on the horns of the altar, appears to be a propitiation for the altar itself, that it may avail for the worshipper. Hence there was propitiation here, not only for the priests and people, but also for the holy things which they had defiled by their sins. *He shall cleanse it and hallow it.* As a good deed begets gratitude in a rightly constituted heart, so expiation, the best of all good deeds, begets repentance and all the kindred affections of an undeceived spirit. This state of mind has its reflection in the mirror of surrounding things. And hence the expiated altar is cleansed and hallowed. The hallowing is simply the exponent of the cleansing. As the altars can have no guilt or impurity in themselves, except in their relation with guilty man, as soon as the repentant worshipper presents the sacrifice that atones for his sin, the altar is not only expiated, but hallowed.

20-28. The scape-goat. 20. *And he shall make an end.* One stage of this day's proceedings, described in the preceding passage, is to be brought to a close before the next begins. *Atoning for the holy place and for the tent of meeting and for the altar.* This recapitulation shows that the three objects mentioned are co-ordinate in this process of atonement. *Present the live goat.* The verb here is that usually rendered offer. Offering does not necessarily imply the slaughter of that which is offered. 21. *Lay his two hands.* There is emphasis and solemnity in laying on both hands. *Confess over it,*

all their sins, and shall put them upon the head of the goat, and send it away by the hand of a set man into the wilderness. 22. And the goat shall bear upon it all their iniquities to a land of excision; and he shall send the goat into the wilder-

as the victim that was to suffer for the things confessed, and take them and their consequences away from the transgressor. *All the iniquities*,[21] violations of law demanding expiation. *All their transgressions*,[21] wrongs done to others demanding redress. These two elements concur in all sins; sometimes the one being prominent, sometimes the other. The former is the main characteristic of sin. *Put them upon the head of*, impute or lay them to the account of. *And send it away*, bearing the iniquity of the whole congregation. *A set*[21] *man*, a man ready for the task at the appointed time. *Into the wilderness*, beyond the limits of the holy community. 22. *Bear upon it all their iniquities.* This is correlative to the phrase, "Hath laid on him the iniquity of all." It is a clear case of imputation and substitution. *To a land of excision*,[22] a land of excommunication, away from the presence and view of the judge. This live goat merely represents the one self-same victim in a new condition, which the slain goat was no longer fitted to exhibit. The victim after death is gone to the place of banishment from God, where it still exists, bearing the perpetual doom of sin. This serves to illustrate the wider meaning of death in Scripture, which is not annihilation, but a state of ill-fare, in contrast with life, which is a state of welfare, not terminated, but only fully entered upon, at the separation of soul and body. As the animal slain and consumed, partly on the altar and partly on the place of ashes, could not represent this essential element of penal death, its second self is introduced to signalize it in a definite and emphatic manner. But another aspect of saving truth is, at the same time, no less clearly illustrated. The one goat represents the death of the substitute for the expiation of sin; the other sets forth the concurrent removal of sin from the object of the divine mercy into the land of forgetfulness, so that it can never come into remembrance against him any more. The one act is involved in the other; but it cannot be presented fully to the mind in a figure without a double

ness. 23. And Aaron shall go into the tent of meeting, and he shall strip off the linen clothes which he put on when he went into the holy place and leave them there. 24. And he shall wash his flesh with water in a holy place and put on his garments; and he shall come forth and offer his burnt-sacrifice and the burnt-sacrifice of the people, and atone for himself

victim. This duplication of the goat for a sin-sacrifice cannot but remind us of the duplication of the bird in the case of the healed leper. There is a marked difference between them. The latter contains an allusion to the leper reviving from the mortal disease, and exhibits propitiation inseparably associated with expiation. The slain bird represents the death of the substitute because he bears the sin of another; the live bird, the resurrection of the substitute because he has fulfilled all righteousness. The two, therefore, combine to exhibit the Redeemer bearing death and earning life for the sinner. This involves the resurrection, and introduces naturally the trespass-offering, of which it is a striking precursor. The goat, in the former case, is a sin-sacrifice, and its duplication merely symbolizes the two effects of the sin-sacrifice — the death for sin and the coincident removal of the penalty forever from the object of the divine forgiveness.

23–25. These verses give the occupation of Aaron, while the set man is sending off the scape-goat. *Shall go into the tent of meeting.* Having sent away this man, he has completed the sacrifice for sin, which is characteristic of this day, he is to go once more into the tent of meeting. It is probable, as the rabbis say, that he now brings away the censer on which the incense was burning. But this, being a matter of no consequence, is not mentioned, and the return into the tabernacle, if merely for this purpose, would probably have been left unnoticed. The main reason for this return is that which is stated in the text, to take off the linen garments, and put on the splendid robes of the high-priest. This act, from the care with which it is stated, is shown to be not merely incidental, but, on the other hand, highly significant. The expiation has now been accomplished. He who has made it was all through perfect in holiness and righteousness, and now that it is finished is entitled on the ground of his unblemished

214   THE DAY OF ATONEMENT.

and for the people. 25. And the fat of the sin-sacrifice he shall burn upon the altar. 26. And he that sent off the goat for a scape-goat shall wash his clothes and wash his flesh with water; and afterwards he shall come into the camp. 27. And the bullock for sin and the goat for sin, whose blood was brought in to atone in the holy place, shall one carry out of the camp; and they shall burn with fire their skins and their flesh and their dung. 28. And he that burneth them shall

integrity to the rewards and honors of perfect obedience. He is, therefore, directed to assume the robes of the just and holy one. This is a fitting act to take place in his Father's house. Accordingly, he is to enter, strip off the mitre, girdle, and coat, the garb of lowliness and destitution, and *leave them there*, never, the rabbis say, to be resumed; but it may be to be resumed only the next year. 24. He shall there *wash his flesh*, namely, his hands and feet, with water, thereby cleansing himself from the ceremonial uncleanness of the sin-victim; *in a holy place*, some place convenient to the laver appointed for the purpose, *and put on* his state garments, and *come forth*, no longer as the lowly sufferer, but as the exalted mediator of the new covenant. He is now to offer the burnt-sacrifice for himself and for the people. *And atone for himself and for the people.* This sacrifice denotes propitiation or atonement in the fullest sense, including not only the bearing of the penalty, but the rendering of the obedience for those who are represented. 25. *The fat of the sin-sacrifice.* The burning of this is only another symbol of propitiation. If the description here be strictly chronological, the fat of the sin-sacrifice is burned on the altar after and upon the burnt-sacrifice; a hint of the paramount importance of the burnt-sacrifice. 26. *And he that sent off.* The set man who has led away the goat with the sins of the people upon it is defiled by contact with the bearer of sin, and is to make the customary ablutions before he returns into the camp. 27. *And the bullock for sin.* The victims for sin, inasmuch as their blood has been brought into the sanctuary for atonement (Lev. vi. 23), are to be carried without the camp to the place of ashes, and there consumed by fire. 28. *And he that burneth them*, being thereby defiled, shall wash his clothes and wash his flesh with water, and afterwards he shall come into the camp.

29. And it shall be unto you a statute forever: in the seventh month, on the tenth day of the month, ye shall afflict your

make the usual ablutions before returning into the camp. This at length completes the history of the sacrifices for sin on this unparalleled day. We learn, thus, the whole of that which is implied in the sacrifice for sin. The prominent point is expiation for sin, denoted by the blood, the burning of the body in the place of ashes, and the exile of the scape-goat. The blood denotes death, the penalty of sin or disobedience to the Author of our being. The burning denotes destruction, or the defeat of all the proper ends of being. The exile denotes the second death, or the experience of the perpetual sufferings of a just doom. When all these befall the substitute, the object of the divine mercy is redeemed, or released from the penalty of sin. Less prominent in the sin-sacrifice is propitiation, the necessary concomitant of expiation, which is indicated, however, by the burning of the fat on the altar. This stands in the background in the present rite. We can now estimate the striking contrast between the sin-sacrifice and the trespass-offering. The former is the sin-bearer for another, and therefore dies, bears the destruction of all the hopes of life, and enters upon the experience of the second death, shadowing forth in vivid detail the equivalent of suffering which the substitute has to bear. The latter is the right-doer for another, who therefore, though he die for him, yet earns and rises to eternal life and liberty, exhibiting in an equally striking figure the resurrection unto life of the Mediator who has died and lived for others. Here death is necessary, as before; but it falls into the shade behind the glory of the resurrection. Expiation must precede; but it wanes before the surpassing excellence of propitiation.

29-34. The day of celebration and the perpetuity of the ordinance. 29. *A statute forever*, lasting as long as the present economy continues in form, and throughout all generations and ages in principle. When the substance comes the shadows will flee away. *In the seventh month.* According to Josephus (Antiq. i. 3, 3) this was the first month of the

souls, and do no work, the home-born and the stranger that sojourneth among you. 30. For on this day shall he atone

year in the order of the calendar existing before the exodus from Egypt (Ex. xii. 2), and of the civil year even after that event. The state of nature described in Gen. ii. 6, the numeration of the month in the history of the deluge (Gen. vii. 11) and the out-going and turn of the year (Ex. xxiii. 16 ; xxxiv. 22), corroborate this tradition. As the sacred year began exactly six months after the other, the first month of the civil year was the seventh of the sacred year. The special observances connected with the first day of the seventh month favor the supposition that it was the old new year's day of Israel. *On the tenth.* The festival of the atonement is naturally suited to be the initial rite of a new life. The civil year of the holy people is consecrated to God, and this ordinance was well fitted to express this thought. Why the tenth day was selected we are not informed. If the fall of man took place on the tenth day it would afford an adequate reason for fixing on this day. Those who mark coincidences will observe that the paschal lamb was set apart on the tenth day of the first month (Ex. xii. 3). *Ye shall afflict your souls.* The soul is pre-eminently the susceptible part of man's nature. To afflict the soul is to give free scope to the convictions of sin and to the shame, sorrow, and indignation which it awakens. The revelation of the mercy of God in the gospel of the Old Testament was the only thing fitted to awaken repentance in the sensitive conscience of the sinner. This gospel of promise is not only announced in words, but symbolized in all possible forms in the ceremonial of Leviticus. The more clearly the sinner apprehends the mercy of God, announced in this manifold way, the more keenly will he feel the exceeding sinfulness of sin. And the more fully he comprehends that God has provided a victim and a priest to satisfy justice in order that he might be at liberty to show mercy, the more deep and contrite will be his repentance towards him. It is worthy of note that the Spirit of truth in the unaffected simplicity of a primeval time dwells on the state of the soul alone, and condescends on no outward manifestations of the inward feeling. The rabbis and doctors interpret affliction of soul by fasting, because such was the formal mode in their day. A deep sense of

for you to cleanse you; from all your sins before the LORD ye shall be cleansed. 31. It shall be a sabbath of rest unto you,

sorrow for sin will naturally lead to abstinence from the delicacies of the table and even from food altogether for a season. But it is to be remembered that the sorrow of the heart is the only genuine repentance, and that outward fastings and other forms will only be an abominable hypocrisy where that is wanting. *And do no work.* This was to be a strict sabbath, as is stated in vs. 31. This is a more genuine and trustworthy effect of heart-sorrow than formal fasting. *The home-born and the stranger.* We here incidentally learn that the sons of Israel were to welcome the stranger of another race to their home and to their God. (See Ex. xii. 49.) 30. *For on this day, shall he atone for you.* The expiation for sin was to be made on this day in the grandest and most comprehensive form. *To cleanse you.* The affliction of the soul, the right disposition in which the worshipper entered upon the appointed ordinance, the repentance, trust, gratitude, and devotion which the thought of its import called forth, was the indication of a cleansed heart. And therefore, as in the case of the healed leper, the priest by the very offering of the atoning sacrifice for the penitent congregation pronounced them clean. It is remarkable that no symbol of purification is enjoined on this occasion, because the reality itself is enjoined in the affliction of soul which was to be manifested on this day. Thus the day of atonement combined purification with propitiation, and this chapter unites the seven chapters on sacrifice to the five on cleansing by the intervening three on the priest. *From all your sins before the Lord.* The sins of his own people are in a peculiar sense before the Lord, because they dwell in his presence, and the light of his countenance is upon them. 31. *A sabbath of rest.* This phrase is twice applied to the day of atonement (here and in xxiii. 32), and once to the sabbatical year (xxv. 4), but elsewhere only to the weekly sabbath. It denotes resting from all work, servile or other than servile. The day of atonement is therefore the only day agreeing with the weekly sabbath in entire abstinence from work. It differs from it, however, as strikingly in being a day of affliction, while the weekly sabbath was a day of rejoicing. The fifty-two sabbaths of gladness, instituted

and ye shall afflict your souls; it is a statute forever. 32. And the priest, whom he shall anoint and whose hand he shall fill to be priest in his father's stead, shall atone; and he shall put on the linen garments, the garments of holiness. 33. And he shall atone for the holy of holies, and he shall atone for the tent of meeting and for the altar; and he shall atone for the

before the fall, are a pleasing indication that man was originally designed for holiness and happiness. The one anniversary sabbath of penitence is an humbling token of his fallen state. *Ye shall afflict your souls.* The text of the divine law is moderate in demanding only the one day of humiliation throughout the year. Its assertion of the fundamental principles of moral rectitude and announcement of the merciful provision of an atonement were alone fitted to awaken this feeling. 32. *The priest whom he shall anoint*, whom the proper party, not here mentioned, shall anoint and consecrate to the office of the priesthood. This has reference to the perpetuity of the statute for the day of atonement. The perpetuity of the high-priesthood provides for the perpetual observance of the ordinance. *He shall put on the linen garments.* The mention of this regulation here shows the deep significance of it. The high-priest is to be afflicted in the affliction of his people. But above all he is to be the sin-bearer, and as such to make himself of no reputation, to be numbered with the transgressors, and pour out his soul unto death in the form of the victim. *The garments of holiness.* Amidst all his humiliation and debasement it is never to be forgotton that he is holy and without blemish, and pre-eminently so in that act in which he bare the sins of many. 33. *Atone for the holy of holies.* These figures of the true holy places are all defiled with sin, for they came from the hands of man, and are in daily contact with human things. Hence they need the great and true and only propitiation to atone for them. *And for the priests and for all the people.* Not only the holy places, but the priests themselves need atonement, since they are but men of like passions and infirmities with all their fallen race. They cannot then be the real mediators. Along with the priests, as it is put here, atonement is made for the people; and the self-same victims that

priests and for all the people of the congregation. 34. And this shall be to you a statute forever, to atone for the sons of Israel from all their sins once a year. And he did as the LORD commanded Moses.

atone for priest and people in the very same act atone for the holy places. Atonement for the one is atonement for the other. 34. *A statute forever.* For the third time this is repeated in order to impress upon priest and people the necessity of the perpetual celebration of this anniversary ordinance. *To atone for the sons of Israel from all their sins.* Atonement is one thing needful for salvation; affliction of soul is another; the mercy of God is the third, or rather the first, from which the others flow. Atonement is the theme of this chapter from first to last. *Once a year.* It is thus at one and the same time a type of the one all-sufficient atonement and by its annual recurrence a witness to its own intrinsic inefficacy. *And he did.* Aaron did as the Lord commanded Moses, by abstaining from entering the holy of holies within the vail in the intervening time between one tenth of the seventh month and another, and of course, when the set time came by entering in the prescribed manner. The compliance with the negative part of the command is all that is to be done at present.

This completes the third section and the first part of the Book of Leviticus. In this sole anniversary of humiliation and soul-affliction the prominent part of atonement is expiation, and the leading sacrifice is that of the victim for sin. This is quite in accordance with a day in which the guilt of sin as an offence against holiness is brought to remembrance. The profound significance of the sin-sacrifice is here brought to light by expanding the ordinance into an elaborate detail, and by reduplicating the victim in order to give a complete analysis of its effect. Hence we are made to see with our eyes that death taketh away sin. Sin is on this day the burden of the afflicted soul; the taking away of sin the relief given by the main victim of the day. But while the special nature and effect of the sin-sacrifice is thus made conspicuous, it is incidentally taught that expiation is never parted from propitiation. The fat of the sin-victim is burned upon the altar; this is always a symbol of propitiation. The expiatory nature of the sin-sacrifice is further indicated by the severe simplicity of the priestly dress on this occasion. This is quite in harmony with the endurance of the penal consequences of sin, but not with receiving the honorable rewards of obedience. The day is not closed however, without assigning its due place to the propitiatory sacrifice. After the expiation has been made, with all solemnity of form, the priest resumes his robes of state and offers the burnt sacrifice for himself and the people. This is the symbol of the great propitiation, by which the penitent worshipper is not only delivered from the wrath to come, but restored to the grace and glory of the eternal inheritance. This chapter fitly closes the present section. It speaks of uncleanness, the uncleanness of the congregation of Israel, the uncleanness of which that of the beast of the field, the woman that has borne a child, the leper, or the patient that has an issue, is only a figure. It enjoins, in the presence of the only constraining motives, the obligation of the moral law and the expiation provided for sin, affliction of soul, expressive of humble and confiding repentance toward God, which is the removal of the moral disease and the return of spiritual health. And it thereupon prescribes the appropriate offerings for priest and people on their recovery from the malady of the will and their restoration to the cleanness of the heart. And in the offering of these sacrifices the high-priest is authorized to pronounce them clean. This is the topstone to the doctrine of the clean and the unclean. The present section unites the first sixteen chapters into a compact whole. In it we have uncleanness involving guilt. While we have the agent of all spiritual cleansing plainly indicated in the oil and the water, we have also the means of all atonement for sin brought forward in the priest discerning the disease, recognizing the recovery, and offering the sacrifices which make atonement. The priest and the victim are one mediator. The water and the oil are one sanctifier. And above all is the one God of mercy and Father of all, the great Forgiver, from whom come the Redeemer and the Regenerator. These sixteen chapters, with their seventeen or eighteen divine communications, are made really one by the marvellous combining power of their inspired compiler.

LEVITICUS XVI.

NOTES.

2. *Mercy-seat*, כַּפֹּרֶת, ἱλαστήριον, *propitiatorium*.

8. *Scape-goat*, עֲזָאזֵל, obviously, goat departing, going away: Sept., ἀποπομπαῖος, εἰς τὴν ἀποπομπήν v. 10, εἰς ἄφεσιν v. 26: vulg. *caper emissarius*; Mishna, שָׂעִיר מִשְׁתַּלֵּחַ; Joseph. ἀποτροπιασμός. All these explanations have the advantages of simplicity and consistency. They suggest two ideas, that the goat is sent away, *emissarius*, and that it bears sin away, ἀποτροπιασμός. These harmonize with the whole text. The former, however, is the prominent idea in the name. In proceeding to investigate the meaning of a term occurring only four times, and all in the one context, we must abide by the principle that it must be something simple and obvious to the minds of the people. This excludes from consideration all interpretations that have their rise in a vain philosophy and a still more delusive mythology. Azazel cannot be a place, because this would be no proper contrast to the Lord in v. 8, and moreover הַמִּדְבָּרָה in v. 10, sufficiently indicates the place. It cannot mean the devil or any evil demon, because we have not the slightest hint of such a meaning in the text, nor even in the Sept. or Josephus; and surmises of such a meaning in the later writings, such as the book of Enoch, and the Rabbinical, Patristic, and Mahometan literature are mere subjective fancies, on which the interpreter cannot lay any stress. Besides the goat is placed before the Lord to atone upon it, and this is quite at variance with being afterwards sent to an evil spirit. The only other meaning is the scape-goat, and this alone is suitable. Patrick saw no objection to this rendering but the one, that עֵז is feminine. But this objection does not hold, as the word is properly masculine (Lev. iii. 12; xxii. 27), though inclusive of the feminine.

10. *To atone upon it*, לְכַפֵּר עָלָיו. This usually means to atone for him or it. But the passage quoted in the text clearly shows it is capable of the other meaning. And "to atone for it" cannot be applied to the goat, but only to the people, an antecedent so remote as to seem harsh, though it gives the meaning of the passage.

12. *Handsful*, מְלֹא חָפְנָיִם. The full of the gowpens in old English phrase. The word occurs six times. *Spices*, סַמִּים, aromatic plants scenting the air.

16. *Abiding*, שֹׁכֵן. From this is formed the Rabbinic term שְׁכִינָה expressing the glory of the Lord dwelling above the mercy-seat in the holy of holies.

21. *Iniquities*, עֲוֹנֹת, ἀνομίας. *Transgressions*, פְּשָׁעִים, ἀδικίας. *set*, עִתִּי, timely, provided for the occasion: ἕτοιμος.

22. *Excision*, גְּזֵרָה, cutting off; ἄβατος, a land from which there is no return.

SECTION IV.—RULES CONCERNING CIVIL MATTERS.

XVII. CONCERNING ANIMAL FOOD.

XVII. 1. AND the LORD spake unto Moses, saying, 2. Speak unto Aaron and to his sons and to all the sons of Israel, and say unto them, This is the thing which the LORD hath commanded, saying, 3. Any man of the house of Israel that slayeth an ox or sheep or goat in the camp, or that slayeth it out-

The following eleven chapters form the second part of Leviticus. As the former part relates to the birth of the nation as a spiritual commonwealth, so the present part relates to the progress of their social life as the people of God. Four chapters treat of civil affairs; four, of religious; and the remaining three of matters having both a civil and a religious bearing. The present section includes the first four chapters, which refer to animal food, chastity, holiness, and the penalties by which many of the preceding regulations are to be enforced. The seventeenth chapter relates to animal food, and regulates the slaughter of oxen and small cattle (1–7) and the use to be made of blood (8–16). It is addressed to Moses, by whom it is to be communicated to the priests and to all Israel.

1–7. Oxen and small cattle to be slain only at the altar. 1, 2. The minute, circumstantial details of these introductory verses are quite suitable and requisite in documents that are historical and legal. The commands received from the Lord must be duly attested. 3. *Any man of the house of Israel.* This is expressly limited to the house of Israel. *In the camp.* The definition in the camp, or outside the camp, limits this regulation in its present form still further to the temporary arrangements of the wilderness, while the people were in camp, a state of things which might have terminated in another year.

side of the camp, 4. And bringeth it not to the door of the tent of meeting to make an offering to the LORD before the tabernacle of the LORD, blood shall be counted to that man; he hath shed blood; and that man shall be cut off from among his people: 5. To the end that the sons of Israel may bring their sacrifices which they are making in the open field, and bring them to the LORD to the door of the tent of meeting unto the priest, and offer them as sacrifices of peace unto the LORD. 6. And the priest shall sprinkle the blood upon the altar of the LORD at the door of the tent of meeting, and burn

4. *And bringeth it not.* The slaying of these animals is not forbidden. Only, so long as they are in the wilderness, it is to be performed at the door of the tent of meeting. *To make an offering.* This seems to imply that no animal was to be slain for food without presenting an offering to the Lord. But, from what follows, it may simply apply to the slaying of animals of which it was the custom of the people to make some part an offering. It is not improbable that this was the general custom, which had grown up among them in Egypt. It was not the custom, however, of their ancestors. Abram had a calf killed and dressed to entertain his guests (Gen. xviii. 7) without any trace of such a custom. *Blood shall be counted to that man.* This favors the view that slaying for sacrifice in an unlawful way is the thing here forbidden. The blood which is set apart for atonement, and so for deliverance from death, avails for man's life. To misapply it, or apply it in an unlawful way or to an idolatrous purpose, is to destroy life, and thus to shed blood. Hence it is said *he hath shed blood*, which is the life of man, as it should have served for expiation. Hence this man is to be excommunicated. 5. *To the end.* The end of the prohibition is here stated. The sons of Israel are in the habit of making their sacrifices in the open field. Before the setting up of a national altar this was allowable, provided the offerings were made to the true God. But now their sacrifices are to be brought to the door of the tent of meeting, and presented as sacrifices of peace unto the Lord. This, also, leans to the idea that the slaying for sacrifice elsewhere is

the fat for a sweet smell unto the LORD. 7. And they shall no more offer their sacrifices to the he-goats, after whom they lust. This shall be a statute for ever unto them for their generations.

8. And thou shalt say unto them, any man of the house of Israel or of the strangers that sojourn among you, who offereth a burnt-sacrifice or a sacrifice, 9. And bringeth it

here forbidden. 7. When they are offered as peace-sacrifices, the blood is sprinkled on the altar, and the fat is burned for a sweet smell, and the rest is at the disposal of the owner. In the ordinary sacrifice of peace, the wave-breast and the heave-leg (Lev. vii. 34) were assigned to the priests. *The altar of the Lord* is contrasted with any other place, and also with the altar of any false god. 7. The further end of the prohibition appears in this verse. Some of the people were privately sacrificing to false gods. 7. *The he-goats.* They had contracted this habit in Egypt, where the goat was an object of worship (Joseph. cont. Ap. 27). It was called Mendes, corresponding to Pan, was reckoned among the eight principal gods, and was worshipped in Lower Egypt, particularly in the Mendesian Nome, which was not far from Goshen. The Israelties were therefore acquainted with this form of idolatry. *After which they lust.* The breach of the seventh commandment is the standing figure for idolatry, as lawful wedlock is the favorite emblem of the worship of the true God. The prohibition, then, is designed to counteract the false training of Egypt. *A statute forever.* To offer sacrifice no more to idols of any kind is a perpetual statute. The mode in which animal food is to be lawfully used will vary with the circumstances of the people (See Deut. xii.).

8–16. Regulations concerning other sacrifice and concerning blood. *And thou shalt say unto them.* This is the second part of this message. It begins with a similar prohibition to offer either burnt-sacrifice or peace-offering anywhere but at the altar of God, under pain of excommunication. This is directed against any sacrifice to the true God being offered elsewhere than at the national altar; whereas the former prohibition was mainly against sacrificing to false gods. This regulation also, extends not only to Israel, but to the stranger who sojourns with him, and becomes a proselyte to the worship of the true God.

not unto the door of the tent of meeting to offer it unto the LORD, even that man shall be cut off from his people. 10. And any man of the house of Israel, or of the strangers that sojourn among them, who eateth any blood, I will even set my face against the soul that eateth the blood, and will cut him off from among his people. 11. For the soul of the flesh is in the blood, and I have given it to you upon the altar to atone

Strangers who were still aliens from the commonwealth of Israel do not come under its regulations, and hence they are not included in the former prohibition which was only for those who professed to have forsaken idolatry. 10. Then follows the vehement denunciation of the Israelite or the proselyte that eats blood. The eating of blood was forbidden as early as the days of Noah (Gen. ix. 4). It is repeated in Lev. vii. 26, 27. It is here in place among a series of regulations concerning food. *I will even set my face*, oppose and reject. *Against the soul*, the voluntary agent, who is susceptible of pleasure as well as of pain. The term appears to be used here on purpose in contrast with the soul or vital principle of the animal. *Cut him off*, by the act of the lawful authorities or by a special visitation. 11. The reason of this stern prohibition is now given. *The soul of the flesh is in the blood.* The soul is the vital principle that has desire, will, and activity as its prominent qualities, which corresponds with the will and its kindred powers in the human soul. In this department of the human spirit lies the moral faculty, by which it is capable of obedience or disobedience and conscious of right and wrong. The soul *of the flesh* is that which gives life to the flesh. This is said to be in the blood, because it is so intimately connected with the circulating blood that it leaves the flesh or the body and ceases to animate it whenever the blood is shed. This is the preliminary fact establishing the essential connection of the blood with the soul. On this rests the mystical or moral fact conveyed in the words, " I have given it to you upon the altar to atone for your souls." This fact is called mystical because it springs from the purpose and exists in the determination of God that so it should be. And it is moral, inasmuch as the soul of the victim is given for the soul of the redeemed. This is the principle of sub-

for your souls; for it is the blood that atoneth for the soul. 12. Therefore I have said unto the sons of Israel, No soul of you shall eat blood, nor shall the stranger that sojourneth among you eat blood. 13. And any man of the sons of Israel or of the strangers that sojourn among you who hunteth any beast or fowl that may be eaten, he shall pour out its blood and cover it with dust. 14. For in the soul of all flesh, its blood is in its soul; and I said unto the sons of Israel, ye shall not eat the blood of any flesh; for the soul of all flesh is its blood: all that eat of it shall be cut off. 15. And every soul that eateth a dead or a torn body, be he home-born or stranger, he shall wash his clothes and wash in water and be unclean until the even: then shall he be clean. 16. And if he wash them not, nor wash his flesh, then he shall bear his iniquity. ¶

stitution, which lies at the root of the scheme of salvation revealed in the book of God. The soul of the victim is in the blood. The blood is therefore to be scrupulously withdrawn from any unworthy or inferior use. We see here the close relationship between the representative and the represented. The soul of man is the spirit regarded as the seat of desire, of will, and therefore of conscience. The soul of the brute is pre-eminently the seat of appetite and will. The will is that part of the vital principle which is most closely connected with the blood. Hence the blood is the life "which atoneth for the soul" of man. 12. Hence the prohibition, "no soul of you shall eat blood." 13. *Who hunteth any beast or fowl.* The blood of any animal that may be eaten, but cannot be offered in sacrifice, is to be poured on the ground and covered with dust. 14. *For in the soul of all flesh.* The reason assigned for this is the universality of the fact that the blood is in the soul of all flesh. The phrase is remarkable. The blood is so intimately connected with the soul, that the removal of the blood is the removal of the soul from the flesh. 15. *Eateth a dead or a torn body.* That which has died of itself or is torn by wild beasts is not to be eaten, because the blood has not been properly drained from it, and it is defiling. He that partakes of it unwittingly is to wash his clothes, wash himself with water, and be unclean until the evening. If he do not, he shall bear his iniquity. According to Ex. xxii. 30, that which was torn was to be cast to the dogs.

The deep import of the law concerning blood here comes out in all its force. It is not merely that the soul or the life is in the blood, but that in consequence of this natural connection the blood has been given of God to atone for him whose life is forfeited through sin. But even the blood of the inferior animal is only a type of that blood which expiates the guilt of sin, and the contemplation of which by intelligent faith cleanses from its defilement. Only the blood of a Mediator, who is not only human but divine, can outweigh in intrinsic value the whole human race, and afford an all-sufficient atonement.

NOTE.

7. *He-goats*, שְׂעִירִם, hairy creatures; μάταιοι, *vanities, idols*.

XVIII. ON CHASTITY.

After purity of diet comes purity of sexual intercourse, which is regulated in the present chapter. It contains an admonition to avoid the evil customs of other nations (1–5), a statute determining the degrees of kindred that are too near for chaste wedlock (6–17), a prohibition of other kinds of incest (18–23), and a warning to beware of defiling the land which was to be given to them as their predecessors had done (24–30). The revelation which it makes is addressed to Moses, who is to communicate it to the people whom it concerns. In this and the following two chapters frequent reference is made to the land in which the people were about to be settled.

1–5. An admonition to avoid the vile customs of other nations. 2. *I am the Lord your God;* a sentence of never-to-be-forgotten significance. *The Lord*, Jehovah, the Self-existent, the Author of all existing things, the Performer of promise, is entitled by the very highest right to command. *Your God.* Here the word "your" is emphatic. It implies two things of the utmost personal interest to those addressed: first, the Lord had chosen them to be his people, and second, being moved by the word and by the Spirit of the Lord, they had chosen him to be their God. God is here the only living Almighty, in con-

XVIII. 1. And the LORD spake unto Moses, saying, 2. Speak unto the sons of Israel and say unto them, I am the LORD your God. 3. After the doing of the land of Mizraim, wherein ye dwelt, shall ye not do; and after the doing of the land of Kenaan, whither I bring you, shall ye not do, nor walk in their statutes. 4. My judgments ye shall do and my statutes ye shall keep, to walk in them: I am the LORD your God. 5. And ye shall keep my statutes and my judgments; which the man that doeth shall live in them: I am the LORD. §

trast with all that falsely claim or receive the title. It is necessary to bring these sublime and solemnizing thoughts before the minds of this new-born people, when it is proposed to wean them from the weak and beggarly elements on which they have been tempted in the past or may be enticed in the future to rely. 3. *The doing of the land of Mizraim.* The people have to beware of a twofold evil, that of hankering after the corrupt customs of Egypt, which they have just left behind, and that of falling into the equally vile practices of the land of Kenaan, to which they are advancing. The iniquity of the Amorites was now full, after a growth of four hundred years. *Whither I bring you,* not to follow their example, but to be the instrument of their extirpation from the land. 4. *My judgments,* judicial sentences, affirming the duty of the people, and usually accompanied with an intimation of the good or evil consequent upon compliance or non-compliance. *My,* in contrast with those of the surrounding nations and their false gods. *My statutes,* edicts or decrees, established and published as customs or institutions of the people of God. *To walk in them,* make them the constant ruling motive of your conduct. *I am the Lord your God.* When we consider the transition from bondage to liberty, from compulsion to responsibility, from promise to possession, through which this infant people were now passing, we begin to understand the frequent reiteration of the absolute supremacy of the true God, and of the covenant of grace and peace subsisting between him and them. It needed all the strength of faith to realize the peculiar relation in which they stood, and to resist old and new temptations. 5. *Which the man that doeth shall live in them.* The

6. No man of you shall approach unto any one near of kin to him to uncover the nakedness: I am the LORD. § 7. The nakedness of thy father or the nakedness of thy mother thou shalt not uncover: she is thy mother; thou shalt not uncover her nakedness. § 8. The nakedness of thy father's wife thou shalt not uncover: it is thy father's nakedness. § 9. The

law says, Do this and thou shalt live. Eternal life is the reward of perfect obedience. But all men have sinned and come short of the glory of God. The statutes and judgments, however, to which the men of Israel are here invited to hearken, contain a message of mercy and peace, and hold out an atonement for sin. He has said to them, I am the Lord your God, and they have responded to his call and accepted his promise. This is their life. Being pardoned and accepted they are exhorted, and by grace enabled, to walk worthy of their new-born faith in God and repentance toward him. *I am the Lord.* This one name, the Creator of all that I purpose, is the secure resting-place of faith and the supreme ground of obedience.

6-17. The degrees of kindred that are too near for lawful wedlock. 6. This verse contains the general principle, enforced by the authority from which there is no appeal: *I am the Lord. Any one near of kin.*[6] *Share,* or flesh of flesh, is used to denote a relative who partakes of the same flesh. *To uncover the nakedness.* This phrase for cohabitation is designedly used to denote an act which is to be condemned as incestuous. As carnal intercourse without the bond of wedlock is condemned by the seventh commandment, these precepts must be understood to prohibit marriage within the degrees of kinsmanship here mentioned. A man is not to wed his mother, father's wife, sister by either parent, granddaughter, sister by the father who has married a second time, aunt by either side, wife of father's brother, daughter-in-law, brother's wife, wife's daughter, or granddaughter. It is to be presumed that the law applies to the female as well as the male; and hence a woman is not to wed her father, and so on throughout. 7. *The nakedness of thy father.* This intimates that the law applies to the female as well as the male, changing what needs to be changed 8. *It is thy father's nakedness,* according to the principle

nakedness of thy sister, thy father's daughter or thy mother's daughter, born at home or born abroad, thou shalt not uncover their nakedness. § 10. The nakedness of thy son's daughter or of thy daughter's daughter thou shalt not uncover their nakedness; for they are thine own nakedness. § 11. The nakedness of thy father's wife's daughter, begotten of thy father, being thy sister, thou shalt not uncover her nakedness. § 12. The nakedness of thy father's sister thou shalt not uncover; she is near of kin to thy father. § 13. The nakedness of thy mother's sister thou shalt not uncover; for she is near of kin to thy mother. § 14. The nakedness of thy father's brother thou shalt not uncover: his wife thou shalt not approach; she is thy aunt. § 15. The nakedness of thy daughter-in-law thou shalt not uncover; she is thy son's wife; thou shalt not uncover her nakedness. § 16. The nakedness of thy brother's wife thou shalt not uncover; she is thy brother's nakedness. § 17. The nakedness of a woman and

that husband and wife are one flesh. 9. *Born at home or born abroad.* Birth abroad, or in another home, would most likely take place when the mother having married again would pass into a home where her daughter by a former husband was not born. 10. *For they are thine own nakedness.* As this holds good of granddaughters, so much more of daughters. The latter case is involved in vs. 7, and does not need any further expression. 11. This case might come under vs. 9. It refers to a younger half-sister, while an elder half-sister is included in the verse quoted. 12, 13. These verses include the aunt on both sides. 14. This by parity of reason may be extended to a mother's brother's wife. 16. This is subject to the exception of the wife of a brother who has died childless, according to the custom recognized in Deut. xxv. 5–10. 17. The daughter or granddaughter of a former wife is excluded. The reason assigned is, she is near of kin. The sister of a former wife is excluded on the same ground, even if their connection were not prohibited by vs. 16. *It is lewdness.*[17]

her daughter thou shalt not uncover; her son's daughter or her daughter's daughter thou shalt not take to uncover her nakedness; they are near of kin; it is lewdness.

18. And a woman unto her sister thou shalt not take, by constraint to uncover her nakedness with her in her life.

The connection here in question is pronounced to be wicked and repugnant to right feeling. Thus the general principle stated in the sixth verse is expanded into ten clauses, which being fairly interpreted will include every needful case. The observance of these rules protects the sanctity and peace of the home, and guards against the licentious manners of the surrounding nations.

18–23. A prohibition of some other kinds of incest. 18. *And a woman unto her sister* [18] *thou shalt not take.* The literal meaning of these words is here given. The Hebrew scholar is aware that this is a usual phrase for "one to another." The case of a sister-in-law is, by parity of relation, settled in verse 16. It is to be understood, therefore, that this verse forbids the taking of a second wife while the first is living. So the Karaites understood it. This is borne out by the context. *By constraint.* It is, in general, an act of unkindness and hardship to the first wife. The one is an adversary to the other (1 Sam. i. 6), a rival in the husband's affections, and therefore in influence over his conduct. *With her,* along with her, and consequently against her, as indeed it might fairly be rendered. *In her life.* This leaves it open to a man to marry another wife after the death of the former. At the same time it is not to be denied, as Patrick and others reason, that polygamy was practised, the practice noticed, and certain regulations founded on the practice in Scripture. Jacob and Elkanah, the latter a Levite, had each two wives, and several kings had more than one. It was enacted that the eldest son should have the rights of primogeniture, though his mother were the less favored of two wives (Deut. xxi. 15), and the rights of the former wife should be guaranteed (Ex. xxi. 10). But it is to be replied that Jacob's case was before the law, that no penalty is imposed in chap. xx. on this particular infringement of the law, that kings are forbidden to multiply wives (Deut. xvii. 17), and that the regulations do not give any

19. And unto a woman in her separation by her uncleanness thou shalt not approach to uncover her nakedness. 20. And with thy neighbor's wife thou shalt not lie carnally, to be defiled with her. 21. And of thy seed thou shalt not give to pass through for Molek, nor shalt thou profane the name of thy God : I am the LORD. 22. And with a male thou shalt not lie as with a woman; it is abomination. 23. And thou

countenance or allowance to the connection, which was simply tolerated and occasionally formed. After forbidding the practice the singular moderation of the legislative system is shown in not imposing a penalty on this offence. It simply guarded the rights of the first wife and her offspring. 19. This enactment needs no elucidation except a reference to xv. 24. 20. This is simply one form of the seventh commandment. 21. *Passing through for Molek.*[21] Idolatry is a spiritual adultery (xvii. 7, and elsewhere). Passing of their seed through the fire in honor of Molek was an idolatrous custom of the Kenaanites, whose country the Israelites were going to possess. They needed therefore to be specially warned against this form of idolatry. Molek was the idol of the Phoenicians and Ammonites having some resemblance to the Greek Kronos. It is probable from this passage that there was obscenity as well as cruelty practised in his worship. Passing children through the fire was supposed by some of the rabbis and fathers to be a kind of lustration by which they were devoted to Molek. But from Ps. cvi. 38 ; Jer. vii. 3 ; Ezek. xvi. 20, it is plain that at least at a late period children were burned as victims to the idol. Diodorus Siculus describes the Carthaginian Kronos as a brazen statue, which was heated red, and the child was placed in its arms and so destroyed with great torture, the priests meanwhile drowning its screams by the beating of drums. Molek was considered to be akin to Baal. *Nor shalt thou profane the name of thy God,* by assigning it to an idol, an imaginary being of the most impure and inhuman propensities. *I am the Lord* is the closing watchword here, once more impressing upon the minds of the people the present fact that the lawgiver is the one true, living God of all authority and power. 22, 23. These are the

shalt not lie with any beast to be defiled with it; nor shall a woman stand before a beast to cohabit with it; it is pollution. 24. Defile not yourselves with any of these; for with all these are the nations defiled which I cast out before you. 25. And the land was defiled; and I visited its iniquity upon it, and the land spued out its inhabitants. 26. But ye shall keep my statutes and my judgments, and shall not do any of these abominations, the home-born nor the stranger that sojourneth among you. 27. For all these abominations the men of the land who were before you have done; and the land is defiled. 28. And the land shall not spue you out when ye defile it, as it spued out the nation that was before you. 29. For whosoever shall do any of these abominations, the souls that do so shall be cut off from among their people.

two sins of Sodom, the one of which is declared to be an abomination,[22] and the other a pollution.[23]

24–30. A warning against defiling the land by unnatural crimes. 24. *Defile not yourselves.* Sin is the only real defilement. *With all these are the nations defiled.* This is the reason for specifying these revolting crimes. The people are warned against them while their hearts are still unbiassed, before they see and become familiarized with them, and so fall into them. *Which I cast out before you,* which I am about to cast out. Such is the force of the original. 25. *And the land was defiled.* The crime was completed and past. *And I visited its iniquity.* The visitation in its beginnings, at least, was actually past. *And the land spued out.* This is a strong figure taken from the action of an over-burdened stomach rejecting its contents. So this land was already beginning to be depopulated. The hornet (Ex. xxiii. 28) and the diseases consequent upon a grossly immoral life were already at work. 26. *The home-born nor the stranger.* From the frequent mention of the stranger it is obvious that proselytes to the true God were expected and welcomed. 27, 28. *As it spued out.* This may be literally rendered, as it will have spued out. The future perfect describes an event in the future as completed

30. And ye shall keep my charge not to do any of the abominable customs, which were done before you, and ye shall not defile yourselves with them: I am the LORD your God.

30 ¶ ¶ ¶

29, 30. *Shall be cut off.* Exclusion from the commonwealth of Israel is the natural consequence of defying the God of Israel. *Ye shall keep my charge*, the charge of his sanctuary, of his law and his promise, as the seed of Abraham in which all the families of the earth were to be blessed. This solemn admonition is now concluded with the never-to-be-forgotten word of power: *I am the Lord.*

NOTES.

6. *Near of kin*, שְׁאֵר בְּשָׂרוֹ, οἰκεῖος σαρκός. *The root*, שָׁאַר, signifies *to be over, remain over*. The lexicons give the meaning *to swell* or *grow*, in order to arrive at flesh as the meaning of the noun. But what is over may just as readily come to signify flesh and kindred.

17. *Lewdness*, זִמָּה, plot, evil device; ἀσέβημα, *impiety*; r. *lie in wait, plan evil.*

18. Thus in Ex. xxvi. 3 it is said, five curtains shall be coupled one to another אִשָּׁה אֶל־אֲחֹתָהּ, *woman to her sister*, and so in vs. 5, 6, 17. See also Gen. xiii. 11; xxvi. 31.

21. *Molek*, הַמֹּלֶךְ, the King; ἄρχων in this passage. The article is always prefixed. This is a profanation of the name king, as Baal is of master or lord.

22. *Abomination*, תּוֹעֵבָה, an object of abhorrence; βδέλυγμα.

23. *Pollution*, תֶּבֶל, confusion, unnatural mixture; μυσαρόν.

XIX. ON HOLINESS.

This chapter treats of holiness as the character of the people of God. It states the general principle and enters into a variety of details suggested by the circumstances and immediate prospects of the people. They are in communion with God (1-8), in the communion of saints (9-22), and are about to be in a land of holiness (23-32), and visited

XIX. 1. And the LORD spake unto Moses, saying, 2. Speak unto all the assembly of the sons of Israel, and say unto them, Ye shall be holy; for I the LORD your God am holy. 3. Ye shall fear each man his father and his mother, and keep my

by strangers (33–37). And each of these relations brings out a series of duties peculiar to itself. The communication is made to Moses and concerns the whole assembly of the children of Israel.

1–8. The assembly in communion with God. 2. *All the assembly* are concerned in this duty. *Ye shall be holy.* This is the general principle. The reason follows. *For I the Lord your God am holy.* Two reasons at least wrapped up in this. First, the Author of your being is holy; and the stream should taste of the fountain. Second, the covenant of grace implied in the terms "the Lord your God" forms the most powerful motive to holiness. Other reasons are implied. Reason binds you to be holy; a sanctified reason enforces the obligation by new motives. 3. Two main pillars of holiness are now adduced. These are, fearing parents and keeping the sabbath. They are associated here as they are in the decalogue, where they unite the first and second tables of the law — our duty to God and our duty to man. Reverence to parents is the foundation of all piety and equity. Up to the years of discretion the parent is in the place of God to the child. Reverence for the parents and their faithful lessons will beget reverence for God in the heart. In like manner if we truly respect the parents, we must esteem the children, and these are our brothers and sisters of the whole human family. The sabbath is the appointed season of rest from labor, of leisure for holy converse, of convocation for religious instruction and worship in all our dwelling-places. It is, therefore, man's highest honor and holiest privilege. Its retrospect is God, the Author of man; its prospect is God, the End of man. The sabbath then is the fountain of all social religion, peace, purity, and liberty. In the eyes of him who inspired the legislator it stands on a par with obedience to parents, among the very pinnacles of holiness. And the history of Jew and Christian corroborates the sentence that lays honor to parents and the keeping of the sabbath at the foundation of all morality and religion. The watchword is, as usual,

sabbaths: I am the LORD your God. 4. Turn ye not to idols, and molten gods make not for you: I am the LORD your God. 5. And when ye offer a sacrifice of peace unto the LORD, for your acceptance ye shall offer it. 6. It shall be eaten on the day that ye offer it and on the morrow; and that which is left till the third day shall be burned with fire. 7. And if it be eaten at all on the third day, it is a foul thing; it shall not be accepted. 8. And he that eateth it shall bear his iniquity;

"I am the Lord your God." This infant people need to have this fundamental principle of all piety reiterated, until it is indelibly impressed on the mind. 4. *Turn ye not to idols.* This is the counterpart of the former verse. As the one presented the positive, the other presents the negative side of holiness. To have other objects of worship than the one true God, or to have a false notion of what God really is, forms the sandy foundation of all error, disappointment, and irretrievable ruin. False gods and molten gods refer to the first and second commandments: they are not to be regarded or made. The watchword comes in here again with great point and force. 5-8. *A sacrifice of peace.* As the fear of parents and the keeping of the sabbath are selected as the corner-stone of all morality, so the sacrifice of peace is set forth as the sum and crown of all worship. The burnt-sacrifice presents the great all-sufficient atonement; the oblation is merely an accompaniment or attendant; the sin-sacrifice sets forth expiation, and the trespass-offering propitiation for a sin of inadvertance. The sacrifice of peace presupposes all this. It is the symbol and medium of fellowship with God. It implies that the people have already accepted the atonement; which is the beginning of all practical holiness. Hence it is the only sacrifice suitable to be introduced here. *For your acceptance.* The child of faith and penitence must ever plead the propitiatory sacrifice as the ground of his acceptance. And the peace-offering includes the blood that expiates and the fat that propitiates, as well as the flesh that constitutes the banquet of love and holiness. The particulars here repeated have been already noticed in vii. 16-18 and are inserted here in a new connection for the sake of emphasis. *He hath profaned the holy thing*[8] *of the Lord.*

for he hath profaned the holy thing of the LORD: and that soul shall be cut off from his people.

9. And when ye reap the harvest of your land, thou shalt not wholly reap the corner of thy field nor gather the gleaning of thy harvest. 10. And thy vineyard thou shalt not glean nor gather the leavings of thy vineyard; to the poor and to the stranger thou shalt leave them: I am the LORD your God. 11. Ye shall not steal, nor deny, nor lie one to another. 12. And ye shall not swear by my name to a lie, nor profane the name of thy God: I am the LORD. Thou shalt not oppress thy neighbor nor rob him, nor shalt thou keep the wages of a hireling with thee till the morning. 14. Thou shalt not speak ill of the deaf, nor put a stumbling-block before the blind;

The holy thing may here be preserved in its generality, as it includes both the sanctuary and the sacrifice. By the third day decomposition has set in, and the flesh is no longer fresh or fit for representing that which is holy. The great propitiatory victim did not see corruption, as life returned on the third day.

9–22. Holiness in communion with the saints. 9, 10. Charitable consideration for the poor. *Thou shalt.* From the plural the lawgiver passes to the singular to enforce individual responsibility. *Not wholly reap the corner of thy field.* Thou art not to be exact about the borders of thy field, or the stray stalks that are forgotten, or a grape here and there on thy vine. Leave them to the poor or the stranger. The solemn watchword is then added. The Lord seeth and regardeth. 11, 12. From charity he passes to verity. Among the saints there is to be no stealing, denying a trust, lying, swearing to a lie, or otherwise taking God's name in vain. The reason is decisive: "I am the Lord." The significance of this sentence is never to be forgotten or unheeded. 13, 14. From verity the legislator proceeds to probity of conduct. Overbearing in its leading forms is condemned. Thou shalt not oppress, rob, or keep back wages earned. Speaking ill of the deaf, who cannot hear, and putting a stumbling-block in the way of the blind, who cannot see, are gratuitous and

but thou shalt fear thy God: I am the LORD. 15. Thou shalt not do wrong in judgment, nor respect the person of the poor, nor honor the person of the great: in righteousness shalt thou judge thy neighbors. 16. Thou shalt not go about as a tale-bearer among thy people; nor stand against the blood of thy neighbor: I am the LORD. 17. Thou shalt not hate thy brother in thy heart: thou shalt surely rebuke thy neighbor, and not bear sin for him. 18. Thou shalt not avenge nor

cowardly acts of mischief. The watchword here intimates that there is One who hears and sees, and will requite the wrong-doer and redress the wrong-sufferer. 15, 16. He now advances from the citizen to the magistrate, from private to judicial rectitude. The judge is not to do wrong in judgment, not to lean to the poor man nor to the rich, but to judge his neighbor in righteousness. This is a concise and comprehensive summary of his duty. The tale-bearer and the false witness are here condemned. If the judge on the bench is to be incorruptible, the witness in the box is to be unimpeachable. The watchword here again reminds all of the inevitable day of final account. 17, 18. From outward manifestations of the moral disposition in word and deed the legislator now rises to the disposition itself. Hatred and revenge are here forbidden, and fidelity and love are enjoined. It is to be observed that vengeance, or the vindication of the law, is proper to the magistrate, to whose duties reference is made in verse 15. *Thou shalt surely rebuke thy neighbor.* This is one of the most difficult tasks of friendship. Yet it is a duty of paramount importance and obligation. It is in fact the principle that binds us to preach the gospel of repentance and remission of sins to an ungodly world. It requires both prudence and grace to discharge it with effect. *And not bear sin for him.* If I do not warn my brother when the opportunity offers, I am to be blamed for want of truth and love. *Nor watch for the children,* watch for their halting or for the chance of retaliation. We have no moral standing here; this belongs only to the magistrate who is bound to vindicate the law. *Thou shalt love thy neighbor as thyself.* How simply and unaffectedly, without any blowing of trumpets, comes in this second of the two commandments on which hang all the law

watch for the children of thy people; but thou shalt love thy neighbor as thyself: I am the LORD.

19. My statutes ye shall keep. Thou shalt not let thy cattle gender of diverse kinds; nor shalt thou sow thy field with seed of diverse kinds; nor shall a garment of diverse kinds, linsey-woolsey, come upon thee. 20. And when a man lieth carnally with a woman that is a bondmaid, betrothed to a husband, and not at all redeemed, nor freedom given to her, they shall be scourged; they shall not be put to death, because she was not free. 21. And he shall bring his trespass-offering unto the LORD to the door of the tent of meeting, a ram of trespass. 22. And the priest shall atone for him with

and the prophets. This, as well as each of the preceding groups of two verses each, is followed by the appropriate and authoritative proclamation, "I am the Lord."

19–22. These verses refer to unnatural connections. 19. Three such connections are here forbidden. *Thy cattle gender of diverse kinds*[19]. This is a monstrous confusion. The other two are mainly typical of that distinction of things that morally differ, which must characterize the holy. *Linsey-woolsey*, a web of which the weft and warp differ in kind. 20–22. Another illicit connection is here condemned and its penalty declared. *A bondmaid*, one who is bound to a certain period of service. The position she occupies is described in Ex. xxi. 7–10. *Betrothed*[20] *to a husband*, literally plucked off, separated, not despised or rejected. *Not at all redeemed*, bought back from slavery. *Nor freedom given to her*, bestowed without payment. These were the two ways of being made free. *They shall be scourged*. Correction by scourging, which was limited to forty stripes, shall be administered. This applies to both as we learn from the following words, "they shall not be put to death." The Sept. also makes it plural. *Because she was not free*. Bondage was a disability arising from fault of some kind. The bondage diminished her responsibility, and her degradation lessened his blame. If a man lie with a free damsel that is betrothed, both are to die by stoning (Deut. xxii. 23, 24)

the ram of trespass before the LORD for his sin which he hath done; and he shall be forgiven for the sin which he hath done. ¶ 23. And when ye go into the land and plant every tree for food, then ye shall count the fruit thereof as uncircumcised; three years shall it be uncircumcised to you; it shall not be eaten. 24. And in the fourth year all its fruit shall be holy, a praise-offering to the LORD. 25. And in the fifth year shall ye eat the fruit of it to add unto you its increase: I am the

If not betrothed, he is to marry her (Ex. xxii. 16; Deut. xxii. 29). *His trespass-offering.* The punishment has been inflicted in the way of scourging. As life has been spared, the trespass-offering, which represents compensation or amends, or the righteousness which merits life, is to be made. *Shall atone for him.* While propitiation is in the foreground, expiation must be at least in the background; and hence a complete atonement is made as far as the type is concerned. *For his sin which he had done.* It is the sin that demands expiation, and there is expiation whenever there is blood shed at the altar. *And he shall be forgiven.* The truly penitent who lays his hand on the atoning sacrifice is always forgiven.

23-32. Holiness in regard to the land. 23-25. The fruit-tree. *When ye go into the land*, the land of promise, to which the wanderers in the wilderness looked forward with hope. *And plant.* This regulation refers to young trees. *Count the fruit thereof as uncircumcised*, acknowledge its foreskin on its fruit, regard it as profane and unfit for use. This is a ceremonial arrangement as it stands in the book of the divine law; but it falls in with botanical science, as the fruit for the first three years is inferior, and if the flower-buds be nipped the future fertility will be promoted. *Three years.* This is the number of perfection. *In the fourth year*, it is fit for use. *Holy, a praise-offering*, a holiness of praises. The fruit of this year is to be dedicated to the Lord. *In the fifth year* the fruit is yours to increase your store of provisions. It has been consecrated by the dedication of the fourth year's produce to the Lord. *I am the Lord*, the Author of your being

Lord. 26. Ye shall not eat with the blood; ye shall not take omens nor use charms. 27. Ye shall not round the corner of your head, nor mar the corner of thy chin. 28. Ye shall not make a cutting in your flesh for the dead, nor make a print of branding upon you. 29. Thou shalt not profane thy

and of all the fruits of the land. 26. From the vegetable the transition is to the animal kingdom. *Not eat with the blood.* This phrase recurs in 1 Sam. xiv. 33 in the same sense. It indicates a careless mode of slaughtering the animal, so that the blood is not properly drained off. Three other customs prevalent in the land to which they were going are now prohibited. *Take omens,*[26] observe objects and events, and interpret them as signs of the purpose of heaven or the course of other events. This meaning of the word is confirmed by Gen. xxx. 27; xliv. 5, and 1 Kings xx. 33. *Use charms,* set forms of words whispered or muttered in a mysterious manner, as if they secured the power of a supernatural being to accomplish the end in view. They either invoked the power of other beings than God, or they were unauthorized by him.

27. *Round the corner of your head,* cut off the hair in a circle round the head, leaving a lock on the top. The corner means the border or edge. The round tonsure was practised by the Arabs in honor of their god called 'Οροτάλ, and identified with Bacchus (Herod. iii. 8), and doubtless by their neighbors the Kenaanites. *Mar the corner of thy chin,* cut or shave off the beard. The marring of the beard was of like import. Apart from idolatry, however, the people were not to disfigure themselves by any singularities of the old inhabitants of the land. There is no allusion in this passage to mourning for the dead. 28. *Not make a cutting in your flesh.* This was quite common in the ancient, and especially the Eastern world, and occurs among the Indians still. *For the dead.* For a soul, that is, a dead or departed soul, the body of which has not yet been removed from the sight. This form of mourning was at length used to express any distress of mind. *Nor make a print of branding.* This is the tattooing of the skin, which was customary among the ancients, and is still practised even in Arabia. But the people of God are not in this way

daughter to make her a harlot; that the land be not adulterous, and the land be not full of lewdness. 30. My sabbaths ye shall keep and fear my sanctuary : I am the LORD. 31. Ye shall not turn to familiar spirits, nor seek after wizards to be defiled by them: I am the LORD your God. 32. Thou shalt

to mutilate or mar their faces or persons. 29. *Profane thy daughter.* Fathers were wont, in many ancient nations, to exercise a most cruel and vile power over their daughters.· This was pre-eminently the case in the land of Kenaan. The immoralities of Sodom and Gomorrha were not without their parallel throughout the land. 30. *My sabbaths.* The only effectual counteraction against the vices and impurities of the land was to be found in the sabbath and the sanctuary. The weekly return of the holy convocation, with its lessons and its devotions, was a strong check upon the temptations without, and a powerful means of generating habits of purity and piety. *Fear my sanctuary.* The knowledge and worship of the true God had, since the days of Melkizedec, vanished out of the land. The reestablishment of the worship of God and the introduction of the highly expressive service of the tabernacle were the safeguards of the true worshippers against the idolatrous and corrupt manners of the previous inhabitants. This brief admonition to keep the sabbath and fear the sanctuary, as the salvation of the people amidst surrounding apostasy, is enforced by the solemn sentence, *I am the Lord.* 31. *Not turn to familiar spirits,*[31] ghosts supposed to be called up, by those who have the secret power, to answer questions or perform some other service. They are so far the slaves or *famuli* of their masters, and hence have been called familiar spirits. *Wizards,*[31] persons professing to be acquainted with secret, supernatural, or infernal arts. These were common in the land of Kenaan. *I am the Lord your God.* Unto me, your Deliverer, ye are to turn for help and seek for wisdom. 32. Respect for age and reverence for God needed to be inculcated and fostered in that age and land. It is no wonder that the minute and careful warnings of this chapter are set before the people. The iniquity of the Amorites was now at its height. We have a very dark outline of it in the painful details of

rise up before a hoary head and honor the face of an old man; and thou shalt fear thy God: I am the LORD. §
33. And if a stranger sojourn with thee in the land, ye shall not oppress him. 34. As one born among you shall be unto you the stranger that sojourneth with you, and thou shalt love him as thyself; for ye were strangers in the land of Mizraim: I am the LORD your God. 35. Thou shalt do no wrong in judgment, in wand, in weight, and in measure. 36. A just balance, a just weight, a just ephah, a just hin, shall ye have:

this earnest and urgent admonition. The abhorrence with which the Lord regarded their crimes and vices moves him to warn his people with all faithfulness against the special temptations to which they were about to be exposed when they set their eyes upon the manners and customs of the doomed people.

33–37. *Holiness toward the stranger.* There is here a retrospect, as well as a prospect. They had been treated with great harshness and cruelty by the governors of Egypt, where they were strangers. When they should reach a land of their own, they are to be kind to the stranger, and just to all men. *Ye shall not oppress him.* By your recollection of the wrongs of the oppressed, be ye far from oppression. 34. *As one born among you.* Treat the stranger as the home-born, and love him as thyself. This is a spirit entirely contrary to the principles of conduct which have been often ascribed to the descendants of Israel. The Roman poet affirms that they were taught *non monstrare vias eadem nisi sacra colenti.* This, however, is a pure calumny on the Hebrew legislator. *I am the Lord thy God.* This is the watchword of the covenant of grace. It comes in here to touch the heart. Ye must be like me. The appeal becomes more frequent and fervent as we advance. 35, 36. Even-handed justice is to characterize your whole dealings. *In wand,* in measure of length. *In measure,* of capacity. *A just weight,* a just stone, a term which we retain to this day among our weights. The paramount reason for your integrity is that you are the holy people of the Lord. Hence it is repeated, "I am the Lord your God, who brought you out of the land of Mizraim." The conclusion of the whole is : "And ye shall

I am the LORD your God, who brought you out of the land of Mizraim. 37. And ye shall keep all my statutes and all my judgments, and do them: I am the LORD. ¶

keep all my statutes and all my judgments, and do them. I am the Lord." It must be confessed that this people had ample instruction and abundant warning to wean them from the bad habits of Egypt, and guard them against the worse temptations of Kenaan.

NOTES.

4. *Idols*, אֱלִילִם, vanities, negations; εἴδωλα, *spectres, shadows*.
5. *Holy thing*, קֹדֶשׁ, τὰ ἄγια.
6. 19. *Of diverse kinds*, כִּלְאַיִם, two things of different kinds: ἑτεροζύγῳ, διάφορον, ἐκ δυό ὑφασμένον; r. *shut up, off*. *Linsey-woolsey*, שַׁעַטְנֵז, κίβδηλον, *adulterate*. The word appears to be of Coptic origin.
20. *Betrothed*, נֶחֱרֶפֶת, plucked off, διαπεφυλαγμένη.
26. *Take omens*, תְּנַחֲשׁוּ, οἰωνιεῖσθε. The word occurs only in eleven places. *Use charms*, תְּעוֹנְנוּ, ὀρνιθοσκοπήσεσθε. This is rendered "observe times" by Maimonides. But the word signifying time is of later origin. The Rabbis understand by it fascinating with an evil eye. But this rests on a questionable etymology. The word is found about nine times.
31. *Familiar spirits*, אֹב, ἐγγαστρίμυθοι, *ventriloquists; r. a bottle or bag*. *Wizards*, יִדְּעֹנִים, ἐπαοιδοί; r. *know*.

XX. PENALTIES.

This chapter lays down the penalties for the breach of certain regulations, mostly contained in the two previous chapters. The worship of Molek and disobedience to parents are treated of in one paragraph, (1–9). Sins of incest have sentence pronounced upon them in another (10–21). An earnest admonition followed by a judicial sentence on dealers with infernal powers completes the chapter (22–27). This communication is made to Moses for the people.

XX. 1. And the LORD spake unto Moses, saying, 2. And thou shalt say unto the sons of Israel, Any man of the sons of Israel, or of the strangers that sojourn in Israel, who giveth of his seed to Molek shall be put to death; the people of the land shall stone him with stones. 3. And I will set my face against that man, and will cut him off from among his people; for of his seed he hath given unto Molek to defile my sanctuary and profane my holy name. 4. And if the people of the

1-9. *Worshippers of Molek and dishonorers of parents.* 2. *Of the sons of Israel or of the strangers.* All who dwell in the land come under this law. The strangers are proselytes to the true religion. *Who giveth of his seed to Molek.* This has its explanation in xviii. 21. *Shall be put to death.* The act is a breach of the first commandment, high treason against heaven. It is not merely departing from God but doing homage to a false god. It is, further, an outward act, which could most easily be avoided. It is, moreover, an offence against this state of which God himself is the sovereign. *The people of the land*, the inhabitants of the district to which he belongs. Those who take part in executing the sentence will beware of themselves committing the offence. *Stone him with stones.* This was the ordinary mode of capital punishment among the people of Israel. The criminal was stripped and his hands bound. He was then thrown violently down a steep twice the height of a man by one of the witnesses. If this proved fatal the sentence was executed. But if not, he was turned on his back, and a large stone dashed on his breast by the other witness, and all the people that stood by threw stones on him till he died. This was a very solemn and awful mode of punishment, as all the bystanders took part in it, and thereby signified their condemnation of the crime. 3. *I will set my face against that man.* This is done in the preceding doom. The Judge of all the earth cannot do otherwise than cut off the man who not only denies God, but sets up another as God. *To defile my sanctuary*, by setting up and honoring a rival sanctuary. *And profane my holy name*, by applying it to anything else real or imaginary. The name is the sign of the essence of God. To ascribe it, therefore, to any creature of God or of the human fancy

land do hide their eyes from that man, when he giveth of his seed to Molek, and do not kill him, 5. Then will I set my face against that man and against his family, and will cut him off and all that lust after him, to lust after Molek, from among their people. 6. And the soul that turneth to familiar spirits and to wizards to lust after them, I will even set my face against that soul, and will cut him off from among his people. 7. And ye shall sanctify yourselves and be holy: for I am the LORD your God. 8. And ye shall keep my statutes and do them: I am the LORD who sanctifieth you. 9. When any man curseth his father and his mother, he shall be put to death;

is to profane it. This shows the heinousness of this crime. 4, 5. Those who abet or screen or fail to punish the worshippers of Molek partake of his guilt and are to share in his doom. *And against his family*, who are tainted with his crime. *And all that lust after him*, that follow his adulterous example in lusting after Molek. The extreme barbarity as well as the abject impurity of this form of idolatry rendered it peculiarly offensive. 6. Familiar spirits and wizards have been already noticed in xix. 31. Those who commit spiritual fornication with them are to be similarly punished. 7. *And ye shall sanctify yourselves.* Quickened into a new spiritual life they are able, as well as bound, to sanctify themselves in practice and be holy in character. Many of the people were still doubtless in a carnal state. But they had the outward call of mercy and the outward privilege of the covenant; and if they were living insensible to these advantages and opportunities, it was at their own peril. *For I am the Lord your God*, your Deliverer and Quickener as well as your Creator and Preserver. Such he really is to the truly believing portion of the people. 8. The natural consequence of sanctification is a holy life, a spontaneous obedience. *Keep my statutes.* Ye shall give heed to my written ordinances. *And do them*, not merely hear, attend, and approve, but obey. *Who sanctifieth you*, the Lord, who quickens you unto a new life of holiness and happiness, has the right to your absolute obedience. 9. Cursing, dishonoring, disobeying father and

he hath cursed his father and his mother; his blood shall be upon him. 10. And he that committeth adultery with a man's wife, that committeth adultery with his neighbor's wife, the adulterer and the the adulteress shall be put to death. 11. And he that lieth with his father's wife hath uncovered his father's nakedness; they shall both be put to death; their blood shall be upon them. 12. And if a man lie with his daughter-in-law, they shall both be put to death; they have wrought pollution: their blood shall be upon them. 13. And if a man lie with a male as one lieth with a woman, they have both committed an abomination; they shall be put to death; their blood shall be upon them. 14. And if a man take a wife and her mother, it is lewdness; they shall burn with fire him and them; and

mother is a crime nigh unto ungodliness. Hence it stands next our duty to God in the ten commandments and is here subjoined to a warning against idolatry. The condemnation of disobedience to parents comes in also appropriately after the injunction to be holy. The penalty is death. His blood shall be upon his own head.

10–21. Penalties laid upon various kinds of incest. 10. Adultery with another man's wife (xviii. 20). *That committeth adultery with a neighbor's wife.* The repetition of the phrase marks the enormity of the offence. They are both to be put to death in the customary way, that is, by stoning. 11. Adultery with a father's wife (xviii. 7, 8). This is a more revolting form of the generic crime. The penalty is the same. 12. Adultery with a daughter-in-law (xviii. 15). This is declared to be pollution, an unholy mixture or confusion. 13. Sodomy is the crime here condemned (xviii. 22). It is termed an abomination, a thing to be regarded with abhorrence, and to be punished with death. 14. To take a woman and her mother (xviii. 17) is an act of lewdness, a vile and wicked deed. The partners in it are to be burned with fire. It appears from Josh. vii. 15–25, that the burning followed stoning to death. We find another case in which this punishment was inflicted, in the following chapter.

there shall be no lewdness among you. 15. And the man that shall lie with a beast shall be put to death; and the beast ye shall kill. 16. And if a woman approach to any beast to copulate with it, thou shalt kill both the woman and the beast; they shall be put to death; their blood shall be upon them. 17. And if a man take his sister, his father's daughter or his mother's daughter, and see her nakedness, and she see his nakedness, it is shame; and they shall be cut off in the sight of their people: his sister's nakedness he hath uncovered; he shall bear his iniquity. 18. And if a man lie with a sick woman and uncover her nakedness, he hath made bare her fountain and she hath uncovered the fountain of blood, and they shall both be cut off from among their people. 19. And the nakedness of thy mother's sister or of thy father's sister thou shalt not uncover; for he uncovereth his near kin; they

15. Carnal connection with a beast (xviii. 23). The perpetrator of this horrid crime is to be put to death, and the beast to be killed. 16. The other form of this unnatural crime (xviii. 23) is to be punished in the same way. 17. Incest with a sister (xviii. 9, 11). This is called shame or infamous lust. Both shall be cut off from their people by stoning. 18. Lying with a woman in her monthly sickness (xviii. 19) is regarded as a crime deserving of the penalty of death. For all the forms of unnatural lust above enumerated the penalty of death is required, and for one the additional dishonor of being burned after death.

19. We now come to a series of forbidden connections for which the penalty is not defined. It is merely stated that they shall bear their iniquity or sin, and in two of the cases that they shall be or die heirless. The first is carnal connection with an aunt (xviii. 12, 13). Such a marriage is condemned. This is a singular instance of impartiality or the total absence of personal bias in the legislator, as he was the son of Amram who married his aunt. It is merely said of those who became so connected that they should bear their iniquity. But in what way they were to be punished we are not informed, and

PENALTIES.

shall bear their iniquity. 20. And if a man lie with his wife's uncle he hath uncovered his uncle's nakedness; their sin they shall bear; they shall die heirless. 21. And if a man take his brother's wife, it is uncleanness; he hath uncovered his brother's nakedness; they shall be heirless.

22. And ye shall keep all my statutes and all my judgments and do them; and the land, whither I bring you to dwell in it, shall not spue you out. 23. And ye shall not walk in the

cannot decide. 20. Here a matrimonial connection with an uncle's wife is forbidden (xviii. 14). The parties to it shall bear their sin. They shall die heirless. This does not mean that they shall be put to death, which is otherwise expressed in the previous verses; nor that they shall be destitute of offspring by the visitation of heaven; but that their offspring, if any, shall not be counted to them, called by their name, or admitted as their heirs. The meaning heirless is corroborated by Gen. xv. 2 and Jer. xxii. 30. 21. To take a brother's wife is termed uncleanness. Those who form this forbidden connection shall be heirless. Their children, if they have any, shall be heirs to others, and they themselves shall be without heirs. Their name would thus perish out of Israel, which was accounted a disgrace and a calamity. Even in the excepted case of a brother dying childless the children of the widow to the surviving brother would be heirs, not to him, but to his deceased brother. The only cases in chap. xviii. left unnoticed here are those of marriage with a granddaughter and of marriage with a second wife while the former one was still alive. The granddaughter may be reasonably included under the daughter. In this way the only forbidden connection to which no penalty is expressly annexed is that with more than one wife at the same time. Considerable checks, however, were put upon the practice by the law which secured all their rights to the first wife and her offspring.

22–31. A closing admonition founded on the preceding legislation. 22. This contains an injunction often repeated (xviii. 4, 26; xix. 9, 37; xx. 7). The warning is added that the land may spue them out if disobedient, as it did their predecessors. 23. The corresponding prohibition now follows. *The statutes* of the former inhabitants are

LEVITICUS XX. 23-27. 251

statutes of the nations which I cast out before you; for they have done all these things, and I loathed them. 24. And I said unto you, Ye shall possess their ground, and I will give it unto you to possess it, a land flowing with milk and honey: I am the LORD your God who have separated you from the nations. 25. And ye shall separate between the clean beast and the unclean, and between the unclean fowl and the clean; and ye shall not contaminate your souls with beast or with fowl or with anything that creepeth on the ground, which I

their evil customs, for which they were in the act of being cast out, because their iniquity was now full. *They have done all these things,* which are denounced in the preceding chapters. When we cast a glance over the black catalogue, it is no wonder that the perpetrators excited the abhorrence and indignation of the High and Holy One. 24. *Ye shall possess,* acquire by conquest, or gain possession of their soil. The word denotes grasping or violent seizing. *I will give it unto you to possess it.* I give you the authority and the ability to obtain possession of it. *A land flowing with milk and honey,* and therefore abounding in the rich pastures and fragrant flowers which afford nourishment for cattle and bees. The watchword of their covenant with God is now introduced with the addition " who have separated you from the nations." God had twice made known his mercy and proclaimed his invitations and warnings to the whole human family, first to Adam and then to Noah, and twice they had forsaken him and despised his mercy. Now he has done a new thing. He has chosen a peculiar people and separated them from all the nations, to be unto him a royal priesthood and a holy nation, bearing testimony in the midst of the nations to his name and grace. What an inestimable honor, what a paramount obligation to be or belong to such a people. 25. *And ye shall separate.* As I have separated you from all nations, you are to separate the clean from the unclean in all things according to my word. *Ye shall not contaminate your souls,* your sensuous, susceptible part, which is the inlet of all temptations and from which, therefore, comes the danger of all sin. *Which I have separated* for you. This raises the distinction above all mere·will-

have separated for you as unclean. 26. And ye shall be holy unto me, for I the Lord am holy: and I separated you from the nations to be mine. 27. And the man or woman that shall have a familiar spirit or be a wizard shall be put to death; they shall stone them with stones; their blood shall be upon them. 31 ¶ ¶ ¶

worship and puts it upon the ground of compliance with a divine command, a command which contains within it a deep spiritual significance. 26. The precept of holiness is now repeated as the conclusion of the whole matter. *Separated you from the nations to be mine.* To be his is the very essence of the great honor of being separate. It touches the heart and awakens the affections. 27. Nothing could be more adverse to such lofty devotedness to God, than seeking after familiar spirits or the infernal arts of the wizard (xix. 31). Such were very prevalent in the country to which they were advancing. The stern sentence is that they should be put to death by stoning, and their blood will be upon their own head. These emphatic and affectionate lessons to the chosen people were not in vain. They did not, indeed, extirpate evil from the hearts of all. But they effected a mighty change in the moral nature of the great bulk of the nation. They told also on the successive generations of Israel and produced beautiful and attractive examples of piety towards God and goodwill to men. And they are telling to this day on a constantly increasing portion of the race of man.

This completes the series of regulations applying chiefly to the civil life of the Israelites in the country to which he was going. With the exception of some reference to the camp in chap. xvii., they all look forward to the land of the nations whom they were to dispossess on account of their abounding iniquity. These chapters, we see, are arranged on a regular plan. Purity in food, purity in wedlock, holiness in converse with God and man follow in orderly succession. To these chapters is added a fourth embodying the sanctions of the enactments which they contain. The whole has pointed reference to the vice and immorality of the country to which they were approaching, and forms a seasonable and faithful warning to the people on the eve of coming into contact with a nation that had filled up the measure of its iniquity

SECTION V. — RULES CONCERNING RELIGIOUS MATTERS.

XXI. CONCERNING THE PRIESTS.

XXI. 1. And the Lord said unto Moses, Say unto the priests, Aaron's sons, Say thus unto them, none shall be defiled for the dead among his people. 2. But for his kin that is

This section consists of four chapters relating to religions matters. They follow a plain and natural order, treating of the priests, the offerings, the days, and the dwelling of God. They are preparatory, like the preceding four, for the settled life of the people when they have entered into possession of the land of promise. The present chapter contains two brief communications addressed to Moses for Aaron and his sons. The first refers to the sanctity to be maintained by the priests in their personal relations to others, and consists of two parts; the first applying to the priests in general (1–9); the second to the high-priest in particular (10–15). The second communication refers to the personal qualities of the priests (16–24).

1–9. Regulations guarding the sanctity of the priests in their intercourse with others. 1–6. These verses refer to the avoidance in certain cases of defilement by a dead body. 1. *No one*, priest. *Defiled for the dead*, for a soul departed (xix. 28), whose body defiled not only him who touched it, but the tent in which it lay (Num. xix. 11, 14). *Among his people*, in the circle of his family or neighborhood. The ties of kindred and the civilities of social life call for services in the case of a death which often involve ceremonial uncleanness. But the priests, on account of their office, are to be excused from these. 2. Six cases are expressly excepted, in which he may take part in the duties owing to the dead. His wife is added

near unto him, for his mother and for his father and for his son and for his daughter and for his brother: 3. And for his sister, the maiden that is near unto him, who hath not a husband, for her he may be defiled. 4. A master among his people he shall not be defiled, to profane himself. 5. They shall not make baldness upon their head, and the corner of their chin they shall not shave off, nor make any cut in their flesh. 6. They shall be holy unto their God, and not profane the name of their God; for the fire-offering of the LORD, the

by some (Keil) as a seventh, on the ground that she is his own flesh (Gen. ii. 24), and is therefore included in himself, and nearer than all other relatives. 3. An unmarried sister who still dwells with her father is included. But when married and away she belongs to another home and kin. 4. *A master among his people*, the head of a house, and there surrounded by servants, relatives, and neighbors, who would have a natural claim on his kind attentions. But, being a priest, he is to refrain from all unnecessary contact with the dead, lest by incurring defilement he should profane himself, and so be rendered unfit for the discharge of his sacred duties. This appears to be the obvious meaning of this much-contested sentence. It is that given by Willet. 5. Disfigurement of the person on account of the dead is forbidden to the priests. Three kinds of it are mentioned. *Baldness upon their head.* Making a bald place on the front of the head between the eyes is again mentioned in Deut. xiv. 1. *The corner of the chin.* Shaving the corner of the chin and making cuts in the flesh have already been forbidden to all Israelites (xix. 27 f.). 6. *They shall be holy.* The great principle is now enunciated that the priests shall be holy unto their God. They could not otherwise be fit to present the symbols representing the great atonement. They could not be suitable types of the true High-Priest between God and man. *And not profane the name of their God.* The essence of God and all that is connected with his will and worship must be kept from profanity. *The fire-offerings.* These represent propitiation. Everything burnt on the altar is a sweet smell, a thing acceptable. *The*

bread of their God, they offer, and they shall be holy. 7. They shall not take a wife that is a harlot or profane, nor shall they take a woman put away from her husband; for he is holy unto his God. 8. And thou shalt sanctify him; for he offereth the bread of thy God: he shall be holy unto thee: for I the LORD who sanctify you am holy. 9. And the daughter of a priest, when she profaneth herself to be a harlot, she profaneth her father; she shall be burned with fire. §

10. And the high-priest among his brethren, upon whose head the anointing oil was poured, and whose hand was filled

bread of God, a parallel phrase, importing the same thing. 7–9. This passage refers to purity in the family relations. A priest is not to marry a harlot, a profane or dishonored woman, or a divorced woman. He is therefore restricted to a virgin or a widow of irreproachable character from any of the tribes of Israel (xxii. 12). He is holy unto his God, and must therefore form a holy affinity. 8. *Thou shalt sanctify him.* This is addressed to the governing power in sacred things for the time being. *He offereth the bread of thy God.* This is a matter of vital consequence to the Israelite. The priest was his present mediator with God. He must be kept pure. Hence this admonition seems to be addressed to the magistrate in this theocratic state, who was to protect the priest in all the rights of his office, and take order that due diligence was shown in the discharge of its duties. *He shall be holy unto thee.* Thou shalt see to it that he is holy, so far as it lies in thy power to further this end. *I the Lord who sanctify you.* This state is a holy nation, a kingdom, indeed, of priests. It is bound to take measures that its priesthood be holy. 9. The daughter of a priest, if she play the harlot, is especially guilty. She profanes her father, as well as herself. She brings dishonor and reproach upon him and his office. She is to be burned with fire, that is, put to death by stoning, and the body then burned.

10–15. The sanctity of the high-priest. 10–12. These verses guard against defilement by the dead. 10. The high-priest is here distinguished by two properties. The anointing oil was poured upon

CONCERNING THE PRIESTS.

to put on the garments, shall not bare his head nor rend his garments; 11. Nor shall he go in to any dead body; for his father or for his mother he shall not defile himself. 12. Nor shall he go out of the sanctuary nor profane the sanctuary of his God; for the consecration of the anointing oil of his God is upon him: I am the LORD. 13. And he shall take a wife in her virginity. 14. A widow and a divorced woman and a profane one and a harlot, these he shall not take; but a virgin of his people shall he take to wife. 15. And he shall not pro-

his head (viii. 12), pointing to his moral perfection. *Whose hand was filled to put on the garments.* Two qualities are here curiously combined into one. The filling of the hands (viii. 22–28) was the ordination of the high-priest to his office. He was thereby entitled to put on the garments of his royal priesthood. This prophetic and regal priest was not to bare his head nor rend his garments in mourning for the dead (x. 6). These acts would be inconsistent with the holiness of his character, as well as with the very purport of his office, which was to abolish death, and make an end of sin by an all-sufficient propitiation and an everlasting righteousness. 11. He shall not defile himself, even for his father or his mother. The transcendent interests of salvation, which depend on his purity and perfection, are not to be endangered or abandoned for the outward forms of an earthly affliction. 12. He shall not leave his sacred duties in the sanctuary, nor profane it by incurring any defilement which would mar their efficacy or acceptance. *The consecration*[12] *of the anointing oil.* He is consecrated unto God, a holy mediator. To desecrate him is to defeat the mediation, and leave the breach between God and man still unrepaired. 13–15. This paragraph relates to sanctity in entering the married state. There is no greater proof that marriage was regarded as holy than the permission extended to the high-priest to marry. 13. He shall marry a virgin. 14. Not a widow, a divorced, or a profane woman, nor a harlot, but a virgin of his own people, of any of the tribes of Israel (xxii. 12). 15. He shall not profane his seed by contracting an unsuitable marriage, or otherwise.

fane his seed among his people; for I the LORD do sanctify him. §

16. And the LORD spake unto Moses, saying, 17. Speak unto Aaron, saying, No man of thy seed in their generations that hath any blemish shall draw near to offer the bread of his God. 18. For no man that hath a blemish shall draw near, blind or lame or flat-nosed or long-eared. 19. Or a man that hath a broken foot or a broken hand. 20. Or hump-backed or wasted or pearl-eyed or scurvy or scabby or broken-stoned. 21. No man having a blemish of the seed of Aaron the priest

I the Lord do sanctify him. He owes his high and holy position to me. He owes himself in the highest possible relations to me.

16–24. Personal defects that excluded from the priestly office. 16. This is a distinct communication. 17. *That hath any blemish.* If the victim was to be perfect, so must the priest be. In the great High-Priest, victim and priest are one, and must be holy, harmless and undefiled. *Draw near.*[17] Only the holy can approach the holy. The victim is offered, made to draw near. The priest draws near. The great High-Priest being both priest and victim, is both active and passive in his work of mediation. *To offer the bread.* The bread is the food, that which is burned on the altar or eaten by the priests of the offerings, whether animal or vegetable. It represents the perfect righteousness which is acceptable to God, and effects propitiation as distinct from expiation. Hence it comes in here appropriately. 18–20. The blemishes are now enumerated. *Blind or lame.* About these there is no dispute. They are manifest disqualifications. *Flat-nosed or long-eared.*[18] These are by some made more general; having any member too small or too great. These are disfigurements. *A broken foot or a broken hand.* These render a man unfit for service. *Hump-backed or wasted.*[20] The latter is contrasted with the former, and is understood to refer to extreme thinness or leanness of flesh or limb. *Pearl-eyed,*[20] having a speck or stain in the eye. *Scurvy or scabby.* These terms denote those who are affected with cutaneous diseases. 21. None of these is to take part in the presentation of the fire-offerings of the Lord. The fire-offerings, like the bread, denote that which

shall come nigh to offer the fire-offerings of the LORD; he hath a blemish; he shall not draw nigh to offer the bread of his God. 22. He shall eat the bread of his God, of the most holy and of the holy. 23. Only unto the veil he shall not go, nor draw nigh unto the altar; for he hath a blemish; and he shall not profane my holy things; for I the LORD do sanctify them. 24. And Moses spake to Aaron and to his sons and to all the sons of Israel. ¶

propitiates. They constitute "a sweet smell" unto the Lord. 22. But he is permitted to eat of the most holy and the holy parts of the offerings which are assigned of the Lord to his priests. 23. *Unto the veil,* however, or unto the altar he shall not go, because he has a blemish. A priest with a blemish would profane the holy things and places, the veil and the altar. 24. Moses communicated these regulations to the priests and the people.

The priests are thus guarded from defilement by the dead, from dishonor by an unworthy affinity, and from unfitness by personal defect. These qualifications are all proper in themselves, and especially becoming in those who are to bear the vessels of the Lord, who are to be distinguished by an unblemished moral character. They point, however, to the spiritual characteristics of holiness, patience and activity, which are to distinguish the true servant of God and Redeemer of his people. Absolute holiness must be found in him who is to mediate with the Holy One for the unholy. Patience is an indispensable quality of him who is to submit to die for sinners, to suffer the loss of all things, endure the contradiction of sinners, and be at length the victim for the sins of others. Activity is also a needful quality in him who is to volunteer the performance of all the duties of a kinsman and of a righteousness which earns the blessings of eternal life.

NOTES.

12. *Consecration,* נֵזֶר, separation, ἅγιον; r. *separate.*
17. *Draw near,* יִקְרַב; *offer, bring near,* יַקְרִיב; *offering,* קָרְבָּן.
18. *Flat-nosed,* חָרֻם, contracted, κολοβόριν; r. *shut in, contract, withhold from common use. Long-eared,* שָׂרוּעַ, stretched, ὠτότμητος.
20. *Hump-backed,* גִּבֵּן, bent, bowed, κυρτός. *Wasted,* דַּק, ἔφηλος. *Pearl-eyed,* תְּבַלֻּל בְּעֵינוֹ, stained in his eye, πτίλλος τοὺς ὀφθαλμούς.

XXII. CONCERNING THE OFFERINGS.

XXII. 1. And the LORD spake unto Moses, saying, 2. Speak unto Aaron and to his sons, and they shall separate themselves from the holy things of the sons of Israel, and not profane my holy name in what they hallow unto me: I am the LORD. 3. Say unto them, Any man of all your seed in your generations that draweth nigh to the holy things which the sons of Israel hallow unto the LORD, having his uncleanness upon him, that soul shall be cut off from before me: I am the LORD.

This chapter is parallel to the former. As that refers to the priest, so this to the offering. It consists of three communications made to Moses for Aaron and his sons, and the last two for the people also. The first determines, on the one hand, who of the priests are not to touch the offerings (1–9), and, on the other hand, who besides the priests are to partake of them (10–16). The second determines the qualities of the victims suitable for offering (17–25). The third lays down certain conditions to be observed even with suitable victims (26–33).

1–9. Who of the priests are not to touch the holy things of the Lord. 2. *They shall separate themselves*, when they labor under any disability, such as is afterwards described. *From the holy things*, those parts of the sacrifice which were reserved from the fire for the priests (Num. xviii. 11–19, 26–29). *And not profane my holy name.* The holy things consecrated to the Lord by the sons of Israel remained truly and always his. The consuming of certain parts of them by his priests was only one of the ways in which he expressed his acceptance. The eating of them by the priests was therefore a holy and solemn act, in which the Lord accepted the sacrifice of his people and the people themselves. Hence to touch them with unclean hands was to profane the name of the Lord. *I am the Lord.* This is appended as the seal and sanction of the rule. 3. The unclean, therefore, are to stand aloof from the holy food, on pain of excommunication. This

4. No man of the seed of Aaron that is leprous or hath a flux shall eat of the holy things until he be clean; and he that toucheth anything unclean by the dead, or a man whose seed goeth from him, 5. Or he that toucheth any creeper for which he is unclean, or a man for whom he is unclean after all his uncleanness. 6. The soul that toucheth any such shall be unclean until the even; and he shall not eat of the holy things, but shall wash his flesh in water. 7. And the sun shall set, and he shall be clean; and then he shall eat of the holy things; for it is his food. 8. The dead and the torn he shall not eat to be defiled thereby: I am the LORD. 9. And they shall keep my charge, and shall not bear sin for it and die by it, when they profane it: I am the LORD who sanctify you.

10. And no stranger shall eat of the holy thing: a sojourner

is followed as usual by the sign and seal of the Lord. 4. He that is a leper or has an issue is not to partake of the holy things till he be clean, and has gone through the process described in several parts of chapters xiii., xiv., and xv. 4–6. He that touches anything unclean by the dead (xix. 28) or whose seed flows from him (xv. 16, 18), or who touches a reptile or another man that is unclean in any way, shall be unclean until the evening. 7. Having washed his flesh in water he shall be clean when the sun is down, and may eat. 8. The prohibition concerning the dead and the torn (xvii. 15, 16), applies with peculiar emphasis to the priests. 9. *Keep my charge.* This is an old and venerable phrase first addressed to Abraham (Gen. xxvi. 5), then to Aaron and his sons (viii. 35), then to the Levites (Num. iii. 7), and lastly to all Israel as a kingdom of priests (Num. ix. 19). *And shall not bear sin for it,* the holy thing, which would otherwise have been defiled and desecrated. *And die by it.* If the propitiation be made void, the power of death returns, because its right revives against the transgressor. The significant sentence is then added, "I am the Lord who sanctify you."

10–16. Who besides the priests are to partake of the holy things. 10. *No stranger.* A stranger here is one who does not belong to the

with the priest and a hireling shall not eat of the holy thing. 11. And when the priest acquires a soul, the purchase of his money, he shall eat of it; and he that is born in his house; they shall eat of his food. 12. And when the priest's daughter is married to a stranger she may not eat of the holy offering. 13. But when the priest's daughter is a widow or divorced and hath no child, and hath returned to her father's house as in her youth, she shall eat of her father's bread; but no stranger shall eat of it. 14. And when a man eateth of the holy thing in

priestly family. *A sojourner* is not a member of the family; neither is a *hireling*, who merely comes to labor day by day. 11. *A soul the purchase of his money.* Serfdom existed among the Israelites. A man became a serf by the sentence of the judge, by the chance of war, or by the act of his own will. The last mode indicates that serfdom in Israel was something very different from Gentile or modern slavery. Its limitations are laid down in Ex. xxi. 2–11, to the remarks on which we refer, and in Lev. xxv. 10, 39–55. A serf might be transferred from one master to another by purchase. *He shall eat of it.* Hence we find that the serf is counted a member of the priest's family and may partake of the holy fare. The same rule applies to the passover (Ex. xii. 44). *He that is born in his house.* This includes, and indeed specially refers to, the offspring of the serf, 12, 13. *The priest's daughter*, if unmarried, belongs to the priest's family by right of birth, and partakes of his fare; but when married to a stranger she belongs to a family not connected with the priesthood, and therefore is not entitled to partake of the holy things. We learn from xxi. 7, 14 and from the present verse that the priests were permitted to marry a wife out of any of the tribes of Israel, and that a priest's daughter might be married to an Israelite of any tribe. If, however, she returns to her father's house a childless widow, she becomes again a member of his family. If she have children it is to be understood that she has still a home and a possession to which her children are heirs. *But no stranger shall eat of it.* After making the needful exceptions all others are excluded. 14. The layman that eats of the

error, then he shall add a fifth of it to it, and give the holy thing to the priest. 15. And they shall not profane the holy things of the sons of Israel, which they heave up unto the LORD; 16. Nor bring upon them the iniquity of trespass when they eat their holy things: for I am the LORD who sanctify them. ¶ 17. And the LORD spake unto Moses, saying, 18. Speak unto Aaron and to his sons and unto all the sons of Israel,

holy food in error is simply to restore an equivalent for the holy thing with the addition of a fifth part to it. 15. *Not profane the holy things of the sons of Israel.* They were in God's stead in this act. On his part they accepted the offering and the offerer in the act of partaking the former. This solemn and significant act was not to be rendered null and void by any unworthy or unwarranted partaker. *Which they heave up.* They were not laid on the altar and burnt with fire like the flesh of the whole-sacrifice, the fat of the peace-offering, or the memorial of the oblation, but lifted up in token of being dedicated to the Lord, and given to the priests to be eaten. This is called heaving. 16. *Nor bring upon them.* This is a continuation of the preceding verse. Unworthy or inadmissible partakers brought upon the people the *iniquity of trespass* by their partaking. Trespass is righteousness unperformed. The trespass-offering represents this righteousness performed by the substitute. Now such partakers nullified the propitiation, which the proper partakers would have accepted on the part of God. They left the people, therefore, still under the debt of righteousness, which the propitiation was to have discharged. They were bound to make amends for this fatal consequence of their unlawful partaking. The mode of making redress appears to be indicated in vs. 14. The equivalent of the holy thing with an added fifth was to be presented. It is to be presumed that the evil consequence which their act was calculated to produce would fall not on the worshipper, but on the intruder. The inadvertent trespasser is therefore to make amends.

17–25. The qualities of victims suitable for offering. This is the second commmunication of this chapter. 18–20. *And unto all the sons of Israel.* It concerns not only Aaron and his sons, but all the people

and say unto them, If any man of the house of Israel or of the strangers in Israel will bring his offering, for all their vows and for all their gifts which they offer unto the LORD for a burnt-sacrifice, 19. For your acceptance it shall be a perfect male of the herd, of the sheep or of the goats. 20. Any that hath a blemish ye shall not offer; for it shall not be accepted for you. 21. And when a man offers a sacrifice of peace unto the LORD, to set apart a vow, or for a gift, of the cattle or of the sheep, it shall be perfect for acceptance; no blemish shall be in it. 22. Blind or broken or maimed or ulcerous or scurvy

A stranger in Israel, as well as an Israelite, may offer a burnt-sacrifice. The stranger in Israel has either submitted to circumcision, and so has been incorporated into the holy nation as a proselyte of righteousness, or merely acknowledges the true God without being circumcised, in which case he was called a proselyte of the gate. *For all their vows and for all their gifts.* Vows and gifts are introduced under the head of sacrifices of peace in vii. 16. The Sept. renders the words "in all their confession and in all their choice,"[18] which brings the whole into harmony with the closing word "for a burnt-sacrifice." The Rabbis, on the other hand, affirm that Gentiles offering a peace-sacrifice burnt the whole on the altar as a whole or burnt-sacrifice. But this does not meet the case of the son of Israel, nor of the proselyte of righteousness. The real explanation seems to be this: that a vow or gift may be either a sacrifice of peace or a whole burnt-sacrifice, according to the will of the worshipper. In vii. 16 the sacrifice of peace was spoken of; in this verse the burnt-sacrifice is meant and expressed. *For your acceptance*, in order that you and your sacrifice may be accepted. *A perfect male.* A male, because it was a burnt-sacrifice (i. 3). Perfect, because it is to propitiate, or to represent the Holy One who is to propitiate. A perfect male or female was allowed for a peace-offering (iii. 1). An imperfect victim will not in any case be accepted as sacrifice. 21. *A sacrifice of peace*, under which is also included a vow or a gift, must be perfect in order to be accepted. *To set apart*, separate, devote. 22. The blemishes are now enumerated. *Broken* in limb. *Ulcerous*,[22] having an abcess or running sore. *Nor*

or scabby, ye shall not offer these unto the LORD, nor present a fire-offering of them upon the altar unto the LORD. 23. And a bullock or a lamb that hath anything too large or too small, thou mayest make a gift of it, but for a vow it shall not be accepted. 24. And the bruised or crushed or torn or cut ye shall not offer unto the LORD; nor in your land shall ye make such. 25. Nor from the hand of a stranger shall ye offer the bread of your God of any of these; for their corruption in them is a blemish in them; they shall not be accepted for you. §

26. And the LORD spake unto Moses, saying, 27. When an ox, a sheep, or a goat is brought forth it shall be seven days under its dam; and from the eighth day and onwards it shall be accepted for an offering by fire unto the LORD. 28. And

present a fire-offering. This is specially mentioned, because the part burned on the altar represents propitiation by a perfect righteousness. 23. An animal having any member too large or too small may serve for a gift, but not for the payment of a vow, inasmuch as the latter implied a perfect victim. 24. The bruised[24] or crushed[24] or torn[24] or cut[24] are animals castrated in some one of four different modes practised in ancient times. The present passage forbids not only the offering of victims so treated, but also the practice itself. 25. *Nor from the hand of a stranger.* As from no Israelite, so from no stranger would such be accepted as sacrifices. *The bread of your God.* Anything burned on the altar or reserved from it to be eaten by the priests of God came under this head (iii. 11; xxi. 21, 22). It must be derived from a perfect victim to represent that which is acceptable to God, which in moral things is perfect righteousness. *Their corruption.* Any one of the ten or twelve defects here mentioned is a corruption, and therefore a blemish, rendering them unworthy of acceptance.

26–33. Conditions to be observed in the case of an unblemished victim. This is the third communication. 27. First, its age. *Seven days under its dam.* The number here indicates perfection in point of days. *From the eighth day and onwards* it is acceptable. It has

an ox or sheep, it and its young ye shall not slay in one day. 29. And when ye make a sacrifice of praise unto the LORD, ye shall sacrifice it for your acceptance. 30. In that day it shall be eaten; ye shall not leave of it until the morning: I am the LORD. 31. And ye shall keep my commandments and do them: I am the LORD. 32. And ye shall not profane my holy name; but I will be hallowed among the sons of Israel: I am the LORD who hallow you. 33. Who brought you out of the land of Mizraim to be your God: I am the LORD. ¶

got a hold of life, and may be viewed apart from the dam. 28. Secondly, the dam and the young are not to be slain in one day. Even the natural affection of a brute was not to be wounded. Much less is our own sense of propriety and good feeling to be blunted. This was a striking lesson in much higher things. It is in keeping with the precept in Ex. xxiii. 19. 29, 30. Thirdly, the flesh of the sacrifice of thanksgiving was to be eaten on the same day on which it was offered (vii. 15). This comes up here again in a new association for the sake of impression. Thanksgiving and parsimony do not go well together. To reserve any part of a thank-offering when there may be hungry mouths ready to partake of it would savor more of parsimony than praise. The word of authority and power here comes in with great effect, "I am the Lord." 31. *Keep my commandments.* The principle of obedience, as distinct from the intrinsic obligation of a moral law, is here brought into view. 32, 33. Ye are to hallow me in all your offerings and proceedings. And ye have the most powerful motives as well as the most cheering encouragements to aim at this object. "I am the Lord," the God of covenant and of salvation. This is an all-powerful motive. " Who brought you out of the land of Mizraim to be your God." Here is another ovewhelming motive. I have delivered you from bondage; I am your God. " Who hallow you." Here is both motive and encouragement; encouragement, because he who is hallowed of God is thereby endowed with a new life and enabled to glorify God in all things. The chapter is closed with the animating watchword, " I am the Lord."

NOTES.

18. Κατὰ πᾶσαν ὁμολογίαν αὐτῶν ἢ κατὰ πᾶσαν αἵρεσιν αὐτῶν.

22. *Ulcerous,* יַבֶּלֶת, flowing out; μυρμηκιῶντα, *warty.*

24. *Bruised,* מָעוּךְ, pressed; θλαδίας. *Crushed,* כָּתוּת, beaten in pieces; ἐκτεθλιμμένος. *Torn,* נָתוּק, rent; ἐκτομίας. *Cut,* כָּרוּת ; ἀπεσπασμένος.

25. *Corruption,* מָשְׁחָת, marring; φθάρματα. שָׁחַת, *corrupt.*

XXIII. CONCERNING SET DAYS.

There are in this chapter five communications to Moses for the children of Israel in general. The first refers to the weekly sabbath and the passover (1–8); the second to the wave-sheaf and the feast of weeks (9–22); the third to the new moon of the seventh month (23–25); the fourth to the day of atonement (26–32); and the fifth to the feast of tabernacles (33–44). It is an enlargement of the second half of the section on set times in Ex. xxiii. 10–19. It is a chapter of much interest in many respects.

1–8. This communication consists of an introduction (1, 2), and two parts relating to the weekly sabbath (3), and the passover (4–8). First, the introduction. 2. *The set times.*² The original word means a time or place appointed for meeting. *Holy convocations.* These are meetings called together for holy or religious ends. Their purpose is defined by the epithet holy. There were other convocations for secular purposes. *These are my set times.* After giving the first place to the prominent object, the sentence is formed independently and completely. These set times have a sacred purpose and a divine authority. 3. The weekly sabbath. This is here placed at the head of the Lord's set times. *Six days shall work be done.* This is indeed a permission to labor; but it is also an injunction. The proper part of man with his present nature and in his present condition is rational employment. The effect of the fall on him and his surroundings has been to harden this native activity of purpose and endeavor into labor and toil. *But on the seventh day.* The number seven here comes into play. There is, undoubtedly, in the physical constitution of man

XXIII. 1. And the LORD spake unto Moses, saying, 2. Speak unto the sons of Israel and say unto them: The set times of the LORD, which ye shall proclaim to be holy convocations, these are my set times. 3. Six days shall work be done: but on the seventh day is a sabbath of rest, a holy convocation; ye shall do no work; it is a sabbath to the LORD in all your dwellings. ¶

a reason for the seventh day's rest. See on Ex. xx. 10. *A sabbath of rest.* This phrase is applied twice to the day of atonement and once to the sabbatical year (xxv. 4). When applied to a day it denotes a resting from all work in the ordinary sense of the term. *A holy convocation.* This is a most important intimation concerning the sabbath. It was a set day of meeting together for social worship. This was its chief distinction for the people. In the place where God was pleased to record his name no doubt the second morning and evening lamb was offered on this day. But this involved the presence and action of the priest only whose turn it was to officiate. And even if such places had been multiplied, so that every tribe might have its sanctuary, the sabbath offerings might not have been multiplied, and they did not afford to all the people the religious exercises and instruction which they needed. But the holy convocation brought together the multitude who kept the holy day to the stated place of social worship. Speaking to the congregation and addressing God were the essential constituents of this simple worship. The former branched into reading the book of revelation and adding the word of instruction and exhortation; the latter into the song of praise and the voice of prayer. *Ye shall do no work.* Work was of two kinds: labor and business; labor being the toil of the hands, business the exercise of trade. Neither was to be done on the weekly sabbath. *A sabbath to the Lord,* dedicated to him, and therefore to communion with him. *In all your dwellings.* This is a very significant phrase. It distinguishes the convocation of the weekly sabbath from that of the annual festival. In the latter the meeting-place was the sanctuary, whether of the nation or the tribe; in the former the village-green, where public meetings were wont be held, and which was at a conve-

4. These are the set times of the LORD, holy convocations, which ye shall proclaim in their set times. 5. In the first month on the fourteenth of the month between the evenings is the passover to the LORD. 6. And on the fifteenth day of this month is the feast of sweet bread unto the LORD; seven days ye shall eat sweet bread. 7. On the first day ye shall have a holy convocation; ye shall do no servile work. 8. And ye shall make a fire-offering unto the LORD seven days; on the seventh day is a holy convocation; ye shall do no servile work. ¶

nient distance from the surrounding homesteads. These weekly meetings kept alive the knowledge and piety of the simple yeoman in all the land. As the climate was mild they did not need a covered building. Their synagogue was the canopy of heaven, or the wide-spreading tree in the green of every hamlet. This verse therefore provides for the early origin of the primitive synagogue. The origin of the stone and lime synagogue is a matter of comparatively little importance. This single verse affords an interesting prospect of the unwritten history of Israel's rural piety.

4–8. *The passover and feast of unleavened bread.* 4. *These are the set times.* After the weekly sabbath comes a general heading for the annual festivals. 5. *In the first month.* This became the first month on the appointment of the Lord (Ex. xii. 2) at the departure from Egypt. *On the fourteenth.* The paschal lamb was set apart on the tenth and slain on the fourteenth (Ex. xii. 6). *Between the evenings.* The slaying of the lamb took place in the last quarter of the day before sunset, since if it had been after sunset it would not have been on the fourteenth, but on the following day. *Passover to the Lord,* kept in honor of the Lord, and in commemoration of the signal deliverance which accompanied its first celebration (Ex. xii.). 6. *And on the fifteenth.* This is the first of the seven days of sweet or unleavened bread. 7. It is a day of holy convocation. *No servile work.* Servile work is manual labor in contrast with business, such as buying and selling. It is to be observed that this day is not called a sabbath, but a holy convocation in which no servile work is to be done. 8. *A fire-offering,* a propitiatory sacrifice. This is specified in Num. xviii. *Seven days*

LEVITICUS XXIII. 8–11.   269

9. And the LORD spake unto Moses, saying, 10. Speak unto the sons of Israel and say unto them, When ye go into the land which I give you and reap its harvest, then ye shall bring the sheaf of first-fruits of your harvest unto the priest. 11. And he shall wave the sheaf before the LORD for your acceptance; on the morrow of the sabbath the priest shall

are fire-offerings to be made. The seventh day is like the first, a day of holy convocation and abstinence from servile work. It is not called a sabbath. The intervening days have their appropriate sacrifices, but labor is not suspended. It is manifest that on the establishment of the people in the land and their dispersion over a wide territory local sanctuaries would have been needed, if the attendance of the whole community on the national festivals was to be secured.

9–14. The second communication begins with the wave-sheaf. 10. *When ye go into the land.* These directions are preparatory to their settlement in a country of their own. The passover itself had no necessary connection with landed property; but the harvest had. *The sheaf of first-fruits of your harvest.* This, as it came from the hands of a grateful nation, was a sheaf of newly-reaped barley. At a later period it was parched, rubbed out, winnowed, and bruised in a mortar, and then a portion of it burnt on the altar; but this does not comport with the simplicity of the early custom. The barley was ripe about the middle of April and the wheat about three weeks later in the warmer parts of Palestine. 11. *And he shall wave the sheaf.* Communion with one another in this offering is prominent. This is the sheaf of the commonwealth of Israel. *For your acceptance.* This acknowledgement of God as the Giver of the harvest is acceptable to him. It is typical of the great propitiation, on the ground of which all are accepted. *On the morrow of the sabbath.* The small minority of interpreters, Rabbinical and Christian, are certainly right in maintaining that the sabbath here mentioned is the weekly sabbath, and not the first day of unleavened bread, for the following reasons: 1. This section is a new communication, distinct from that relating to the feast of unleavened bread. It is worthy of remark that the sabbath here is left undetermined, in order to suit the harvest. It cannot

wave it. 12. And ye shall offer in the day of your waving the sheaf a perfect he-lamb of the first year for a burnt-sacrifice to the LORD. 13. And its oblation, two tenths of fine flour

be proved that it belonged at first to the seven days of unleavened bread, however probable it may appear, though afterwards it actually did. In Deut. xvi. 9 the feast of weeks is reckoned simply from the putting of the sickle to the standing corn. 2. The first day of unleavened bread is not called a sabbath, but simply a day of holy convocation, in which no servile work was to be done. 3. The feast of weeks was on the morrow of the sabbath (vs. 15), and this sabbath can only be the weekly sabbath. But it was the fiftieth day from the day of the wave-sheaf, inclusive, and hence this also must have been the day after a weekly sabbath. Moreover they were expressly to count seven sabbaths from the morrow of the sabbath to the morrow of the sabbath; and as the latter can only be a weekly sabbath, so must the former. This argument is decisive of itself. The only way of evading it, is by assuming that the sabbath means in vs. 15 not even a week, but a period of seven days beginning with any day. 4. And therefore it is to be observed that the sabbath in the Old Testament does not mean a week, and nowhere does it mean any seven days beginning on any day of the week. Josephus, it is true, (Antiq. iii. 10, 5), states that the sheaf of first-fruits was presented on the sixteenth of Nisan; but this is merely the interpretation or the practice of his time and of his party. The Sept. also by the rendering "on the morrow of the first,"[11] and Onk. by the phrase "after the good day," are supposed to countenance the statement of Josephus. But neither of them has given an exact version of the original words, and they are both too late to outweigh the reasons assigned. 5. It must be added as a fifth reason, that the only sabbath mentioned in the New Testament in connection with the feast of unleavened bread is the weekly sabbath which fell on the day after the first day of the feast, that several things were done on this first day which were not consistent with a strict sabbath, as, a judicial investigation (Matt. xxvi. 57), a crucifixion (John xix. 31), buying fine linen and buying and preparing spices (Mark xv. 46; xvi. 1; Luke xxiii. 56). Hence the day of presenting the wave-sheaf was the first day of the week, according to the original

mingled with oil, a fire-offering to the LORD for a sweet smell; and its libation of wine, the fourth of a hin. 14. And bread or parched corn or fresh ears ye shall not eat until this same day that ye bring the offering of your God; it is a statute forever for your generations in all your dwellings. §

15. And ye shall count for you from the morrow of the sabbath, from the day that ye bring the wave sheaf; seven sabbaths shall be complete. 16. Unto the morrow of the seventh sabbath ye shall count fifty days; and ye shall offer a new oblation unto the LORD. 17. From your dwellings ye shall bring bread of waving, two cakes of two tenths; they shall be of flour; with leaven shall they be baken; They are

institution. 12, 13. Along with the sheaf is offered a perfect lamb for a burnt-sacrifice, with its oblation and libation. Two tenths of an ephah are here prescribed, instead of one, for a lamb (Num. xxviii. 31), perhaps because it accompanied the oblation of first-ripe grain. 14. *And bread.* No part of the new crop was to be used for food until this sheaf was offered. *In all your dwellings.* This was a rule to be observed in every household.

15-22. The feast of weeks is the second part of this communication. It is evidently connected as a continuation and completion with the wave-sheaf at the beginning of harvest. *And ye shall count.* The counting is made simple by the seven squared. *Seven sabbaths shall be complete.* The seventh sabbath shall be fulfilled. 16. *Until the morrow of the seventh sabbath.* This will be the fiftieth day from the sabbath of the feast of unleavened bread. *A new oblation.* The wave-sheaf was an oblation at the beginning of harvest, and this was a new oblation at the end of the wheat harvest. It is made of the new wheat, as the former was of barley. 17. *From your dwellings,* not from the field, as the wave-sheaf was brought. This too was a national offering. *Two cakes of two tenths,* double that which accompanied the wave-sheaf. *With leaven,* because it is to be the ordinary bread of your homes. *The early fruits.* These are different from the sheaf of first-fruits. The latter was the first sheaf of the barley

the early fruits unto the LORD. 18. And ye shall offer with the bread seven perfect lambs of the first year and one bullock of the herd and two rams; they shall be a burnt-sacrifice to the LORD with their oblation and their libation, a fire-offering of a sweet smell unto the LORD. 19. And ye shall offer one kid of the goats for a sin-sacrifice, and two lambs of the first year for a sacrifice of peace. 20. And the priest shall wave them with the bread of the early fruits for a waving before the LORD upon the two lambs; they shall be holy unto the LORD for the priest. 21. And ye shall proclaim this same day, a holy convocation shall it be unto you, ye thall do no servile work; it is a statute forever in all your dwellings for your generations. 22. And when ye reap the harvest of your land,

harvest. The former was the early wheat manufactured into fine flour. 18. The sacrifice consists of the sacred number of lambs, a bullock and two rams for a burnt-sacrifice, accompanied with their oblations and libations according to Num. xxviii. The great propitiation is represented here in a very significant manner. This is peculiarly appropriate when the grain harvest is completed. Bread is the staff of life. And it is the propitiatory sacrifice that guarantees life and all its blessings to those who are ready to perish. 19. *A sin-sacrifice* for any inadvertence was the suitable acknowledgement of personal defect and the typical pleading of the true expiation for sin. *A sacrifice of peace* comes appropriately from the nation now in communion with God. 20. *Shall wave them*, the two lambs with the bread of early fruits upon them. The peace-offering is evidently the crowning act to which the others led the way, as peace with God is the unspeakable privilege of the nation this day. *They shall be holy unto the Lord for the priest.* The peace-sacrifice was usually eaten by the offerer. As the holy nation is here the offerer the priest acts as its representative. 21. *Ye shall proclaim this same day.* The nature of the proclamation follows. The Pentecost is a day of holy convocation in which no servile work is to be done. This is a perpetual custom. 22. In this new connection the injunction of xix. 9

thou shalt not clear out the corner of thy field when thou reapest, and the gleaning of thy harvest thou shalt not gather; to the poor and to the stranger thou shalt leave it: I am the LORD your God. ¶
23. And the LORD spake unto Moses, saying, 24. Speak unto the sons of Israel, saying, In the seventh month in the first of the month ye shall have a rest, a memorial of the

is with a kindly impressiveness repeated. The interval between the offering of the wave-sheaf and the wave-cakes was the time of grain harvest. The latter was therefore the completion of the former. It is obvious that the immediate reference of these festivals is to the operations of the harvest. At the same time it is manifest that we have now completed a cycle of festivals which have a most intimate and profound union among themselves. The passover represents death; the wave-sheaf and the wave-loaves symbolize life. The Messiah is priest, king, and prophet. As priest he is the Lamb of God that taketh away the sin of the world. As king, he is the wave-sheaf, the first-fruits from the dead. This has peculiar force when we remember that he rose on the first day of the week and the very day of the wave-sheaf being offered. As prophet, when the day of Pentecost was fully come he sent the promise of the Father, the Spirit of Truth and of utterance upon the disciples, the full harvest of their waiting and praying, the bread of eternal life for their hungering souls. In this brief period of seven times seven days there is a typical epitome of the history of salvation.

23-25. The feast of the blowing of the trumpet. This is the third communication. 24. *In the seventh month.* Like the seventh day this month has a sacred significance. As the first month of the civil year it has also a distinct importance. *On the first day of the month.* This was the new year's day of the primeval year. It was therefore the anniversary of the first day of that creation to which man belongs. *Ye shall have a rest.* This, as we shall see, is not a full sabbath, but a rest from labor. *A memorial of the trumpet blast.* It was commemorative of creation, an event of paramount importance and gladness, which was celebrated by the blowing of the trumpet. *A holy*

trumpet blast, a holy convocation. 25. Ye shall do no servile work; and ye shall make a fire-offering unto the LORD. §

26. And the LORD spake unto Moses, saying, 27. But on the tenth of the seventh month is the day of atonement: it shall be a holy convocation to you, and ye shall afflict your souls; and ye shall make a fire-offering to the LORD. 28. And ye shall do no work on this same day; for it is a day of atonement, to atone for you before the LORD your God. 29. For every soul that shall not be afflicted on this same day shall be cut off from his people. 30. And every soul that doeth any work on this same day, I will destroy that soul from among his people. 31. Ye shall do no work; it is a statute forever for your generations in all your dwellings. 32. It is a sabbath of rest unto you, and ye shall afflict your souls:

convocation. As this was not one of the great festival occasions, on which the people were to appear before the Lord, we may presume that it was celebrated not only in the tabernacle, but in all the dwellings of the people. It was an occasion of universal interest. A holy convocation for thanksgiving and prayer would be most suitable. 25. *No servile work.* Though work not servile was permitted, the son of toil was to be released from his labor. *A fire-offering.* This is prescribed in Num. xxix 1–6.

26–32. The fourth communication refers to the day of atonement. The account of this solemn day is given here to complete the series in a form abbreviated from chap. xvi. with some additions. 27. *A fire-offering.* This always denotes propitiation and acceptance. The peculiar rite of this day is described in chap. xvi. and the fire-offering in addition is given in Num. xxix. 7–11. 28. It has been already noticed that this is the only day of abstinence from all work beside the weekly Sabbath. The peculiarity of the day, as a time of atonement, is explained in chap. xvi. 29, 30. He that neglects to afflict his soul or to abstain from all work on this day is to be excommunicated. 31. This restriction is to be observed throughout the country in the homes of the people. 32. The sabbath of rest for humiliation

LEVITICUS XXIII. 32–37. 275

on the ninth of the month at even, from even unto even, ye shall keep your sabbath. ¶

33. And the LORD spake unto Moses, saying, 34. Speak unto the sons of Israel, saying, On the fifteenth day of this seventh month is the feast of tabernacles seven days unto the LORD. 35. On the first day shall be a holy convocation; ye shall do no servile work. 36. Seven days ye shall offer a fire-offering unto the LORD; on the eighth day ye shall have a holy convocation, and ye shall offer a fire-offering unto the LORD; it is a solemnity; ye shall do no servile work.

37. These are the set times of the LORD, which ye shall proclaim to be holy convocations to offer a fire-offering unto

and mourning is to be a complete day from sunset on the ninth to sunset on the tenth.

33–36. This part of the fifth communication refers to the feast of tabernacles. 34. *On the fifteenth day.* This corresponds to the feast of sweet bread in the first month. *Seven days.* There were seven days of unleavened bread preceded by the pasch. 35. *On the first day,* as on the first day of sweet bread, a holy convocation and no servile work. 36. In Num. xxix. 12–34 we have a minute regulation concerning the fire-offering of each day of the seven. *On the eighth day.* As the seven days of sweet bread were preceded by the paschal meal, so the seven days of tabernacles are followed by an eighth day, which is a day of holy convocation with its appropriate fire-offering prescribed in Num. xxix. 35–38. It is called the great day of the feast in John vii. 37, and has special reference to the ingathering (Ex. xxiii. 16). *It is a solemnity.*[36] This word is used of the last day of the feast of unleavened bread Deut. xvi. 8 and in Josephus, Antiq. iii. 10, 6, of the day of pentecost, which is the closing day of the first cycle of festivals in the second year. This accords with the rendering of the Sept., assembly of closing or dismissal. The idea of restraint or sacred obligation is not inconsistent with this.

37–44. A recapitulation, with an appendix on dwelling in booths. 37. *These are the set times.* From this chapter it appears that there

the LORD, a burnt-sacrifice and an oblation, a sacrifice and libations, each in its day. 38. Besides the sabbaths of the LORD and beside your gifts and beside all your vows and beside all your free-gifts, which ye give unto the LORD. 39. But in the fifteenth day of the seventh month, when ye gather in the produce of the land, ye shall keep the feast of the LORD seven days, on the first day a rest, and on the eighth day

were seven days on which labor or servile work was suspended: the first and seventh days of the feast of sweet bread, the day of the feast of harvest, the new moon of the seventh month, the day of atonement, and the first and eighth days of the feast of ingathering. Of these the day of atonement alone was a sabbath of rest, in which all kinds of work were to cease. Hence we perceive that the Supreme Governor, who demanded the weekly sabbath, was very far from multiplying other days of cessation from labor, and required only one other day of absolute rest from all business. *A fire-offering unto the Lord.* These are all specified in Num. xxviii., xxix. The different kinds are the burnt-sacrifice, the oblation or meat-offering, the sacrifice, including the peace-offering, the sin-sacrifice, and the trespass-offering, with the libation or drink-offering. Hence it appears that some portion or memorial of the libation was cast upon the fire of the altar. 38. *Beside the sabbaths.* These form a class by themselves, the weekly set times. *Beside your gifts,* which are not sacrifices at all. *Beside all your vows.* The vows and free gifts come under the head either of peace-offerings or of burnt-sacrifices. 39. *But.* Another aspect of the feast of tabernacles is now presented. *When ye gather in the produce.* It is the feast of ingathering. Ripe grapes can be found in July; but the general vintage of Palestine is in September. The whole produce of the ground may therefore be gathered in at the feast of ingathering, which was at the full moon next the autumnal equinox. *On the first day a rest.*[39] The rest here is not the word sabbath, which applies only to the weekly sabbath, the day of atonement, and the sabbatical year. It is the partial rest — the rest from labor or servile work — which characterizes all the other days of holy convocation, as we see from the following verse. 40. *Take unto you*

a rest. 40. And ye shall take unto you on the first day the fruit of goodly trees, shoots of palms and branches of leafy trees and willows of the brook; and ye shall be glad before the LORD your God seven days. 41. And ye shall keep a feast unto the LORD seven days in the year; it is a statute forever for your generations; in the seventh month ye shall keep it. 42. In booths ye shall dwell seven days, all that are born in Israel shall dwell in booths. 43. That your generations may know that I made the sons of Israel dwell in booths, when I

on the first day. The taking of branches and forming of booths were not work to be done on the strict sabbath, but only on those festive days on which abstinence from servile work only was required. *Fruit of goodly trees,* branches with leaves, blossoms, and whatever fruit was upon them. *Shoots of palms.* These are the spreading leaves of the palm. This tree, of which there are said to be a thousand kinds, is the characteristic tree of Palestine. *Leafy trees,* abounding in intertwining shoots and leaves. *Willows of the brook,* that grow by the watercourses in the meadows. *Ye shall be glad.* This is the season of rejoicing, because the products of the labor of the year have been gathered, and in the order of a kind Providence it satisfies the wants and gratifies the tastes of the rational and susceptible race. *Seven days,* as usual, the time of perfection. 41. This is to be a perpetual ordinance. 42. *In booths.* The booth is a hut made of branches of trees, with the green leaves on. The tabernacle is a structure of boards, and therefore more permanent. The tent is an awning of goats' or camels' hair cloth, supported by a pole or poles. *All that are born in Israel.* They are all entitled to take part in this solemnity, and all that can and will are certain to join in it. To insist on absolute universality is to become the bond-slave of the letter. 43. *That your generation may know.* Commemoration is suited to the genius of humanity. History is the memory of moments or turning-points in the progressive development of mankind. And these moments are pregnant with instruction for all coming generations. *Dwell in booths.* This festival is commemorative of the Israelites dwelling in booths at Succoth (booths), when they came out of Egypt.

brought them out of the land of Mizraim: I am the LORD your God. 44. And Moses spake of the set times of the LORD unto the sons of Israel. ¶

Hence we see that several ends and lessons may coincide in the same solemnity. This is the feast of ingathering because the increase of the field was now gathered in, and the feast of tabernacles in remembrance of the deliverance from Egypt. The seven days referred especially to the commemoration of the past (Deut. xvi. 13, 14); the eighth day to the crowning of the year with the goodness of the Lord in the ingathering of the harvest.

Hence we are led by an easy path to a higher significance of all these set times. This arises from the reference not merely to natural and historical events, but, above all, to the God of nature and history. We recognize in the cycle of the seventh month the primeval religion of universal man. The day of the new moon of the original beginning of the year is the stated anniversary of the six days' creation. The dawn of human history is celebrated by the blowing of the trumpet. After this, on the tenth of the month, comes the day of atonement, the day of confession of sin and repentance toward God; the origin of which is to be found in the fall of man, if it do not call to remembrance the date of that first disobedience. It speaks of self-condemnation, but at the same time of pardon and acceptance through the mercy of God. The day of ingathering would have been the meet sequel of the day of creation, if no fall had intervened to disturb the moral order of things. The holy soul in the full tide of its happiness would have poured forth its spontaneous notes of gratitude to the God of light and right and love. When Adam yielded to temptation, however, the mystery of mercy came forth in a word of invitation from the holy breast of God; and so hope awoke in the guilty breast of man, and faith still stepped forth to celebrate the feast of ingathering, the earnest of all blessings in time and in eternity from the hands of God through the mediation of the great High-Priest.

On this ancient stock of the catholic church of Adam and Noah was grafted the vine brought out of Egypt with its peculiar ordinances, its new beginning of the year, its passover, feast of unleavened bread, and feast of weeks. These, also, only rise to their true significance when we remember their relation to God. The paschal lamb and its accompanying seven days festival bring out into a new prominence the propitiation for sin. The feast of first-fruits and the pentecost after seven times seven days, like the circumcision after seven days, celebrate the second great element of salvation, the spiritual resurrection and purification of the soul, the first-fruits of the Spirit, by which it is determined to accept the atonement and realize the blessedness of freedom and peace. In the unsearchable wisdom of the provident Disposer of all events the solemnities of the second half of the second year now fall into one compact whole, foreshadowing the full enjoyment of pardon, the third part of the great salvation, in itself the source and sum of all the rest, and inclusive of perpetual acceptance, adoption, and inheritance. Thus the revolution of every sacred year presents before the sanctified imagination, in orderly succession, the atonement, the new birth, and the inheritance of the saints in the kingdom of God. And this remarkable chapter shows that the set times of the Lord are the several stages of the kingdom of God here on earth.

NOTES.

2. *Set time* מוֹעֵד, appointed time or place : ἑορτή. חַג, vs. 6, feast; ἑορτή.

11. Τῇ ἐπαύριον τῆς πρώτης. The statement in Josh. v. 11, " they ate of the corn of the land on the morrow after the passover unleavened cakes and parched corn in the self-same day," refers to the first day of unleavened bread when they began to eat of the bread of the land, on which the manna ceased, and has no bearing on the question of the wave-sheaf. The view of this question given in the text is that of the Baithusians, who were akin to the Sadducees and the Karaites, and alone serves to harmonize the different accounts of the crucifixion.

36. *Solemnity* עֲצֶרֶת assembly of restraint, detention, or conclusion: ἐξόδιον, closing meeting ; r. *shut in, restrain*. It is applied in Isa. i. 13 and Joel i. 14 to a suspension of servile work for a religious solemnity, and in Jer. ix. 1 to a confederacy of wicked men. It occurs about ten times; in four of which it applies to the last day of the feast of ingathering.

39. *A rest* שַׁבָּתוֹן; ἀνάπαυσις. שַׁבָּת; the sabbath, applied only to the weekly Sabbath, the day of atonement and the sabbatical year: σάββατον, σάββατα.

XXIV. OF THE HOUSE OF GOD.

XXIV. 1. And the LORD spake unto Moses, saying, 2. Command the sons of Israel, and let them fetch the pure olive oil beaten for the light to kindle a continual lamp. 3. Without the veil of the testimony in the tent of meeting, Aaron shall order it from evening to morning before the LORD continually; it is a statute forever for your generations. 4. Upon the clean candlestick he shall order the lamps before the LORD continually. ¶
5. And thou shalt take fine flour and bake it into twelve cakes; two tenths shall be the one cake. 6. And thou shalt set them in two piles, six in the pile, on the clean table before the

In this chapter are two communications; one concerning the house of God (1–9), and another concerning the honor of his name (10–23). They are both made to Moses. The first communication contains two parts, one for the sons of Israel concerning the light for the candlestick (1–4), and another concerning the bread for the table in the house of the Lord (5–9). The second communication is prefaced by a narrative of the occasion on which it was given (10–12).

1–4. The light for the golden candlestick. This is repeated in a new connection, having been already given in Ex. xxvii. 20, 21, where it has been already explained. 4. *The clean candlestick*, made of pure gold, and free from all soil. See on Ex. xxxi. 8. On this second communication being made it is probable that the provision and preparation immediately followed. It may have been given before the consecration of the priests along with the following regulation.

5–9. The bread for the table. This is now specified for the first time. 5. *Fine flour.* Of this there must be twenty-four omers, as there are two omers in each cake. An omer was the portion of manna gathered by each Israelite in the wilderness. It contained about three and one-half pints. The two omers are a double portion, and indicate the abundance of blessing in God's house. 6. *In two*

Lord. 7. And thou shalt put upon the pile pure frankincense; and it shall be on the bread for a memorial, a fire-offering unto the Lord. 8. Every sabbath-day he shall lay it before the Lord continually, from the sons of Israel it is a perpetual covenant. 9. And it shall be to Aaron and his sons, and they shall eat it in a holy place; for it is most holy unto him of the fire-offerings of the Lord by a statute forever. §

piles. The table was two cubits long and one broad. A pint contains about 34.6 cubic inches, and therefore two omers, or seven pints, are equal to 242.2 such inches. Hence a cake of two omers of flour would be about 9 by 9 by 3 inches or 12 by 7 by 3 inches, if there was no increase by kneading and baking. It is obvious, therefore, that the arrangement must be a pile, which would be eighteen inches high. *The clean table.* It was made of acacia wood and overlaid with pure gold (Ex. xxv. 23–30), and, of course, free from any stain. 7. *Pure frankincense.* The bread was placed on two plates or trays, and the frankincense in two bowls. These vessels were of pure gold. Frankincense is an emblem of acceptance for the suppliant. *A memorial,* calling to mind the whole table fare, of which it was the part that was eventually burned upon the altar. *A fire offering.* The burning of that which was placed on the altar was the sign of the offering being accepted; and the burning of incense was the token of accepted prayer. Every victim burned on the altar was transformed into a perfume, a sweet smell unto the Lord. 8. *Every sabbath-day* the bread was to be renewed. It was a work of necessity which might be performed even on the sabbath (Ex. xii. 16). *From the sons of Israel it is a perpetual covenant.* The people had evidently a special connection with the bread. There were twelve cakes, as there were twelve tribes in Israel. Bread, the staff of life, is a fit emblem of the blessing of the covenant. The benefit implied the fulfilment of the covenant, that is, the righteousness which gave the legal title to eternal life. Hence this bread on the table of the Lord from the twelve tribes of Israel is an appropriate token of the perpetual covenant between the Lord and his people. 9. *It shall be to Aaron and his sons.* The bread when taken away was to be eaten by the priests in

10. And the son of a woman of Israel and of a man of Mizraim came out among the sons of Israel; and the son of the woman of Israel and a man of Israel strove in the camp. 11. And the son of the woman of Israel blasphemed the name and cursed; and they brought him to Moses; and his mother's name was Shelomith, daughter of Dibri, of the tribe of Dan. 12. And they put him in ward, that he might expound unto them from the mouth of the LORD. ¶

13. And the LORD spake unto Moses, saying, 14. Bring forth him that cursed without the camp, and let all that heard

a holy place, within the precincts of the tabernacle. The frankincense was doubtless burned upon the altar of incense. The bread is the emblem of the blessings of life, as the seven lamps are of the light of life. The incense on the golden altar standing between the table and the candlestick is the memorial of the ransom of life. The first speaks to us of the Father, the second of the Spirit, and the third of the Messiah.

10–12. These verses record the occasion of a new communication from the Lord. 10. *Came out among the sons of Israel.* Being an Egyptian by the father's side, he had no place among the Israelites, except as a stranger, a proselyte to the true God. He seems to have intruded into the camp of Israel. This may have been part of the occasion of the strife. 11. In the heat of the struggle he blasphemed the name. This is the exclusive name of God, Jehovah, which was not even pronounced by the Jews of a later period, and which is usually rendered "the LORD" in the English version. This man inherited from his father at least a wavering mind, and in the fury of his resentment provoked his antagonist in the highest degree by blaspheming the name of God and cursing; thus adding imprecation to blasphemy. This led to the prompt interference of the bystanders, who brought him to Moses. 12. He is put in ward until a definite sentence is obtained from the Lord. This is revealed to Moses in a new communication.

13–23. General directions for cases of strife. 14. *Bring forth.* The blasphemer is by the very act excommunicated, and therefore

lay their hands upon his head; and let all the assembly stone him. 15. And to the sons of Israel thou shalt speak, saying, Whosoever curseth his God shall bear his sin. 16. And he that blasphemeth the name of the LORD shall be put to death; all the assembly shall stone him; as the stranger, so the home-born, when he blasphemeth the name shall die. 17. And he that smiteth a man's life shall be put to death. 18. And he that smiteth a beast's life shall make it good, life for life. 19. And if a man cause a blemish in his neighbor, as he hath done so shall it be done to him. 20. Breach for breach, eye for eye, tooth for tooth; as he causeth a blemish in the man so shall it be done to him. 21. And he that smiteth a beast shall restore it; and he that smiteth a man shall die. 22. Ye shall have one judgment; as the stranger so shall the home-born be; for I am the LORD your God. 23. And Moses spake to the sons

removed from the camp. *All that heard.* The witnesses are solemnly to identify and lay on him the guilt by laying on their hands. *All the assembly.* They, as well as the witnesses, by their judicial acts practically abjure all participation in his guilt. 15. *And to the sons of Israel.* Here we have further instructions called forth by the occasion. 16. He that curses God or blasphemes the sacred name, whether stranger or homeborn, is to be stoned by the assembly. 17. *He that smiteth a man's life,* smiteth him so as to take his life, is to be put to death. 18. He that killeth another man's beast must give a beast of equal value. 19. He that causeth a blemish in another shall suffer the like blemish on himself. 20. The *lex talionis,* or law of retaliation, is here repeated (Ex. xxi. 24), for the guidance of the civil magistrate. It is not lawful for the subject to take the execution of the law into his own hands. But it is his right to appeal to the magistrate, who is to administer the law of equity. 21, 22. The law of distributive justice is here reiterated for the sake of emphasis, and applied equally to the native and the stranger. 23. The sentence on the blasphemer is now executed according to the word of the Lord, on whose authority the whole administration of justice in Israel rests.

of Israel, and they brought forth the blasphemer out of the camp and stoned him with stones: and the sons of Israel did as the LORD commanded Moses. 32 ¶ ¶ ¶

Even the judicial procedure of this chapter belongs to religion. It belongs, moreover, to the house of God, which is the seat of justice. The name of the Chief Ruler has been blasphemed in his very court. His attendants report the case to him in the tent of meeting, consult him and receive instructions from him in this earthly home how to deal with the offender. The chapter has therefore a fundamental unity, and the compiler is warranted in the arrangement of its apparently incongruous parts. The present section has a logical sequence in the whole of its topics. It treats of the priests, the offerings, the set times, and household arrangements of the Lord. It enters into a series of details which could not have been so clearly brought out in any other connection. The ingenuity of this arrangement is much more apparent when we consider that the whole section consists of a series of pieces, which the writer received from another and was only authorized to put in order.

SECTION VI. — MATTERS PARTLY CIVIL, PARTLY RELIGIOUS.

XXV. SABBATICAL YEARS.

IN this section there is a mingling of the secular and the sacred. It contains only two communications, of which the one occupies two chapters and the other one. The subject of the former is the sabbatical year. It falls into two parts, of which the one contains a code of regulations for its observance and provisions concerning liberty and property, and the other an admonition setting forth the blessings attendant upon its observance and the evils consequent upon its neglect, in the form of promises and warnings. The topic of the latter is the vow, which comes naturally after the sabbatical year, as some of its regulations depend on the jubilee. It appears from the commencement and close of the first communication, and from the close of the second that they were both made in Mount Sinai, and therefore antecedent to some of those in the intervening sections, and about the same time with those in the first section of this book. They are both designed for the whole nation.

The twenty-fifth chapter begins with the institution of the sabbatical year (1–7). The remainder of the chapter is occupied with the jubilee and its legal effects on property and liberty. After a definition of the jubilee (8–12), the legal return of every man to his land, with its effect on contracts, is described in 13–34, and the emancipation of the serf, with its consequent arrangements, is set forth in 35–55.

1–7. The sabbatical year. 1. *In Mount Sinai.* This communication must have been made either during the forty days while Moses was on the mount with God, or afterwards, in the temporary tent of meeting, which may have been on the slope of the mount. The date is a clear proof that the sacred penman, who received these various

XXV. 1. And the LORD **spake unto Moses in Mount Sinai, saying, 2. Speak unto the sons of Israel, and say unto them, When ye go into the land which I give you, then shall the land keep a sabbath unto the** LORD. **3. Six years thou shalt sow thy field and six years prune thy vineyard and gather its produce. 4. But in the seventh year the land shall have a sabbath of rest, a sabbath unto the** LORD **: thou shalt not sow thy field nor prune thy vineyard. 5. The self-growth of thy harvest thou shalt not reap, nor gather the grapes of thy nazarite**

messages from heaven in a certain order of time, was yet moved to put them together according to a certain order of thought. Until we have descried the principle that governed his arrangement we are not in a condition to judge of its propriety. 2. *When ye go into the land.* This and the following communication, like most of those in the preceding two sections contemplate the state of things not in the wilderness but in the future land. *Then shall the land keep a sabbath.* Man's surroundings are modified by his moral nature. As the rational agency of man for a proposed end is something beyond the instinctive activity of the mere animal nature, and requires a special rest on the seventh day, so the cultivation of the field accomplished by such agency causes an extraordinary growth beyond the spontaneous effort of nature ; and the ground that is so treated requires a special period, a seventh year, of rest, beyond the mere repose of the winter. See on Ex. xx. 10. Hence a cultivation for six years is to be followed by a cessation on the seventh year. The cultivator of the soil is aware of the necessity of this arrangement in all countries. It is the fundamental principle of a rotation of treatment. 3, 4. *Six years* of agricultural industry. *A sabbath unto the Lord.* Though a physical reason lies at the root of this regulation, the sacred writer consistently with his principle and purpose, refers it to the God of the physical universe, from whose intelligent will the laws of nature ultimately proceed. On this year intelligent man is not to sow his field nor prune his vine, if he be in covenant with his God on the terms of the chosen people. 5. *The self-growth,*[5] that which grows of itself without sowing or tilling the soil. *Thou shalt not reap*, reaping for the purpose

vine: it is a year of rest unto the land. 6. And the sabbath of the land shall be to you for food, to thee and to thy servant and to thy maid and to thy hireling and to thy guest, that sojourn with thee. 7. And to thy cattle and to the beasts that are in thy land shall all its produce be food. §
8. And thou shalt count unto thee seven sabbaths of years, seven times seven years; and the days of the seven sabbaths of years shall be to thee nine and forty years. 9. And thou shalt blow the trumpet of glad sound in the seventh month, on

of ingathering is not to take place. *Thy nazarite vine,* left unpruned, having all its tendrils hanging untouched, like the unshorn locks of the Nazarite. The poet speaks of the *viridis coma* of the vine. *A year of rest unto the land,* in which it is released from the operations of tilling, sowing, and ingathering. 6, 7. *The sabbath of the land,* that which grows spontaneously when the land, undisturbed by culture, enjoys a sabbath. *To you for food, to thee.* The owner and all others were to be on a footing of perfect equality. Each was permitted to gather for the present need, but not for store or sale. *Thy guest* is to be on a par with all thy other inmates. *That sojourn with thee.* This applies to the servants and the guests alike. *And to thy cattle and to the beasts.* To manifest the thorough return to the state of aboriginal liberty not only the cattle, but the wild animals are to share in the natural growth of the land. The wild animals would be merely those which are innoxious to man, and are allowed to exist in a land of civilization. It is not our part to estimate the result of such a regulation as this. It is enough to observe that the children of God would be secure from want under his beneficent providence, and that a considerable check would be put upon human cupidity. Certain results of this enactment are indicated by the legislator himself.

8–12. The jubilee. *Thou shalt count unto thee.* Counting is a rational process, and reminds us that we are in the sphere of man communing with his Maker. *Seven sabbaths of years,* seven sabbatical years. A sabbath of a year is a sabbath that lasts a year, in contrast with a sabbath-day. These seven sabbath-years involve seven times seven years, or nine and forty years. *The trumpets of glad sound,*[9]

the tenth of the month; in the day of atonement ye shall blow the trumpet in all your land. 10. And ye shall hallow the fiftieth year, and proclaim liberty in the land to all its inhabitants: it shall be a jubilee unto you, and ye shall return every man to his possession, and return every man to his family.

of clangor, or joyful acclaim. *In the seventh month.* It appears that the sabbatical and jubilee years began in the seventh month, the first month of the primeval year. This is required by the natural history of the year. The sowing time in Palestine is about November, and therefore a month or two after the beginning of the original year, which was a little before the autumnal equinox. The reaping time is after the vernal equinox, terminating in the month of May, and the vintage in September. Now, if the sabbatical year began in Abib, about the vernal equinox, it would be the sowing of the preceding year that would be left unreaped, instead of the spontaneous growth of the sabbatical year, which is contrary to the text. But if it begin with Tisri, about the autumnal equinox, everything is in its natural order. The sowing is omitted in the second month, and the natural growth is unreaped in the eighth or ninth month. But it is to be observed that the sacred writer reckons the months according to the sacred year; and, as the civil year began six months earlier, the first half of the seventh civil year would be the second half of the sixth sacred year. *On the tenth of the month,* on the day of atonement the trumpet was to sound. The day of expiation, of ransom for sin, of release from doom, of restoration to life, liberty, and inheritance, was singularly appropriate for the opening of the jubilee. 10. *And ye shall hallow the fiftieth year.* The sabbatical was the forty-ninth year; the jubilee is the fiftieth It is hallowed by its peculiar ordinances concerning liberty and property. *And proclaim liberty.* Liberty from bondage was secured to every Israelite at the end of six years by the civil law (Ex. xxi. 2). The jubilee, however, gave liberty to the serf in Israel whose term was not otherwise completed, so that at one and the same time for this year men were free all over the land. *A jubilee*[10] *unto you,* a trumpet-note of deliverance, a twofold deliverance — every man to his possession and every man to his family.

11. A jubilee shall that fiftieth year be unto you; ye shall not sow nor reap its self-growth nor gather its nazarite vine. 12. For it is the jubilee, it shall be holy unto you; out of the field ye shall eat its produce. 13. In this year of the jubilee ye shall return every man unto his possession. 14. And when thou makest a sale to thy neighbor or buyest from the hand of thy neighbor, oppress ye not one another. 15. By the number of years after the jubilee thou shalt buy of thy neighbor; by the number of years of the crops he shall sell to thee. 16. According to the multitude of the years thou shalt increase its price, and according to the fewness of the years thou shalt diminish its price; for the number of crops he

All family rights of liberty and property are restored; all the breaches and disturbances of the last forty-nine years are healed and repaired. 11. *That fiftieth year* shall be like the forty-ninth and all seventh years before: there shall be no sowing nor pruning, no reaping nor gathering. 12. *It is the jubilee,* a holy year in its restitution of all temporal things. *Out of the field,* in common with all animated nature, not out of the private store gathered in this year, for there shall be none such, ye shall eat its produce. Such is the peculiar institution of the jubilee.

13–34. This portion of the chapter treats of the inalienable inheritance of an Israelite, under two heads, sale and redemption. First, of sale (13–24). *In this year of the jubilee,* the first privilege of every Israelite is to return to his patrimonial estate. 14. *Oppress ye not one another.* In buying or selling there is to be no fraud or violence, no taking advantage of the necessities of any party. 15. The number of years after the last jubilee is to be deducted from the full number of forty-nine, and the number of crops for the remainder of the year is all that can be bought or sold. The buyer naturally looks to the number of years to be abated; the seller, to the number to be reckoned in the price. 16. The price is to be in proportion to the number of intervening years. So the land was not bought, but only the use of the fruit for a given number of years. 17. The fear of the Lord

selleth unto thee. 17. And ye shall not oppress every one his neighbor, but thou shalt fear thy God: for I am the LORD your God. 18. And ye shall do my statutes and keep my judgments and do them; and ye shall dwell in the land securely. 19. And the land shall yield its fruit, and ye shall eat enough, and ye shall dwell on it securely. 20. And if ye say, What shall we eat the seventh year? Lo, we shall not sow nor gather in our produce: 21. Then I will command my blessing upon you the sixth year, and it shall yield

is to deter from oppression. 18. *Keep my judgments and do them*, give heed to them with the intent of doing them, and carry this intent into effect. *Dwell in the land securely*, relying on the immutable promise of him who is holy, just, and true. 19. *Yield its fruit.* Happiness, consisting in the full enjoyment of all things needful, will be the invariable consequence of holiness. 20. *And if ye say.* This is the question of him who looks no further than the laws of nature, and is prone to conceive them absolutely immutable, or amenable to no higher law than he has observed. *We shall not sow.* We are required not to take the only means known to us of providing for our daily wants. 21. *I will command my blessing.* This is the higher law, to which nature yields obeisance. Moral ends transcend physical. Above nature is the God of nature who has a moral creation to which the natural creation is merely subservient. *Upon you*, who bear my moral image, for whom the earth was made. *The sixth year*, of which they had a weekly illustration in the double manna of the sixth day. *Produce for three years.* The question in the letter regarded merely the sabbatical year. The answer reaches to the year of jubilee. It must be remembered, as has been noticed on vs. 9, that the first half of the seventh civil year was the second half of the sixth sacred year. In the language of the sacred year, then, which is that of the text, while the reaping of the sixth sacred year was also that of the sixth civil year, occurring in the first half of the one and in the second half of the other, yet, on the other hand, it was the sowing of the sixth sacred year that was to be omitted for the seventh or sabbath year; for this was the sowing of the seventh

produce for three years. 22. And ye shall sow the eighth year, and eat of the old produce until the ninth year; until its produce come in ye shall eat the old. 23. And the land shall not be sold out and out: for the land is mine; for ye are strangers and sojourners with me. 24. And in all the land of your possession ye shall grant redemption for the land. §

25. If thy brother fail and sell part of his possession, his redeemer that is near of kin shall come and redeem that which

civil year. In like manner, it was the sowing of the seventh sacred year that was to be omitted for the eighth or jubilee year; for this was the sowing of the eighth civil year. And for the same reason still the sowing of the eighth sacred year, which is spoken of in vs. 22, is that of the ninth civil year, which is, accordingly, as it ought to be, the year after the jubilee. We now understand produce for three years. The crop of the sixth sacred year is blessed so as to suffice, along with the spontaneous growth, for three years. There is no sowing in the sixth sacred (seventh civil) year, and in the case of the jubilee no sowing in the seventh sacred (eighth civil) year. 22. But *ye shall sow in the eighth year*, that is, the eighth sacred year, or the first half of the ninth civil year. Hence, the crop of the sixth sacred year serves from the opening months of that year to the opening months of the ninth year. "Until its produce come in, ye shall eat of the old. 23. *Sold out and out.* It cannot be alienated beyond redemption. *For the land is mine.* It belonged not to the people, but to the Lord, who did not therefore allow the father to alienate from the son, as if it were his own absolutely. He could not encumber it beyond the fiftieth year, and seldom so long. *Ye are strangers and sojourners with me.* The land is for you, while you are on it, but no longer. It must then go to your descendant of the next generation. 24. The purchaser is even bound to restore it to the real owner, if he can pay the proportion of the purchase-money for the years that have yet to run till the jubilee.

25–28. Land always redeemable. *If thy brother fail,* be reduced to poverty, and forced to sell some of his land. *His redeemer.*[25] This interesting term, which occurs so early as Gen. xlviii. 16, where it is

his brother hath sold. 26. And if a man have no redeemer and his hand reach and he find enough to redeem it, 27. Then he shall count the years of its sale, and restore the surplus to the man to whom he sold it; and he shall return to his possession. 28. And if his hand find not enough to restore to him, then that which is sold shall remain in the hands of the buyer until the year of jubilee, and it shall go out in the jubilee, and he shall return to his possession. §

29. And if a man sell a dwelling-house in a walled city, then it may be redeemed until the end of the year after its sale; for a term of days it may be redeemed. 30. And if it be not redeemed until the whole year is fulfilled, then the house which is in a walled city standeth out and out to the buyer for his generations; it shall not go out at the jubilee. 31. But the houses of villages that have not walls around

applied to the Supreme Being, comes from a root signifying to loose, release, deliver, redeem. Redeemer is the term least open to objection; but it is too narrow for the original, which includes the functions of redeeming the land, ransoming the person, avenging the death, and perpetuating the line of him to whom he is next of kin. The obligation of the next of kin to discharge these functions was held to be most solemn and inviolable. 26. *No redeemer,* no near kinsman, such as is described in vs. 48, 49, or none having the means of redemption. He may himself, by his industry, earn the means of redemption. 27. The purchaser is bound to accept the part of the price which is proportional to the remaining years till the jubilee, and return the land *to the owner.* 28. In the third place, he may have neither redeemer nor means of redemption; in which case the land remains with the purchaser till the jubilee, and then returns to him or his heir without purchase.

29–34. A house when redeemable, and when not. 29. *A dwelling-house in a walled city,* if sold, may be redeemed within a year. *For a term of days.* Any period up to a full year is simply a number of days. 30. *Standeth out and out,* with a silencing, cutting off, or ex-

them shall be counted as the field of the country: such may be redeemed, and they go out at the jubilee. 32. But the cities of the Levites, the houses of the cities of their possession, may the Levites redeem at any time. 33. And whosoever may redeem from the Levites, the sale of the house and city of his possession shall go out in the jubilee; for the houses of the cities are their possession among the sons of Israel. 34. And the field of the suburb of their cities shall not be sold; for it is their perpetual possession. §

35. And if thy brother fail and his hand shake with thee, thou shalt hold him up, a stranger and sojourner he shall live with thee. 36. Thou shalt not take of him usury nor increase, but shalt fear thy God, and thy brother shall live with thee.

tinction of all claim on the part of the seller. 31. *The houses of villages*, that are not walled. These are to be counted as the field. They may be redeemed, or they go out at the jubilee. 32. The houses of the cities of the Levites are redeemable at any length of time or in perpetuity. The reason of this is obvious. They have no part in the land, and these houses are their only inheritance, without which they would have no habitation in the land. 33. *May redeem from the Levites.* The cities and houses of the Levites were given by the tribes to them out of their own inheritance. To buy back any part of that which was so given was therefore to redeem it. But the sale on the part of the Levite could only be for the number of years till the next jubilee. 34. *The field of the suburb.* The town parks assigned to the Levites could not be permanently alienated, as they were necessary to those who inhabited the town.

35–55. Concerning the serf and his emancipation. 35–38. The treatment due to a poor brother. *If thy brother fail*, fall into poverty. *And his hand shake*, if any inability to earn his bread befall him. *Thou shalt hold him up*, receive him as a stranger and sojourner into thy house, giving him food and clothing, and receiving from him whatever work he can do. 36. Neither interest nor increase is to be required of him. *Fear thy God.* The fear of God is the

37. Thy money thou shalt not give to him on usury; nor give him thy food for increase. 38. I am the LORD your God, who have brought you out of the land of Mizraim, to give you the land of Kenaan, to be your God. §

39. And if thy brother fail with thee and be sold unto thee, thou shalt not lay a hard service on him. 40. As a hireling, as a sojourner, he shall be with thee; unto the year of jubilee he shall serve with thee. 41. And he shall go out from thee, he and his sons with him; and return to his family and to the possession of his fathers shall he return. 42. For they are my servants, whom I brought out from the land of Mizraim; they shall not be sold into bondage. 43. Thou shalt not rule over him with rigor, but shalt fear thy God. 44. And thy bond-

motive to brotherly kindness. He that loveth his Heavenly Father should love his brother, who is the son of that Father. 37. The precept of disinterested kindness is repeated for the sake of emphasis. 38. The reason is presented again in a still more impressive form. *I am the Lord your God.* The God of performance, who brought you out of the land of bondage; the God of mercy, who forgave and accepted you; your God, who is in covenant with you, and conducts you to the land flowing with milk and honey. Go thou, and do with like good-will toward thy brother.

39–46. Kindness to the serf. The impoverished man that sells himself to his brother is to be treated not as a bond-servant, but as *a hireling* or *a sojourner*, a laborer hired from day to day, or a sojourner who labors with thee for a longer period while he is free. And he is to go out free at the jubilee. According to Ex. xxi. 2, the Hebrew serf was to go free after six years of serfdom. The approach of the jubilee might shorten this period to any extent. 41. *He and his sons.* They shall recover liberty and inheritance at the same time. 42. *My servants.* No other man may treat them as his slaves. They shall not be sold into perpetual bondage. 43. The fear of God will constrain thee to treat his servants with gentleness and consideration. 44–46. *Shall be of the nations.* The nations have forsaken their Maker.

man and thy bondmaid, which thou shalt have, shall be of the nations that are around you; of them shall ye buy bondman and bondmaid. 45. And also of the sons of the sojourners that dwell among you, of them shall ye buy, and of their families that are with you, which they have begotten in your land; and they shall be your possession. 46. And ye shall bequeath them to your sons after you to hold as a possession; ye shall be served by them forever; but over your brethren, the sons of Israel, thou shalt not rule, one over another, with rigor. §

47. And if the hand of a stranger and sojourner with thee avail, and thy brother fail with him and be sold to the stranger and sojourner with thee, or to the stock of a stranger's family, 48. After he is sold he may be redeemed; one of his brethren

They are in a state of rebellion against him. To treat them as slaves is a measure of punishment for this crime of treason against heaven, which the God of heaven is warranted to inflict by his servants. Hence the children of Israel were allowed to purchase and hold slaves of the Gentiles, whether belonging to other lands or residing among them, and to bequeath them to their descendants. It is to be remembered, however, that if they were incorporated into the nation by circumcision, they were to be treated as natives; and also that no other nation, much less church, has ever received a similar commission concerning the rest of the human race. Now that the Gentiles under the Christian dispensation are invited to accept the life, inheritance, and liberty of the gospel of salvation, such a commission would be altogether incongruous with the spirit of the message, and can never be renewed. See on the law of serfdom in Israel, Ex. xxi. 1-11.

47-55. The law regarding an Israelite who had become a serf to a Gentile. 47, 48. *If the hand.* Hence it appears that a stranger sojourning among the Israelites might attain to wealth, while an Israelite might sink into poverty. This indicates that the civil polity of Israel was not adverse to the prosperity of Gentiles residing among them. The Israelite sold to a foreigner may be redeemed at any time. The foreigner must be residing in the land of Israel, in order

may redeem him. 49. Or his uncle or his uncle's son may redeem him, or any of the near kinsmen of his family may redeem him; or if his hand avail he may redeem himself. 50. And he shall reckon with his buyer, from the year of his sale to the year of jubilee; and the price of his sale shall be according to the number of years; as the days of a hireling shall he be with him. 51. If there be yet many years, according to them he shall restore his ransom out of the money of his purchase. 52. And if few years remain until the year of jubilee and he reckon with him, according to his years he shall return his ransom price. 53. As a yearly hireling shall he be with him; he shall not rule over him with rigor in thy sight. 54. And if he be not redeemed by these, then he shall go out in the year of jubilee, he and his sons with him. 55. For unto me are the sons of Israel servants; they are

to be amenable to the laws of Israel. 49. A brother, uncle, cousin, or other near kinsman may in this case undertake the function of the *goel*. This obligation appears to extend to the next of kin, however remote. *If his hand avail.* This implies that the serf, even under a Gentile, might have some means of realizing money. 50. *As the days of a hireling.* The Israelite serf was to be redeemable at any time, so that his term of service might end like that of a hireling. 51, 52. The ransom price will vary according to the number of years the state of bondage has yet to run; and it cannot run beyond the jubilee. 53. The master is to be merciful to his serf. He is to deal with him as with a free man who is hired from day to day. *In thy sight.* This is addressed to the magistrate, who is to have his eyes open to the treatment of the serf, and take measures that it be dictated not by rigor, but by kindness. 54. *Not redeemed by these* friends or means. If he have no kinsman or none able to redeem him, and do not attain the means of redeeming himself, he shall go out free at the jubilee, and his children with him. 55. The Israelite is God's servant, and therefore no other can have the right of a master over him. *They are my servants.* He has brought them out of bondage to the heathen.

my servants, whom I brought out of the land of Mizraim; I am the LORD your God.

I am the Lord your God. This pregnant sentence needs to be again and again repeated, that this infant people may at length come to understand its import. It involves the obligations of power, love, and reason. You should know him; for he has made you rational and intelligent. You should love him; for he is your God, your Father, Deliverer, Quickener. You should obey him; for he has the right of creation and preservation over you.

The jubilee rises over the sabbatical year, as the day of Pentecost was over the weekly sabbath. Each was the fiftieth after seven sabbaths. As the sabbath-day was a day of release from the payment of debt, because no business was to be transacted on that day, so the sabbath-year was a year of release from the payment of a debt (Deut. xv.), because a debt could not ordinarily be paid when there was no sowing or reaping. As the sabbath-day was an occasion of rejoicing in the liberty of rest from labor, so the day of Pentecost was an occasion of rejoicing in the liberty of abundance of the means of life in the harvest reaped. As the sabbath-year affords a release at the same time from toil and from the demand of the creditor, so the year of Pentecost affords the unmeasured blessings of freedom from bondage, and restoration to all the rights of property. But the whole economy of Israel was a type of higher things, of things in the church on earth in its wider range, and of things in the general assembly and church of the first-born who are written in heaven. So it is with the jubilee. It affords to the prophetic seer a fine figure of the advent of Messiah and of the effect of his mission. The Lord hath sent him to bind up the broken-hearted, to proclaim liberty to the captive and the opening of the prison to the bound, to preach the acceptable year of the Lord and the day of vengeance of our God, and to restore them by a new birth to an inheritance incorruptible and undefiled and that fadeth not away, reserved in heaven for those who are kept by the power of God through faith unto salvation.

It may be said with truth that these ordinances, the primitive simplicity of which awakens in the unsophisticated heart some touch of romance and enthusiasm, failed to produce all the holy and happy results which they were calculated to effect. The sabbath-day, the cycle of annual festivals, the sabbath-year, and the jubilee fell into oblivion and neglect, and the chosen people, during a long history of more than twenty centuries, again and again forsook the Lord God of their fathers and served other gods, or served the true God with a show of wisdom in will-worship which came to be contrary to the main spirit and letter of divine revelation. Nevertheless, by these significant institutions, and the written revelation in which they were embodied and illustrated, a seed of divine truth was planted in the heart and memory of man which has not died out after the space of twenty-four centuries. Through these years of struggle and persecution it has brought to the birth of a new and holy existence all that have adorned the profession of an Israelite or a Christian indeed, in whom is no guile. And at this day it maintains the spiritual life of all Christendom, fills and extends the boundaries of civilization, and makes its benign influence felt to the utmost limits of the human race. It has not therefore been sown in vain; and it is destined eventually to accomplish the whole purpose for which it was sent.

NOTES.

5. *Self-growth*, סָפִיחַ, that which grows spontaneously; αὐτόματα; r. *add, pour out*. *Nazarite*, נָזִיר, separate, solitary, undressed; ἁγίασμα; r. *separate, consecrate*. The original is retained, as it is by the English version in Num. vi., to indicate the connection.

9. *Glad sound*, תְּרוּעָה, trumpet blast; φωνή; r. *ring, clang, shout*.

10. *Jubilee*, יוֹבֵל, acclaim, joyful sound; σημασία, *signal*; r. *cry, shout for joy*.

23. *Out and out*, לְצְמִתֻת, to extinction; εἰς βεβαίωσιν; r. *cut off, silence*.

25. *Redeemer*, גֹּאֵל, releaser, upholder, avenger; ἀγχιστεύων.

XXVI. AN ADMONITION.

This chapter stands to the book of Leviticus as Ex. xxiii. 20-33 to the code of civil law contained in Ex. xxi.–xxiii. It holds out a promise of protection and prosperity in the land, as the latter passage gives an assurance of guidance on the way to it. It opens with a prohibition of idolatry (1, 2), puts on record a glowing promise of prosperity to those who obey the law (3–13), pronounces a solemn

XXVI. 1. Ye shall not make for you false gods nor rear up for you a graven image nor a pillar, nor set up a figured stone in your land, to bow down to it; for I am the LORD your God. 2. My sabbaths ye shall keep and fear my sanctuary. I am the LORD.   33 ¶ ¶ ¶

sentence of chastisement on the disobedient, arranged in an ascending scale of five successive stages (14–33), and closes with a statement of the end sought by the corrective judgments accumulated on the people, namely, that the land may enjoy its sabbaths and the people may be brought to repentance (34–46). This remarkable warning turns out to be a no less remarkable foreboding of the future history of the people down to the times of the New Testament. It stands here as a part of the communication begun in the preceding chapter, to which it contains many allusions.

1, 2. The prohibition of the worship of false gods. *Ye shall not make for you.* They were made either by the imagination of the worshippers or by the hands of the artist. *False gods*, gods of a misguided imagination that have no reality, or relics of a traditionary idea of God which have gained many elements of falsehood and lost the essentials of truth. This is the breach of the first commandment. *Nor rear up.* There is to be no making nor rearing up, much less worshipping, of idols. Some think that they may use the image, if they do not worship it. That is not the doctrine or demand of Scripture. *A graven image.* This is the breach of the second commandment. The debased mind cannot rest satisfied without a visible figure of the deity, or at least a typical object of worship. The former is the graven image which aims at giving some analagous conception of the deity, and soon falls into the error of confounding the substance with the shadow. The latter is the pillar, which belongs to a ruder and severer mode of deviating into error. *A figured stone.* The image was probably of wood. The figured stone differs from the pillar in being carved into the form of an idol, or with figures or symbols on its surface. *For I am the Lord your God.* I, who have given you all this instruction concerning my essence and purpose, am the Lord your God. This sentence expresses the fundamental principle of all religion, and has often been explained. It must be stamped in letters

3. If ye walk in my statutes and keep my commandments and do them, 4. Then I will give your showers in their season, and the land shall yield its increase and the tree of the field shall yield its fruit. 5. And the threshing shall reach for you the vintage, and the vintage shall reach the seed-time ; and ye shall eat your bread to the full, and dwell securely in

of light on the mind of the Israelite. Hence it is repeated again and again. It contains the reason for avoiding all idolatry. *My sabbaths, my sanctuary;* the time and place of worship. The weekly sabbath and the day of atonement were to be celebrated by a total cessation of business. The other six days of holy convocation released the laborer from his toil, while they did not require the abandonment of lighter occupations. The sabbatical and jubilee years are equally in favor of the men of toil. And hence the sabbath of the land was truly to it a sabbath of rest. The holy place was the tabernacle and its precincts. But the place of convocation in all their villages and the home of every family had each its own peculiar sanctity which was to be truly revered. The sabbaths and the sanctuary mean here, all the sacred lessons, exercises, and habits which are connected with the time and the place.

3–13. The promise to those who keep the law. 3. The condition stated. The people have been accepted. They are now to be regarded as a holy nation, circumcised in heart, and therefore fitted by divine grace to walk in the statutes of God. To such the condition is proper. 4. *Your showers.* Rain is the source of vegetable growth. It is therefore the antecedent of corn and wine. *In their season.* The autumnal rains begin usually in the end of October or beginning of November when the seed was sown. They continue at intervals during November and December. The spring rains cease in the month of March. These are called the early and the latter rains which water the newly-sown fields and the full-grown grain. Rain ceases during the harvest in May and all the summer. By these showers in their season the land yields its increase and the tree its fruit. 5. *The threshing* beginning in May or June will reach to the vintage beginning in July, and that to the seed-time in October and

your land. 6. And I will give peace in the land, and ye shall lie down and none make you afraid; and I will rid the evil beast out of the land, and the sword shall not pass through your land. 7. And ye shall chase your enemies, and they shall fall before you by the sword. 8. And five of you shall chase a hundred, and a hundred of you shall chase ten thousand; and your enemies shall fall before you by the sword. 9. And I will regard you and make you fruitful, and multiply you, and establish my covenant with you. 10. And ye shall eat old store, and bring out the old because of the new. 11. And I will set my tabernacle among you, and my soul shall not abhor you. 12. And I will walk among you, and I will be your God, and ye shall be my people. 13. I am the LORD your God who have brought you out of the land of Miz-

November. Plenty and security are the promised blessings of this verse. 6. *And I will give peace.* The wonted state of your land will be peace in the pregnant sense of the absence of the violent man, the evil beast, and the sword. 7, 8. *And five of you shall chase a hundred.* Victory will crown your army when an enemy appears. 9. *I will regard you,* have my eye upon you for good. Here are four blessings in this verse: favor, fruitfulness, multiplication, and stability of covenant from God. 10. Superabundance. The old store will yet be unexhausted when the new fruits come in. 11. *I will set my tabernacle.* He will dwell among them, holding daily intercourse with them. *My soul shall not abhor you;* a very singular phrase, intimating that there is moral deformity in them on account of which they might be justly abhorred, but at the same time implying that propitiation has been made and purification begun. 12. *I will walk among you,* have personal and practical intercourse with you. The covenant relation is expressed in the affecting words, "I will be your God, and ye shall be my people"; your God, forgiving and accepting you; my people, penitent and confiding towards me. 13. The promise now closes with the standing watchword, "I am the Lord your God," and the historical appeal to what he had already done for them, which was a pledge of

raim from being their bondmen; and I brake the bars of your yoke, and made you walk upright.

14. And if ye hearken not unto me nor do all these my commandments, 15. And if ye despise my statutes, and if your soul abhor my judgments, so that ye do not all my commandments, but break my covenant, 16. I also will do this unto you, and I will appoint over you terror, decay, and fever, consuming the eyes and wasting the soul; and ye shall

the performance of all that was now promised. *Brake the bars of your yoke, and made you walk upright.* A strong and impressive figure to exhibit to them the new-born liberty into which they were now introduced. It is taken from the bar of wood which was bent round the necks of oxen and fastened to the pole or yoke. The breaking of this yoke off the necks of the Israelites enabled them to walk uprightly. There is a regular gradation in these ten verses of promise. First are placed the material blessings in seven verses and then the spiritual in three. Rain, peace, and the favor of Providence, with their natural consequences make up the temporal blessings. To dwell with them, walk with them, and be their covenant God are the spiritual blessings.

14–33. The threat against disobedience. 14–17. The first correction for disobedience. 14, 15. The case of disobedience put in four successive stages: if ye hearken not, do not my commandments, despise my statutes, and your soul abhor my judgments. Here is evidently a climax in sinful habit going on from simple inattention to the abhorrence of the inmost soul. Again, the object is first "me," then my commandments, the moral law especially, next my statutes, the positive enactments of the theocracy, and, lastly, my judgments, the decisions which affirm principles and afford precedents for future guidance. The result of this state of the moral habit is disobedience and consequent breach of covenant. 16. The following two verses contain the corrective judgments which will in this case be sent upon them. *Terror*, a mental affliction, the sure consequence of an evil conscience. *Decay and fever*, contrasted kinds of bodily disease. *Consuming the eyes.* The dull eye is the invariable mark of wasted

sow your seed in vain and your enemies shall eat it. 17. And I will set my face against you, and ye shall be smitten before your enemies; and they that hate you shall rule over you, and ye shall flee when none chaseth you.

18. And if on this ye hearken not unto me, then I will yet chastise you seven times for your sins. 19. And I will break the pride of your strength; and I will make your sky as iron and your land as brass. 20. And your strength shall be spent in vain, and your land shall not yield its increase, nor the tree of the land yield its fruit.

21. And if ye walk against me and do not wish to hearken unto me, then I will add seven strokes unto you for your sins.

powers. *And wasting the soul*, wearing out the animal life, which is the effect of fever. *Sow your seed in vain*. The seed sown either does not ripen or is devoured by the enemy. 17. *I will set my face against you*. Then all things work together against them. They shall be smitten by the enemy, ruled over by their foes, and shall even flee when no man pursueth.

18–20. The second correction, if disobedience be continued. 18. *And if on this*, notwithstanding all these chastisements. *Seven times*, a complete number of judgments, leaving no excuse from insufficient warning or rebuke. 19. *Break the pride*. It is pride of strength that tempts to self-confidence and self-will. It is the great antagonist of God, and must fall. *Your sky as iron*, and therefore no showers in their season. *Your land as brass*, and therefore no growth of seed sown, nor budding of the vine. 20. *Your strength shall be spent in vain*. The simple withholding of one blessing, rain, will make all your strength be spent in vain. The land will yield no increase, the tree no fruit.

21, 22. The third correction, if they still persist in backsliding. 21. *If ye walk against me*. Hitherto it has been, "if ye hearken not unto me"; now it is, "if ye walk against me," implying no longer inattention, but active opposition to God. *Then I will add*. The judgments are cumulative. *Seven strokes*. Another complete series

22. And I will send upon you the wild beast and it shall bereave you, and cut off your cattle and make you few, and your highways shall be desolate. 23. And if on this ye be not chastened for me, and walk against me, 24. Then I also will walk against you, and I also will smite you seven times for your sins. 25. And I will bring upon you a sword that will avenge the covenant; and ye shall be gathered in your cities, and I will send a pestilence among you, and ye shall be delivered into the hand of the enemy. 26. When I break the staff of your bread ten women shall bake your bread in one oven and return your bread by weight; and ye shall eat and not be satisfied. §

of chastisements will be inflicted. 22. *The wild beast.* This indicates the wasting of their strength and the decrease of population. *Bereave you*, rob you of your children, cut off your cattle, diminish your numbers, and cause your roads to be unfrequented.

23-26. The fourth correction, on persisting in apostasy. 23. *And if on this ye be not chastened.* If the accumulated troubles of the past have not the effect of humbling you and awakening repentance, as they might have done, other measures still are to be tried. 24. *I also will walk against you.* Punishment is retributive. *Smite you seven times.* This is a sevenfold stroke of retribution, in which their opposition only encounters a mightier opposition. They run only on the thick bosses of his buckler. 25. *A sword that will avenge the covenant.* This is the sword of a mighty conqueror whom the Lord will now raise up against them. This is the walking against them of which he speaks. It will avenge a broken, down-trodden covenant, the covenant of the God of mercy, which they have dishonored. The usual calamities of war are now depicted. They will be beseiged in their cities, visited with the pestilence, and delivered into captivity. 26. *I will break the staff of bread.* In addition to the sword, famine will desolate the land. Ten women will prepare the bread for a whole city. *In one oven*, which will be sufficient for the scanty supply. *By weight*, on account of the scarcity of the means of life. " Ye shall

LEVITICUS XXVI. 27-30. 305

27. And if on this ye hearken not unto me, and walk against me, 28. Then I will walk against you in fury, and I, even I, will chasten you seven times for your sins. 29. And ye shall eat the flesh of your sons and the flesh of your daughters shall ye eat. 30. And I will destroy your high places and cut down your sun-stocks, and cast your carcasses upon the carcasses of your blocks, and my soul shall abhor you. 31. And I will

eat and not be satisfied." Here is an accumulation of miseries on the head of the obstinately disobedient people.

27-33. The fifth and final correction. Its consequences are depicted in the remainder of the chapter. 27, 28. *I will walk against you in fury.* If, in this weakened, wasted, vanquished condition, they still walk against God, they will be visited by a still more severe retribution, a walking in fury, and a sevenfold chastisement for their sins. 29. The dire necessities and extremities of famine are here described. Such revolting acts are recorded in the seige of Samaria by the Syrians (2 Kings vi. 28, 29), in the seige of Jerusalem by the Chaldeans (Lam. ii. 20; iv. 10), and in the seige of the same city by Titus (Joseph. Bell. Jud. v. 10, 3). The seer has his eye upon the dark scenes of the future. 30. The cause of all their disaster is unveiled in the next stroke. *I will destroy your high places.* The false gods in whom they put their trust will be destroyed. The high places were the altars and other religious erections on hills, at which either the true God was unlawfully worshipped, or idolatry was openly practised. *Sun stocks*[30] were cones, pyramids, or other figures representing the sun as worshipped under the title Baal-chammon, or lord of heat. The Phenicians and Persians were votaries of a deity of fire under different forms. *Blocks,*[30] or logs or stones. These were pieces of wood or stone resembling or representing some object of idolatrous worship. The worshipper and the worshipped are here involved in the same ruin. It is very significant to find this word so familiar in the time of Ezekiel. *And my soul shall abhor you.* This is the contrast to the promise in vs. 11. The absolute Fountain of reason must abhor all such unreason in opinion or intention as is involved in the worship of stocks or stones, as well as in the practice of any form of presump-

make your cities waste and desolate your sanctuaries, and I will not smell your sweet odors. 32. And I will desolate the land; and your enemies that dwell in it shall be amazed at it. 33. And I will scatter you among the nations and draw out a sword after you; and your land shall be desolate and your cities waste.

tuous sin. 31. The scene of dreary desolation rises more and more plainly before the eye. *I will make your cities waste.* The siege is at an end, the inhabitants are gone. *And desolate your sanctuaries.* Apart from its importance in the scene of ruin, this plural term has an interest of its own. It contemplates a plurality of sanctuaries to meet the requirements of the nation when settled in the country assigned to it, and covering an extent of territory and having an amount of population which would render it inconvenient or impossible for all to fulfil their religious obligations at the one central sanctuary. Only the national representative worship could be duly performed at one centre even for so small a country as Palestine. The private duties of religion needed local sanctuaries at least as numerous as the tribes; and in the event of the extension of the commonwealth of Israel by internal growth and by the accession of proselytes from the nations, new local sanctuaries would have to be continually added. It is evident from this passage that it was not designed to confine the offering of sacrifices on the part of individuals and families to one sole, central place. *I will not smile.* This is an intimation that he will no longer be propitious. The time of acceptance is past. They have trodden under foot the blood of the everlasting covenant. There remaineth no more sacrifice for sin. 32. *I will desolate the land.* As the Amorites before them, so now the chosen people are swept away from the land. The conquerors who possess and dwell in it are amazed at its desolation. 33. This verse gives the last stroke to the picture. *I will scatter you among the nations.* While their land lies waste and their cities in ruins, they themselves are dispersed among the nations and the sword unsheathed against them. More than once has this description been realized in the history of this people. They were carried away into captivity in part by Tiglath-pileser (2 Kings xv. 29), by

34. Then shall the land enjoy its sabbaths all the days of its desolation, while ye are in the land of your enemies; then shall the land rest and enjoy its sabbaths. 35. All the days of its desolation it shall rest, because it did not rest in your sabbaths, when ye dwelt upon it. 36. And upon them that are left among you I will send a faintness into their hearts in the lands of their enemies, and the sound of a falling leaf

Shalmaneser (2 Kings xviii. 29), and by Nebuchadnezzar on three several occasions. Returning after seventy years of captivity they remained in their own country with various fortune until the siege of Jerusalem by Titus, which terminated in the razing of the walls and the burning of the temple. For eighteen centuries from that event they have been without a country, and are at this day scattered among the nations. The prophetic picture, melancholy though it is, has been fully borne out by the reality.

34–46. The ends contemplated in these multiplied chastisements. These are chiefly two. The land is to enjoy its sabbaths and the people are to be brought to repentance. The present aim, to admonish the infant people for their real and perpetual welfare, precludes anything more than the most distant allusion to the more comprehensive purpose for which the peculiar people were called into existence, namely, that all the families of the earth might be blessed in the seed of Abraham. 34. *The land enjoy its sabbaths.* What a touching appeal there is in this to the infant people in their first love! It pictures to them a people become so besotted with worldliness and idolatry as to neglect the sabbatical and jubilee years, if not the weekly sabbaths. The long years of desolation, during the exile of the people, are to compensate for this neglect. The statement is repeated to enhance its affecting impression. 35. The prophetic event is a third time repeated, with the reason for it expressly annexed. 36. From the land he passes to the people, who should be far away from it. *A faintness*,[36] (Deut. xxviii. 65). This is an exact description of the mental state of the Jews in the captivity, and in their dispersion after the Christian era. *The sound of a falling leaf,* the feeblest rustle that strikes the ear, breeds alarm and prompts to flight. The startled fancy

shall chase them; and they shall take flight as from the sword, and they shall fall when none chaseth. 37. And they shall stumble one upon another as before a sword when no one chaseth, and there will be to you no standing before your enemies. 38. And ye shall perish among the nations, and the land of your enemies will eat you up. 39. And they that remain of you shall pine away in their iniquity in the lands of your enemies; and also in the iniquities of their fathers, with them shall they pine away. 40. And they shall confess their iniquity and the iniquity of their fathers in their transgression which they have committed against me, and also that they have walked against me. 41. When I also walk against them, and have brought them into the land of their enemies, if then their uncircumcised heart be bowed down, and then they enjoy

conjures up a sword, and they fall down as slain when no man pursues. 37. They stumble one upon another; they are far from standing before the enemy. 38. They shall perish in great numbers, because of the oppression and persecution which the nations among whom they dwell in the height of their panic or the intensity of their hate will practise upon them. *The land of your enemies*, as a ravenous beast, will eat you up. 39. *Shall pine away in their iniquity.* Their iniquity and the iniquity of their fathers, their iniquity as individuals and as a nation; will be the source of their decline. 40. The main end of all their chastisements is now brought out. *They shall confess.* A case is here put: if they confess. The whole of the heart-rending description already given is, indeed, put before the people as one long supposition or possibility, for the purpose of making an indelible impression upon their hearts. *And the iniquity of their fathers.* They are a whole of manifold growth and continuity. Their iniquity has been of long standing and wide consequence. They are reaping the fruits of a heritage of crime. *In their transgression* is the fruit not only of their own evil heart, but of the inherited disaffection of their fathers. 41. *When I also walk against*, meet their aggravated sin with sevenfold retribution in five successive stages. This remarkable

their iniquity, 42. Then will I remember my covenant with Jacob, and also my covenant with Isaac, and also my covenant with Abraham will I remember; and the land I will

warning is not constructed upon the principle of an exact and literal adaptation of the outline to the reality. Yet the history of Israel admits of a fivefold division. The times of the judges down to Eli, the intervals from Samuel to Rehoboam, from Jeroboam to the captivity of the ten tribes, from Hezekiah to the seventy years of captivity, from the return to the destruction of the temple, and the dispersion that continues to the present day, are sufficiently marked. To note one mark of these periods, "terror" grew to the time of Eli, "the pride of their strength" was broken in the time of Rehoboam, "the wild beast" figures again in the desolation of the land on the exile of the ten tribes (2 King xvii. 25), the "sword" becomes very prominent in the time of Josiah and his three sons, and the eating of human flesh in the famine of a siege, the desolated sanctuary, the literal ceasing to smell the sweet odors, and the scattering among the heathen, stand out very conspicuous in the conquest of Titus and its consequences. An elaborate essay on this whole passage would tend very much to illustrate the structure of prophetic composition and the mode of its interpretation. *If then their uncircumcised heart be bowed down.* This refers to the "pride of power" which is the leading characteristic of a fallen spirit. *And then they enjoy their iniquity.* To enjoy is here to feel that they are reaping the bitter fruit of their evil doings. This is a very bold, but still perfectly intelligible, figure. 42. *Then will I remember my covenant.* The threefold establishment of the covenant is here made prominent, and is significant of its perpetuity. It is very remarkable that in the fivefold hypothesis of rebellion against God there is not a hint of the final rejection of his people. In the covenant are found the momentous words, "In thee, in thy seed, shall all the families of the earth be blessed (Gen. xii. 3; xviii. 18; xxii. 18; xxvi. 4; xxviii. 14). The covenant was an immutable purpose of God, which is to this day in the process of being fulfilled. *And the land.* The land is to have its sabbaths. A remnant of the captives were brought back to it after the seventy years of exile

AN ADMONITION.

remember. 43. And the land shall be left of them and enjoy its sabbaths, when it is desolate without them, and they enjoy their iniquity, because, even because they despised my judgments and their soul abhorred my statutes. 44. And yet for all this, when they be in the land of their enemies I will not despise them nor abhor them to consume them, to break my covenant with them; for I am the LORD their God. 45. And I will remember for them the covenant of the former men, whom I brought out of the land of Mizraim in the sight of

(Jer. xxv. 11; xxix. 10; Dan. ix. 2; Ezra i. 1). As there are seven sabbath-years and one jubilee in every fifty years, seventy years of rest give a period of five hundred or four hundred and thirty years during which these years of rest were neglected. The interval from the crossing of the Jordan, about 1451, to the captivity of Judah was about eight hundred and forty-five years. Hence it appears that these sabbaths were neglected more than half the time from the conquest to the captivity. After the exile of seventy years the land of Judah, which had not been colonized like that of the ten tribes, was reoccupied by the returning remnant of the people. 43. The desolation is once more sadly attributed to the iniquity of which they were reaping the fruit. 44. *And yet for all this.* This is the counterpart of the oft-repeated "on this." In the land of their enemies they shall not be forgotten. The time of the judges and the period of the captivity afford the historical confirmation of this promise. *To consume them* utterly would be to break the covenant of the Lord, which cannot be done, because it is the immutable counsel of God, and involves in it the eternal purpose of salvation for man. *For.* The reasons now assigned are embraced in that word and seal of the covenant, "I am the Lord their God." At the end of this harassing prognostication it recurs once more. 45. *And I will remember.* God's memory never fails. *The covenant of the former men.* The covenant with Abraham, Isaac, and Jacob was fulfilled to their descendants who were brought out of Egypt, and solemnly renewed with them at Mount Sinai. This great event was transacted in the sight of all surrounding nations. *To be their God.* This is the import of the covenant. *I am the Lord.* This

the nations to be their God: I am the LORD. 46. These are the statutes and the judgments and the laws which the LORD made between himself and the sons of Israel in Mount Sinai by the hand of Moses. ¶

is its warrant. 46. *These are the statutes.* We have here the express testimony of Moses that this communication was made to him on Mount Sinai, and therefore antecedent to the erection of the tabernacle. This section is of so much importance as to warrant the appending of a closing formula. But the comprehensiveness of the terms " statutes and judgments and laws" appears to cover a considerable portion of Exodus as well Leviticus. The first seven chapters and the present section of Leviticus come expressly under the head of the legislation commencing with chap. xx. of Exodus, and communicated from Mount Sinai. And there is nothing to hinder the sections from chap. xvii. to the end of Leviticus being assigned to the same period. Moses having received these communications interposes the history of the making and erection of the tabernacle and of the consecration of the priests among these divine communications in the manner best fitted for their illustration. We shall find him pursuing the same course in the Book of Numbers. Chapters xi.–xvi. of Leviticus appear to have been communicated after the erection of the tabernacle.

NOTES.

1. *Figured stone,* אֶבֶן מַשְׂכִּית, stone of image, λίθον σκοπόν.
13. *Bars,* מֹטֹת, τόν δεσμόν; r. *move, shake.*
30. *Sun-stocks,* חַמָּנִים, the fire idols, τὰ ξύλινα χειροποίητα; r. *be hot.* *Blocks,* גִּלּוּלִים, trunks, logs, εἴδωλα; r. *roll.* This is a frequent word in Ezekiel, who uses it thirty-eight times. It occurs also twice in the Pentateuch, and seven times elsewhere.

XXVII. VOWS.

The vow is the promise to dedicate something to the Lord. It is therefore an act of free-will. But when once the vow has been made it is, in ordinary circumstances, binding (Num. xxx). Hence the vow is treated after matters of intrinsic obligation have been settled.

XXVII. 1. And the LORD spake unto Moses, saying, 2. Speak unto the sons of Israel and say unto them, When a man setteth apart a vow, at thy valuation shall the souls be to the LORD. 3. And thy valuation shall be of the male from twenty years old to sixty years old, even thy valuation shall be fifty shekels of silver, by the shekel of the sanctuary. 4. And if it be a female, then thy valuation shall be thirty shekels. 5. And if it be from five years old to twenty years old, then thy valua-

Reference has already been made incidentally to the vow in Lev. vii. 16 and xxii. 18. In this supplementary chapter the valuation of everything that may be made the object of a vow is determined: of persons (2–8); of cattle (9–13); of houses (14, 15); of land (16–25). All these may be redeemed except clean animals that are fit for sacrifice. The firstling cannot be vowed, because it is the Lord's (26, 27). That which is devoted cannot be sold or redeemed, but must be put to death (28, 29). The tithe is regulated in 30–38. The closing formula is in 34. This communication is made to Moses in Mount Sinai for the sons of Israel. .

1–8. Valuation of persons. 2. *When a man setteth apart*[2] *a vow*, or, as some render it, maketh a special vow. The verb no doubt means to distinguish as wonderful; but this is a distinction of all vowing. *At thy valuation.* At the valuation of Moses as the lawgiver. This only is consistent with the context which fixes the value. The communication is also addressed primarily to Moses. *Shall the souls be to the Lord.* In vows regarding persons the sum at which the person was valued was to be given to the Lord. The Levites, including the priests, were already consecrated to the service of God. It was not therefore necessary or desirable that persons vowed should be actually taken into his service as attendants at the tabernacle. Hence the arrangement of a rate which was to be payable for such persons. 3, 4. *From twenty years old to sixty.* This was the period of active service. *Fifty shekels of silver.* The slave was valued at thirty shekels (Ex. xxi. 32). *By the shekel of the sanctuary.* See on Ex. xxx. 10; Lev. v. 15. The female was valued at thirty shekels. 5, 6 *From five years old to twenty.* This was the period of youth or

tion shall be for the male twenty shekels and for the female ten shekels. 6. And if it be from a month old unto five years old, then shall thy valuation be of the male five shekels of silver, and for the female thy valuation shall be three shekels of silver. 7. And if it be from sixty years old and upwards, if a male, then shall thy valuation be fifteen shekels and for the female ten shekels. 8. And if he fail of thy valuation, then he shall present himself before the priest, and the priest shall value him; according to that which the hand of the vower reacheth shall the priest value him. §

9. And if it be a beast of which they make an offering unto the LORD, all that he giveth of such unto the LORD shall be holy. 10. He shall not alter it nor change it, good for bad, or bad for good; and if he do change beast for beast, both it and

minority. Twenty shekels are here allowed for the male and ten for the female. *From a month old to five years.* This is the period of infancy. The valuation is five shekels for the male and three for the female. This accords with the redemption price for a firstborn son (Num. xviii. 16). 7. *From sixty years old and upwards.* This is the time of old age. The valuation is fifteen shekels for the male and ten for the female. Females being of weaker frame are valued at a lower rate. The valuation is otherwise founded on age, or the capacity for service determined by age. 8. And if he fail of thy valuation, if he be so poor as to be unable to pay the fixed assessment, the priest is vested with authority to abate it according to his means.

9–13. Valuation of cattle. 9. *A beast of which they make an offering unto the Lord,* that is, of the herd or of the flock, is holy, and must be given to the Lord without exchange or redemption. 10. *He shall not alter it nor exchange it.* The former word may refer to the putting of one kind of beast in place of another, the latter to the substitution of a beast of the same kind. *Good for bad, or bad for good.* The animal vowed is holy, and is not to be exchanged in any way from any motive. If the exchange be made, both the animal vowed and its

its exchange shall be holy. 11. And if it be any unclean beast of which they do not make an offering unto the LORD, then he shall present the beast before the priest. 12. And the priest shall value it between good and bad; at the valuation of the priest it shall be. 13. And if he do redeem it, he shall add a fifth of it to thy valuation.

14. And if a man consecrate his house to be holy unto the LORD, then the priest shall value it between good and bad; as the priest valueth, so shall it stand. 15. And if the consecrator redeem his house, he shall add a fifth of the money of thy valuation unto it, and it shall be his.

16. And if of the field of his possession a man consecrate any part unto the LORD, then thy valuation shall be according to its seed; the seed of a homer of barley being valued at

exchange will be holy. This precludes any selfish motive. 11, 12. *And if it be an unclean beast*, that is, not allowed for sacrifice, and so not of the flock or the herd. This is to be presented before the priest, who shall value it "between good and bad," that is, at an average rate, and his valuation is to stand. 13. If the vower redeem it, he must add a fifth to this valuation. This also precludes any unworthy motive.

14, 15. Valuation of a house. Here again the priest shall fix the value. If the consecrator choose to redeem it, he shall add a fifth part to the valuation.

16-25. Valuation of land. 16-21. First, part of the field of his patrimony, which in ordinary circumstances he cannot alienate beyond the year of jubilee. 16. This the priest shall value according to its seed. *A homer of barley.* The homer, equal to ten ephahs or one hundred omers, contains about five and a half bushels of grain. At four or five bushels to the acre, this would sow more than an acre, and at a lower rate it would sow two acres. Fifty shekels at 2*s.* 3*d.* a shekel would amount to £6 4*s.* 6*d.* Fifty shekels for fifty years, or a shekel a year, is the value fixed for a portion of ground containing between one and a half and two statute acres. This

fifty shekels of silver. 17. If he consecrate his field from the year of jubilee at thy valuation it shall stand. 18. And if he consecrate his field after the jubilee, then the priest shall reckon unto him the money according to the years unto the year of jubilee, and abatement shall be made from thy valuation. 19. And if he that consecrates it do redeem the field, then he shall add a fifth of the money of thy valuation, and it shall stand as his. 20. And if he redeem not the field or have sold it to another man, it shall no more be redeemed. 21. And the field when it goeth out in the jubilee shall be holy unto the LORD; as a field devoted, the priest shall have possession of it.

22. And if he consecrate unto the LORD a field of his purchase, which is no part of the field of his possession, 23. Then the priest shall reckon to him the worth of thy valuation unto the year of jubilee; and he shall give thy valuation on that

was of course a moderate valuation. 17, 18. *From the year of jubilee.* The price being fixed for the period from jubilee to jubilee, that for the period from the time of vowing to the next jubilee is to be ascertained by simple proportion, "according to the years unto the year of jubilee." *Abatement shall be made* of the fixed valuation according to the number of years to the next jubilee. 19. If he redeem the field he shall add a fifth as usual, and it shall be his. 20. But if he do not redeem it, or if he sell it to another, and therefore of course do not redeem it, it shall never be redeemed. 21. At the jubilee when it goes out it shall be holy unto the Lord, as a field devoted. It becomes the possession of the priest.

22–25. Secondly, a purchased field. This is no part of his inheritance, and he has only the use of it till the jubilee. 23. The amount of the valuation is to be given *on that day* on which the vow is made. Plainly in this case the obligation could not be discharged by an annual payment, because the field might pass out of his hands at any time. No fifth part is here mentioned, because the use only of the

day as a holy thing unto the LORD. 24. In the year of jubilee the field shall return to him of whom he bought it, to whom the possession of the field belongeth. 25. And all thy valuations shall be by the shekel of the sanctuary; twenty gerahs shall be the shekel.

26. Only the firstling of a beast which belongeth to the LORD, no man shall consecrate it; whether ox or sheep, it is the LORD'S. 27. And if the beast be unclean, then he shall release it at thy valuation and add a fifth to it; and if not redeemed it shall be sold at thy valuation.

28. Only no devoted thing that a man devoteth unto the LORD of all that he hath, of man or of beast or of the field of his possession shall be sold or redeemed; every devoted thing

land till the jubilee was possessed by the vower. 24. The field in this case, according to xxv. 28, returns to him from whom it was bought. 25. The value of the shekel of the sanctuary is here defined. See on vs. 3.

26, 27. The firstling cannot be vowed. It belongs to the Lord already, and therefore cannot be vowed to him by one who does not possess it. It may be released, if unclean, by paying the valuation with a fifth added. If not, it is to be sold at the valuation.

28, 29. *A thing devoted*[23] is not to be redeemed or sold. The *cherem* is mentioned for the first time in this chapter. It means a person accursed or cut off from the communion of God or his people, or from the number of the living, or a thing accursed and so cut off from all common use and given over to destruction. This ban could only come from God or his accredited representative and agent; and could only fall on a person or the property of a person guilty of incorrigible rebellion against God, as an idol (Deut. vii. 26), a city of idolaters (Deut. xiii. 18; Josh. vi. 17), an ungodly people (1 Sam. xv. 3, 21), sinners and transgressors in Israel (Isa. xliii. 28), a heathen rebel against God and his people (1 Kings xx. 42; Isa. xxxiv. 5). That which was thus solemnly devoted to destruction was not to be sold or redeemed. If a living creature, it was to be

is most holy unto the LORD. 29. No devoted thing, which is devoted out of man, shall be redeemed; it shall be put to death. 30. And all the tithe of the land, of the seed of the land or of the fruit of the tree, is the LORD's: it is holy unto the LORD. 31. And if a man do redeem his tithe, he shall add a fifth of it to it. 32. And all the tithe of the herd and of the flock, of all that passeth under the rod the tenth shall be holy unto the LORD. 33. He shall not search between good and bad nor change it; and if he do change it, it and its exchange shall be holy; it

put to death as a thing doomed. If inanimate, it was irrevocably surrendered to the Lord to be disposed of at his will. A ban is therefore to be carefully distinguished from a vow. The subject of the vow was consecrated to the Lord at the will of the vower as an acceptable offering, and if a sacrifice, was either a peace-offering or a burnt-sacrifice of the herd or of the flock. The subject of the ban was devoted to destruction only at the behest of God as an accursed thing, by no means to be offered as a sacrifice, but to be put to death as under the sentence of the ban. *Which is devoted out of man,* which belongs to the race of man, and is devoted on account of incorrigible iniquity. Such devoted men are to be put to death as malefactors in the most awful sense, that is, as impenitent rebels against God. There is not the slightest hint of either parents or masters being at liberty to ban either their children or serfs, in this or in any other passage of scripture referring to the ban. The case of Jephthah is not that of a ban, but a vow, and refers to offering and not to extermination. The daughter of Jephthah had done nothing to bring her under the ban, and human sacrifices were forbidden under the Mosaic code.

30–34. The tithe. The tithe of the fruits of the ground belongs to the Lord. 30. If redeemed, commuted for a money payment, a fifth was to be added to it. 32. The tithe of cattle belongs also to the Lord. 33. *He shall not search between good and bad.* The tenth animal that passes under the rod is marked with ruddle as the tithe, and is not to be changed; or if changed, both it and its exchange shall not be redeemed. 34. These are the commandments which the LORD commanded Moses for the sons of Israel in Mount Sinai.

belong to the Lord. The tithe of animals is not be redeemed. 34. From the last verse it appears that this communication also was made from Mount Sinai before the erection of the tabernacle. It is obvious therefore that the arrangement of these documents is not wholly chronological, but in the first place logical. The first sixteen chapters describe the consecration of the people to the Lord by the ritual of propitiation, by the consecration of the priests, by the ritual of purification, and by the day of atonement, in which all these are combined and consummated. The next eleven chapters portray the preparation of the people for entering into the promised land. They treat of the social life of the people of God, as a state, as a church, and as a state and church coinciding one with the other. There is therefore a perfectly logical arrangement running through the whole. This whole book exhibits the people and their ordinances, civil and religious, as a type of all subsequent stages of the church as constituted on earth. It is the lock of which the Epistle to the Hebrews is the easy key. It is the document which affords a vocabulary for the philosophy of redemption.

NOTES.

2. *Setteth apart*, יַפְלִא, εὔξηται. The verb means to do something extraordinary. A vow is of this nature.

28. *A thing devoted*, חֵרֶם, ἀνάθεμα. The root signifies to cut off, and hence in this case to destroy. The word "harem" comes from this root.

www.ingramcontent.com/pod-product-compliance
Lightning Source LLC
Chambersburg PA
CBHW050336230426
43663CB00010B/1874